Advance Praise for *How'd You Score* That *Gig?*

"Reading this is like having your own career counselor on call. It is, without doubt, the #1 book for anyone who's unhappy in their job, confused about what to do next, or just wonders if they're in the best career for them."

—Barbara Stanny, author, *Secrets of Six-Figure Women: Surprising Strategies to Up Your Earnings and Change Your Life*

"Alexandra Levit has written an ideal book for all those adults who still don't know what they want to do when they grow up. The practical self-assessment that opens the book could point even the most indecisive person toward a realistic and satisfying career path."

—Tom Musbach, editor, Yahoo! HotJobs

"Not excited by the prospect of becoming a cube monkey when you graduate college? *How'd You Score* That *Gig?* gives readers an arsenal of advice and tools that anyone dreading the nine-to-five grind needs to read. Levit has penned the ultimate Gen Y career guide."

—Hannah Seligson, author, *New Girl on the Job: Advice from the Trenches*

"First Alexandra Levit broadens your imagination about what kinds of careers are possible, and then, after tantalizing you, she provides specific tips for breaking into the field. Enormously valuable!"

—Ben Casnocha, author, *My Start-up Life: What a (Very) Young CEO Learned on His Journey Through Silicon Valley*

"This book is fantastic. The self-assessment right at the beginning focuses the reader on where to start. *How'd You Score* That *Gig?* is a must-read for every college graduate."

—Rick Fulton, chief operating officer, GetTheJob.com

"Alexandra Levit provides excellent tools for professionals fed up with vague advice like 'Follow your passion.' The assessments and profiles of real people in real professions can mean the difference between trudging through a decade of workplace misery and actually experiencing fulfillment while earning a living."

—Pamela Slim, blogger, Escape from Cubicle Nation

"A must-read for anyone who's ever woken up on Monday morning and wondered, 'Is this all there is?' Reading this book is like hitting the informational interview jackpot."

—Michelle Goodman, author, *The Anti 9-to-5 Guide: Practical Career Advice for Women Who Think Outside the Cube*

"There are literally thousands of ways to make a living in today's world, and few of them show up in any book or website. Thankfully, in *How'd You Score* That *Gig?*, Alexandra Levit has decided to go exploring for you, opening your eyes to dozens of rewarding careers."

—Peter Vogt, author, *Career Wisdom for College Students: Insights You Won't Get in Class, on the Internet, or from Your Parents*

"*How'd You Score* That *Gig?* is filled with impressively in-depth information about a wide variety of interesting careers. I highly recommend this book for parents seeking to help their children explore fulfilling career opportunities."

—James A. Boyle, president, College Parents of America

"Alexandra Levit is a true insider who really understands what twenty- and thirtysomethings want from their careers. This book is full of inspiring stories, concrete tips, and helpful resources. Read this book, then go score a great gig!"

—Lindsey Pollak, author, *Getting from College to Career: 90 Things to Do Before You Join the Real World*

"A one-of-a-kind manual that helps answer the question 'What do I want to do with my life?' Alexandra Levit's detailed self-assessment tool and comprehensive passion profiles arm you with invaluable information about yourself and potential careers."

—Christine Hassler, author, *20 Something Manifesto: Quarter Lifers Speak Out About Who They Are, What They Want, and How to Get It*

"You won't be able to put this one down! *How'd You Score* That *Gig?* goes way beyond being a reference guide to the coolest jobs. It very comprehensively talks about how to get certain gigs and what it really takes to succeed in them. Fascinating!"

—Jason Alba, chief executive officer, JibberJobber.com

"In *How'd You Score* That *Gig?*, Alexandra Levit breaks down and simplifies the biggest barriers to discovering and living your passion. She provides an easy approach to answering the difficult questions: What should I do, and more importantly, how do I get started?"

—Ryan Healy, blogger, *Employee Evolution*

How'd You Score **That** Gig?

BALLANTINE BOOKS ⛪ NEW YORK

How'd You Score That Gig?

A GUIDE TO THE COOLEST JOBS— AND HOW TO GET THEM

Alexandra Levit

A Ballantine Books Trade Paperback Original

Copyright © 2008 by Alexandra Levit

Published in the United States by Ballantine Books, an imprint of The Random House Publishing Group, a division of Random House, Inc., New York.

BALLANTINE and colophon are registered trademarks of Random House, Inc.

Excerpts from the Princeton Review website: copyright © by The Princeton Review, Inc. Used by permission.

Library of Congress Cataloging-in-Publication Data
Levit, Alexandra.
How'd you score *that* gig?: a guide to the coolest jobs—and how to get them / Alexandra Levit.
p. cm.
ISBN 978-0-345-49629-4
1. Vocational guidance.   2. Occupations.   3. Job hunting.   I. Title.
HF5381.L3563   2008
650.14—dc22   2007041376

Printed in the United States of America

www.ballantinebooks.com

9 8 7 6 5 4 3 2 1

Book design by Nancy B. Field

Contents

Introduction

IF YOU SPEND TIME TALKING to twenty- and thirtysomethings working today, you'll unfortunately hear some unhappy stories. Far too many people hold jobs they don't particularly care about. They commute to work every day and arrive home eight to twelve hours later without a clear sense of where they've been, where they are going, or why. In 2004, after I published a book called *They Don't Teach Corporate in College*, I traveled to universities and corporations around the United States and heard these stories firsthand. The situation left me wondering: How did all of these smart, ambitious, goal-directed young people end up in dead-end or passionless careers?

I believe that part of the answer lies in the college recruiting scene. No matter who you are and what school you're graduating from, the story is usually the same. Despite a major that you thought was going to prepare you for a career in the real world, by the time you're a senior you still have no idea what you want to do with your life. You visit the campus career center and are introduced to a bevy of consulting and banking firms and Fortune 500 staples. You don't want to go to graduate school right away and might not know what to go to graduate school for, so you interview for these jobs and inevitably accept one. You become like every other college student graduating in America today, and before you know it, you're on a career path that may not have anything to do with your true calling.

For previous generations, this setup worked out well enough. They accepted college recruiting for what it was, and to some extent felt that a meaningful career meant a healthy, steady paycheck and not much else. We twenty- and thirtysomethings today, though, are rather different in our expectations regarding job satisfaction. Our parents carefully nurtured our talents and self-esteem from babyhood and told us we could be anything we wanted to be. As adults, our career desires are directed toward finding meaningful work that helps others. In essence, we want to be "paid volunteers," to join an organization not because we have to, but because we want to, because it allows us to do something significant with our lives. We're highly concerned with our professional development and want to have the opportunity to make a significant impact at a young age.

Unfortunately, the college recruiting system isn't changing quickly enough to meet our needs, and even after we've gone through the process and possibly even accepted a position, many graduates yearn for a solution outside the typical channels. We want to discover the hidden road, the one that leads to an exciting, unique, and fulfilling line of work, the one taken by a select few who always get asked the question, "How'd you score *that* gig?" We long to have a job that makes us love getting up in the morning, a job that has our friends talking enviously at their Friday night happy hour gatherings. That's where this book comes in. *How'd You Score That Gig?* is for you, the twenty- or thirtysomething who wants to find and travel that hidden road of your dreams.

The book features sixty cool jobs you may never have thought about pursuing, divided into seven categories based on the broad personality types that are generally best suited to those jobs. I selected the cool jobs via an online survey in which I asked nearly five hundred twenty- and thirtysomethings to tell me about their dream careers. Based on the responses, I generated a list of the top sixty careers and constructed a fairly comprehensive profile of each using the information I gathered from written sources and in-depth interviews with more than a hundred individuals currently holding the jobs. Then, I researched various personality-type measures to develop my seven "passion profiles"—adventurer, creator, data-head, entrepreneur, investigator, networker, and nurturer—and placed the sixty cool jobs into the appropriate categories. In the first chapter, I provide an assessment to help you decide which passion profiles (and therefore which jobs) might be most appealing to you. However, though you may be tempted to skip ahead to your own passion profile, I hope that you will be sufficiently intrigued to read the entire book, because you never know what might spark your interest and prompt you to go out and learn more about a particular job. My goal in writing *How'd You Score That Gig?* was to offer a true insider's glimpse into each and every one of these careers, and to provide you with critical advice you simply can't get in your run-of-the-mill job-reference book—especially as it pertains to how you'd go about getting a job in that field. Congratulations on having the courage to embark on the journey toward career fulfillment. I promise it will be worthwhile.

How'd You Score That Gig?

Self-Assessment

THE COOL JOBS IN THIS BOOK are organized within seven passion profiles, or the core personality types of the individuals who are best suited to them. This assessment is meant to determine which passion profile(s) best describes you, and to help you select the types of careers you might wish to explore. Please answer the questions below by selecting the *one* statement that best applies to you, or is *closest* to what you might consider to be true for yourself.

1. **I am most productive when I am**

   A. following my artistic instincts
   B. collaborating with people who all have different strengths
   C. addressing the personal needs of the people I serve
   D. setting concrete, logical goals and achieving them one at a time
   E. solving problems based on information that I gather
   F. taking risks and seeking out new experiences
   G. trying to address a business need

2. **I find work difficult when**

   A. I feel like I'm being taken advantage of
   B. I lose interest in the task and I want to move on to something else
   C. the carelessness and disorganization of others holds up a project
   D. people try to force me to respond to a task in a certain way, even though I have my own vision
   E. I only think of the big picture rather than carefully considering the task
   F. I worry too much about what other people think of me
   G. I pursue my own solutions to the point of being stubborn

3. **I like to lead by**

   A. persuading people that my way is the best way
   B. having total say over the daily responsibilities of my business
   C. reaching out personally to each person I work with
   D. letting common sense overrule personal considerations
   E. allowing people to have the freedom to fulfill their potential in unconventional ways
   F. developing a unique vision and allowing it to guide me
   G. I'm not a particularly strong leader. I can't deal with the politics

4. **My ideal pace at work is**

   A. slow and one that leaves me breathing room to tinker around on my own

   B. one that I set each day depending on my mood

   C. slow so I can fully help other people

   D. fast and one that puts me into contact with lots of different people every day

   E. fast and one that involves a lot of unanticipated challenges

   F. slow and one that allows time to plan and deliver the best final product

   G. fast and one in which I can do what I want on a whim

5. **My co-workers think I'm**

   A. caring

   B. logical

   C. free-spirited

   D. inquisitive

   E. creative

   F. innovative

   G. social

6. **When I am confronted with a new business opportunity**

   A. I jump in immediately before someone else thinks of it

   B. I jump in immediately—the risk gives me a rush

   C. I make a decision based on the data

   D. I try to understand how it will work out given similar situations that occurred in the past

   E. I take advantage of it if it will allow me to express myself in a new way

   F. I talk to others about the best way to approach the situation

   G. I only pursue it if I feel my participation will serve the greater good

7. **My view on financial compensation is**

   A. It's more important to me to make a difference than to make a lot of money

   B. I want to use my artistic talent, and I'm willing to undergo a little financial hardship if I have to

   C. I want to learn, and I'm willing to undergo a little financial hardship if I have to

   D. I don't want to be disappointed when I talk to my colleagues and find out what they're making

   E. I want my compensation to be directly related to my output

   F. I don't need much, just enough that I can afford to experience the world

   G. I want to make a lot of money, so I'd be willing to lose some at first

8. **When I have a conflict with a colleague**

   A. I avoid confrontation and try to be extra nice in an attempt to smooth things over

   B. I leave it alone since I might not be working with that person for very long

   C. I don't let it stand in the way of what I need to get done

   D. I often don't even realize that the colleague is upset

   E. I wait for the colleague to take the first step in improving the situation

   F. I nip it in the bud—it's essential to maintain a good working relationship

   G. I try to reason with the colleague and keep things from getting too personal

9. **I take the most pride in my work when**

   A. my team pulls together and finishes a difficult project

   B. I've adjusted well to a situation where I'm out of my element

   C. I've improved the quality of someone's life

D. My calculations result in the best possible end product

E. I've succeeded at building an operation from the ground up

F. I've developed something that is aesthetically pleasing, a unique expression of myself

G. My colleagues think I've stumbled across something brilliant

10. Assuming I'm really engaged in a task I like, I usually come across as

A. driven and frenetic

B. focused and rational

C. patient and warm

D. introspective and probing

E. impulsive and fun-loving

F. social and talkative

G. imaginative and expressive

11. When I imagine the perfect work setting, it's

A. my place of business—where I pay the rent

B. a private studio

C. an open office with lots of access to co-workers

D. a different locale every day

E. in front of my computer terminal

F. a place of learning

G. a place where people come for help

12. Work tends to frustrate me when

A. I can't get to all the people who need my help

B. the tasks I'm assigned don't allow for any creativity

C. I'm isolated all day long and don't have anyone to talk to

D. I'm stuck behind a desk for too many days in a row

E. I have too many monotonous, structured tasks that take me away from my projects

F. I realize that I could be out making money for myself instead of someone else

G. I can't figure out the best solution to a problem

13. **As a child, you might have found me**

A. convincing my parents to let me take in the latest stray

B. turning the neighborhood lemonade stand into a fully functioning snack shack

C. putting on shows in the basement

D. writing programs on my parents' computer

E. recruiting my fellow second graders to start a new club

F. outside way more than I was inside—camping, on the ski slope, etc.

G. taking apart the radiator just to see if I could put it back together again

14. **A course I was likely to sign up for in school was**

A. Modern African Culture

B. Computer Programming

C. Principles of Business Planning

D. Research Methods

E. Introduction to Theater Studies

F. Persuasive Communication

G. Child Development

15. **On my day off, I'm**

A. on a plane

B. scoping out business opportunities

C. doing something creative

9

D. playing Sudoku

E. attending the best party whose invite came my way

F. volunteering at my place of worship or community center

G. planning my next home-improvement or research project

16. **If I had an unlimited supply of cash, I would**

A. take the time to research all of the subjects I've always wanted to learn about

B. donate regularly to my favorite causes

C. "do my thing" in Costa Rica for a few months

D. buy a beach house on Nantucket for all of my family and friends to congregate

E. fund the business I've always dreamed of

F. quit my day job in order to pursue my artistic passion

G. seek out the best formula for mastering the stock market

17. **I would sit in traffic all day for the chance to**

A. crack a case that's been plaguing my city's administrators for years

B. write and publish the Great American Novel

C. gain access to the best scuba diving on the planet

D. attend a conference where I'd get to hobnob with the major players in my field

E. change the course of a child's life

F. invent a new product or service

G. predict an important outcome using the right combination of data

18. **My ideal type of lunch at work**

A. tastes home-cooked but is delivered, so I don't have to interrupt my thought process

B. is at the hot new place downtown, where the dishes are arranged with flair

C. involves eating my usual fare, at the usual place

D. involves a big gathering and lots of conversation

E. is paid for by venture capitalists

F. different from the one I had the day before

G. involves having something simple with a few close co-workers

19. **Formal education bought me**

A. something to fall back on in case I don't succeed at my art

B. the opportunity to learn about the best avenues for making the world a better place

C. the chance to learn interpersonal skills in a highly social atmosphere

D. to be honest, I feel like my time could have been better spent out in the world

E. absolutely everything when it comes to my career

F. the opportunity to develop my analytical-thinking ability

G. the credibility that customers and investors are looking for

20. **In a past life, I might have been**

A. a monk or a nun

B. an apothecary

C. an explorer

D. a classical musician

E. a town mayor

F. a robber barron/industrialist

G. a Scotland Yard detective

ANSWER KEY

• •

Score your assessment by circling the letter you selected for each question in the row designated for that question. Then, in each column ("A", "C," "D," etc.), add up the number of circles and write your total at the bottom.

	"A"	"C"	"D"	"E"	"I"	"Ne"	"Nu"
1.	F	A	D	G	E	B	C
2.	B	D	G	E	C	F	A
3.	E	F	D	B	G	A	C
4.	G	B	F	E	A	D	C
5.	C	E	B	F	D	G	A
6.	B	E	C	A	D	F	G
7.	F	B	E	G	C	D	A
8.	B	E	G	C	D	F	A
9.	B	F	D	E	G	A	C
10.	E	G	B	A	D	F	C
11.	D	B	E	A	F	C	G
12.	D	B	G	F	E	C	A
13.	F	C	D	B	G	E	A
14.	A	E	B	C	D	F	G
15.	A	C	D	B	G	E	F
16.	C	F	G	E	A	D	B
17.	C	B	G	F	A	D	E
18.	F	B	C	E	A	D	G
19.	D	A	F	G	E	C	B
20.	C	D	B	F	G	E	A

TOTALS

• •

Number of "A" answers: _____   Number of "I" answers: _____

Number of "C" answers: _____   Number of "Ne" answers: _____

Number of "D" answers: _____   Number of "Nu" answers: _____

Number of "E" answers: _____

• •

If you have more **"A"s** than any other letter, you are an **Adventurer**

The free-spirited adventurer is naturally spontaneous and enjoys taking risks. These individuals seek out experiences and approach each new opportunity with optimism and enthusiasm. Adventurers are frequently jacks-of-all-trades—they have many interests and skills and just don't have enough hours in the day to attend to them all. Adventurers are outspoken and opinionated and don't place too much importance on what other people think. They believe that life is theirs to live, and that it's their responsibility to make the world a better place even if that means wading in dangerous waters. While adventurers will approach tasks with creativity and fearlessness, they may get distracted along the way by unrealistic plans and expectations, and as a result may never finish what they start. Adventurers are at their best in situations that require adjustment to a new way of life and that allow them to go with the flow, and they often feel stifled in traditional work settings.

If you have more **"C"s** than any other letter, you are a **Creator**

Creators place extreme importance on developing products, such as art, music, or physical spaces, which allow them to express themselves and their unique view of the world. Emotional and imaginative, they intuitively see the beauty of things. Known for being open communicators, creators prefer a flexible work environment that encourages originality and allows them to move at their own pace. They dislike conformity and may be impulsive decision makers. The creator can be egotistical at times and always wants to be considered an important contributor. As someone who sees the big picture, the creator may lack organizational skills and the patience to execute projects step-by-step.

If you have more **"D"s** than any other letter, you are a **Data Head**

The data head has a knack for gathering and organizing information. These individuals prefer to work on their own and despise inefficiency and bureaucracy. The data head is happiest setting concrete goals and then achieving them. Usually deliberate and even-tempered, data heads believe that "common sense is king." Their performance standards are high and they will settle for nothing less than the best final product. Data heads' skills may make them strong candidates for leadership positions, but their occasional lack of social graces and their unusual sense of humor can sometimes get in the way of their career growth. They don't like to be micromanaged and will pursue their plans to the point of being stubborn. Their respect can be earned through reason; once you've gotten it, it's for life.

If you have more **"E"s** than any other letter, you are an **Entrepreneur**

Entrepreneurs are experts at observing the world around them and uncovering needs that they can meet. Active and high-energy, they dislike sitting down with a book or being chained to a desk from nine to five. These individuals are always coming up with new ideas, even in their sleep, and they solve tough problems through their flexibility and resourcefulness. Entrepreneurs have the ability to push past fear and take risks in pursuit of a payoff, they have thick skins, and they don't allow difficult people to stand in their way. Although entrepreneurs may sometimes jump into situations without thinking them through, they accept that they don't know everything and willingly seek out mentors to help them achieve their goals. They prefer to have ownership of the important decisions, but are often at their best when they leave the nitty-gritty details to others.

If you have more "I"s than any other letter, you are an Investigator

Investigators place a high value on science, process, and learning. They excel at research, using logic and the information gained through their senses to conquer complex problems. Nothing thrills them more than a "big find." Intellectual, introspective, and exceedingly detail-oriented, investigators are happiest when they're using their brain power to pursue what they deem as a worthy outcome. They prefer to march to their own beat, and they dislike overly structured environments that necessitate a set response to challenges. Investigators are not interested in leadership, and developing the interpersonal skills necessary to fuel collaboration is a hurdle for many of them. They may feel insecure in their ability to "keep up" in their fields and can react badly when forced to put more important work on hold to complete a task that doesn't intrigue them.

If you have more "Ne"s than any other letter, you are a Networker

Networkers always have a ringing phone and a full dance card. They thrive on keeping busy and managing a diverse array of responsibilities. Networkers seek out group relationships and emphasize interpersonal fulfillment. They need personal contact and surround themselves with people who respect them. Networkers are gracious and generous with people who share their values, but, as leaders, they may be critical of those who won't commit or give 100 percent to a task. Though they are generally well liked due to their excellent social and persuasive skills, they can be oversensitive and too emotionally invested in a job, always warding off fears that they don't fit in. The "team player" networker likes to consult a variety of points of view in order to make a decision.

If you have more **"Nu"s** than any other letter, you are a **Nurturer**

The nurturer's top priority is to care for others. These individuals derive satisfaction from helping others in need and making an emotional impact on people's lives. Gentle, reliable, loyal, and warm, nurturers excel at communicating in a way that makes it easy to trust them. They prefer to stay in the background and allow others to take the spotlight, and they dislike confrontation and conflict. Nurturers generally have a positive, healthy outlook, but when they feel taken advantage of or that someone is being insensitive, they may get stressed out or angry. Because they care so much about their jobs, nurturers have issues setting limits with others and can burn out easily. They're not highly motivated by financial compensation, but need to feel appreciated and valued in order to be successful.

Some people will score highly in several passion profiles. For example, it's possible to have 8 "E" answers and 6 "C" answers. You may even have two passion profiles tie for the highest score—for instance, 9 "D" answers and 9 "I" answers. You should make a note of which passion profiles you scored the highest on (I suggest the top three) and pay special attention to the cool jobs in those chapters. I hope you'll find it interesting to read through the whole book, though, for you may discover something unexpected about a career you might enjoy that's not in one of your profiles! Now, with the fairness of alphabetical order, let's start with the adventurers.

The Adventurer

I was one of a very few in Canada to be selected for two outstanding youth programs, one called Katimavik and the other called Canada World Youth. In these programs, I had the opportunity to travel all across Canada and down to Brazil on the Canadian government's dime working in small towns, building up the communities. My participation made me realize that I love to travel, and led me to become an English professor at Qiongzhou University in Hainan, China. I know that I am doing a good thing as I am improving my students' English skills so they can go on to teach others. I feel like I am doing my part in the world.

—Paul, twenty-four, ESL teacher

I AM IN AWE OF ADVENTURERS. Though I encourage all twenty- and thirtysomethings to break out of the narrow-fitting boxes "real life" tends to place us in and to search the world for a vocation they're passionate about, no one is better at it than the individuals profiled in this chapter. Every one of us is acquainted with an adventurer who has effortlessly mastered the lay of a foreign land despite being born in, say, Detroit, or one who has turned away from things like Starbucks and traffic and never looked back. And every one of us knows the feeling of being critical yet envious of her lifestyle, daunted yet impressed by her courage. Adventurers come from a wide range of backgrounds and financial circumstances, and some have little formal education while some have a lot. What they all have in common, though, is a free-spirited, experience-seeking personality style. As the first passion profile of the seven we'll explore in this book, what's the adventurer all about? Let's take a deeper dive.

The hallmark of the adventurous mind-set is spontaneity. Plotting out a routine that changes little from day to day is not a concept with which most adventurers are comfortable, and usually their jobs don't allow for it anyway. Rather, adventurers hunger for fresh experiences and approach each one with optimism and enthusiasm. "The best part of my job is that every day is very different," says Karyn, thirty-one, an outdoor adventure guide. "One morning I'll wake up to see a bear rattling outside the tarp, and then later on a big tree will nearly fall on our shelter. Or I'll be hiking at six A.M. and get totally lost!" Jamie, a thirty-year-old news correspondent, has a job that is, in some ways, the opposite of Karyn's. But she too craves the excitement that comes with not knowing what to expect from a given day at work.

The coolest jobs, for me, are foreign service officer, news correspondent, and photographer. I'm attracted to these because they have a great deal of variety, breadth, and depth. All of these careers allow the individuals in them to really explore issues and do new things every day. Their skills transfer to several different environments, they get to travel widely, and they interact with diverse cultures and people.

—*Evelyn, twenty-five*

"Things are always interesting, and that's why I'm still doing this job," she says. "A story can take me to the projects or to the governor's mansion, or both in the same afternoon. I covered the 2000 presidential recount from the Florida capitol, I've watched as police cart suspects away in handcuffs, and I've met families moments after tornadoes destroyed their neighborhoods." Risk taking is another trait shared by most adventurers. "A willingness to be up for anything is important," claims Darley, twenty-seven, a travel journalist. "And being flexible is vital. On the road, I have come to realize that things just happen and you just have to go with the flow."

The idea of "going with the flow" is one that came up during many of my adventurer interviews, and it's one of the things I most admire about these folks. One of the reasons adventurers are content to lean in whatever direction the wind is blowing is that there is so much about life that they cherish and enjoy. "I don't place all of my energy into my job," says Chris, twenty-five, an oceanographer. "There are many other things that bring me happiness, and that diversity allows me to weather any challenges or setbacks without too much trouble. If work isn't going well, I'll write it off and attempt to salvage what is left, and I'll get some extra surfing done in the meantime!" Adventurers are often jacks- and jills-of-all-trades—they have so many interests and skills that it's sometimes a struggle to fit everything in. Maki, thirty-two, a documentary photographer who also works in the entertainment world, has become an expert in packing as much action into her days as possible. "There will be times when I have to go to the Caribbean for a fashion shoot and I'll take a side trip and do documentary photography," she says.

For the adventurer, being confident and outspoken is a matter of survival, and also a necessity for good self-esteem, as they often find themselves being judged for their unorthodox career choices. "Photographers have to be self-promoters," says Maki. "You can't be shy about your abilities. If you're going to get work, you have to sell yourself to editors." More than other passion profiles, adventurers go their own way and don't worry too much about what other people think. "A lot of people have told me that staying in one job for at least a year is best—and maybe they're right—but I've moved every six months for a couple of years," says Darley, without regret. "My advice is just to live each day fully and take advantage of every opportunity, because you never know where things will lead."

Although the adventurer believes in being empowered to direct

Foreign service officer sounds like the best job—travel, intrigue, and a unique blend of politics, international trade relations, and cultural diversity. I'd also be up for being a travel journalist, because of the opportunity to see the world and tell stories about my adventures.

—*Brad, twenty-nine*

his own life, he also has an innate sense of social responsibility. Some adventurers work daily to preserve and learn about the natural environment, while others focus on social causes. Regardless, most are driven to make the world a better place even if their efforts and dedication place them in harm's way. "The Oregon coast has some of the roughest seas in the world, so there are plenty of chances to get a thrill, or just get sick," says Chris. "But for me, it's rewarding to pursue exciting questions about the way our world works." Peter, a thirty-year-old news correspondent, expressed a similar sentiment. "NBC pays me to personally witness history, and to experience the world, and so it's my job to deliver the most accurate and representative information to my audience. Sometimes, that means I don't need an alarm clock because I can count on being woken up by a nearby explosion in Baghdad."

While the adventurer approaches new tasks with creativity and fearlessness, he has the tendency to get distracted by unrealistic plans and expectations, and as a result may end up changing paths entirely. Most of the adventurers I spoke to mentioned having at least a few different jobs—if not a few different careers. "After college, I took a year off to research whales for a nonprofit in Massachusetts," says Matt, thirty, now a travel journalist. "I was able to live for a while just watching whales and crewing boats, but after eight months, I ran out of funds and turned to an editor for help. She needed a writer for a management column at a technology trade magazine. I knew nothing about the subject but I did my best and she loved it. Then, a little later down the line, I started working in travel writing." Because adventurers tend to be nomadic, a stint in a particular career is often short-lived. "My company has a high turnover rate, and I don't think that's unusual for this field," says Karyn. Jamie claims the same thing about the television news industry. "When I graduated from college, a reporter who graduated a few years before me told me: 'The people who make it in this business aren't necessarily the best, they just stick it out the longest.' He's now a lawyer," she says.

Like entrepreneurs and creators, adventurers often feel stifled in traditional work settings. "I prefer to be master of my own schedule," says Matt. "If I want to take a week off, I can, so long as I meet all of my deadlines. It's up to me." They are at their best in situations that require adjustment to a new way of life. "I moved around a lot when I was a kid, and that definitely helped prepare me for this job, where you're living in a foreign country and have to get used to new environments quickly," says Geoff, thirty, an ESL teacher in Japan. One thing is for certain—for the true adventurer, predictability equals boredom. "After I have been on land for a few months working on proposals and cruise planning, I start to get an itch to be out at sea, doing fieldwork," says Katy, twenty-eight, an oceanographer. "My career allows me to go to fascinating places and to meet amazing people. I have worked on projects in the U.S., Greece, Cyprus, Sweden, and Turkey, and I really enjoy learning about new cultures, languages, and ways of life."

The adventurers featured in this chapter have had experiences that the majority of people living today only dream about. They've traveled to the ends of the earth and back, engaged in jobs that both fulfill them personally and contribute to the well-being of the world's people and resources.

> ESL teacher sounds like the perfect job for me. I love to travel and teach, and this is a career that would bring the two together. At the same time, it would allow me to have an authentic cultural experience in a foreign country where I'd learn so much more than I would just being a tourist.
>
> —*Katie, twenty-three*

In reading about the jobs of the conservationist, documentary photographer, ESL teacher, foreign service officer, news correspondent, oceanographer, outdoor adventure guide, and travel journalist, I hope that those of you with a simmering sense of adventure will be inspired to make a bold career move that could very well change the course of your own life.

CONSERVATIONIST

My parents certainly encouraged me to explore the outdoors as a child. Weekly trips to the state park with my tree ID book made it educational and challenging. By the time I was ready for college, it was my own personal choice to pursue a science degree because it was the field that I was most comfortable in. I've always had enthusiasm and passion for conservation initiatives, and I've developed leadership skills as well. Our volunteers look to aquarium staff to answer questions on wetland ecology, and with a strong leader they feel more confident in returning and in encouraging their friends and families to volunteer. Time is the most valuable donation.

—Charmaine, twenty-eight, conservationist

MOST OF US ARE CONCERNED about the declining state of our environment, but few are in a position to improve the situation on an everyday basis. Conservationists, sometimes known as conservation scientists, are responsible for managing, restoring, and protecting a country's natural resources. Working with government and industry associations as well as landowners, they come up with methods for combating damage and for using the land without injuring the environment. As you would imagine, a lot of conservationists spend a great deal of time working outdoors in remote areas, recording the type and state of the natural resources in an area, and reporting on the environmental impact of human activities such as hunting and logging.

According to the U.S. Bureau of Labor Statistics' *Occupational Outlook Handbook,* the more common conservationists are range managers, soil conservationists, and water conservationists. Range managers in the United States study hundreds of millions of acres of land, mostly in the western states and Alaska, in order to maximize their use. They inventory soils, plants, and animals; develop resource management plans; help to restore degraded ecosystems; or assist in managing ranches. Soil conservationists provide technical assistance regarding erosion and other land preservation issues to farmers, forest managers, governments, and landowners, while water conservationists advise on a broad range of natural resource topics including water quality, groundwater contamination, and water resource management. Conservationists often specialize in one area, such as wildlife management or urban forestry.

Charmaine, twenty-eight, is a conservationist employed by the National Aquarium in Baltimore, Maryland. Her focus is wetland restoration of the Chesapeake Bay, and she spends much of her time in the field, managing a conservation team that includes sixty to a hundred volunteers. A typical project involves traveling on a research vessel to a protected island in the Chesapeake and planting up to a hundred thousand native marsh plants over the course of five to seven days. "I love the flexibility of this job," says Charmaine. "Although I'm doing wetland restoration at the moment, I have also taken an interest in shark conservation and have been able to participate in shark-tagging sessions in Ocean City."

The U.S. Bureau of Labor Statistics' *Occupational Outlook Handbook* reports that conservationists generally hold a minimum of a bachelor's degree in fields such as ecology, agriculture, biology, or environmental science. If you don't have any formal science training, however, your next best option is to volunteer or intern at a government agency or at an environmental or community organization. The Investigate Biodiversity website (investigate.conservation.org) maintains that this is one of the best ways to find out about and secure a part- or a full-time opening, to meet influential contacts, and to gain real-world field experience. It worked for Charmaine. "I'd heard great things about the conservation department at the National Aquarium and it sparked my interest, so I signed up to volunteer," she says. "I helped out during a large-scale debris cleanup of a tidal marsh and the staff got to know me. When one employee moved on I was encouraged to apply for the opening, and was hired shortly thereafter."

If you're interested in breaking into conservation, joining a relevant professional organization can be an excellent vehicle for launching your career. Although many require an annual membership fee, they regularly provide great learning and networking opportunities in the form of conferences, seminars, specialty publications, and chapter meetings. Here are a few that were recommended to me:

- Association of Conservation Engineers (www.conservationengineers.org)
- Conservation International (www.conservation.org)
- National Park Service (www.nps.gov)
- National Wildlife Federation (www.nwf.org)
- Natural Resources Conservation Service (www.nrcs.usda.gov)
- The Nature Conservancy (www.nature.org)
- Sierra Club (www.sierraclub.org)
- Student Conservation Association (www.thesca.org)
- U.S. Fish and Wildlife Service (www.fws.gov)
- The Wilderness Society (www.wilderness.org)
- World Wildlife Fund (www.panda.org)

As you progress in a conservation career, a graduate degree can facilitate efforts to reach more senior positions within government agencies and private-sector consulting firms. A Ph.D. is a necessity for teaching and research positions in academia. Investigate Biodiversity says that it may also help to get certified in a particular discipline, which basically just involves completing formal training and passing a standard industry test. For instance, you could be certified as a wetland scientist through the Society of Wetland Scientists, or as a professional wildlife biologist through the Wildlife Society. "I became a certified scuba diver when I went to work at the aquarium," says Charmaine. "And I found that this enhancement certification helped me get a spot on the R/V *Coral Reef*, a team of just twelve people that travels to the Bahamas annually to collect tropical fish for aquarium exhibits."

Few jobs sound more fun and rewarding for an adventurer, but conservation does have its drawbacks. The field will continue to be competitive, even as land development projects and an emphasis on environmental protection and fire prevention generate additional jobs. You have to be in excellent physical shape, be willing to move where the jobs are, and be prepared to work under adverse conditions. "We have no control over the weather, and conservation teams work rain or shine," says Charmaine. "And since we run entirely on grants, a lack of funding will occasionally set us back a bit." Like most environmental jobs, conservation doesn't offer big salaries either—according to the website CollegeBoard, the U.S. Department of Labor reports that the average conservationist made just under $55K last year. But, as those who love nature know, money isn't everything. "The National Aquarium has so much to offer, including great benefits, and I find the whole package to be better overall compensation than higher pay," says Charmaine.

DOCUMENTARY PHOTOGRAPHER

> I'd been to New York for the first time in February 2004. I came here for a week with my girlfriend. A couple of days before flying back home I decided to call Magnum Photos. I told them that I dig their work and asked if I could come over to look at the office, see how everything works. It didn't work out before I left, but I stayed in touch with Mark, Magnum's New York bureau director. In the fall, I called Mark again to ask him if I could do an internship at Magnum. After sending my résumé and a portfolio, I called back a couple of times and sent a self-promotion piece that I made especially for that internship and was then connected to B.J. and Claudine from the Magnum In Motion department. We talked about our mutual expectations and what we want to do together. After that, I booked my flight and off I went to New York.
>
> —Martin, twenty-seven, documentary photographer

DOCUMENTARY PHOTOGRAPHERS, or those who use compelling images to tell a story, are revered in the photography profession. Documentary photography is often confused with photojournalism, and during my research for this section I often found the two terms used interchangeably. The main difference between the two seems to be that documentary photography is meant to serve as a historical document of a political or social era, while photojournalism documents a specific incident. Both documentary photography and photojournalism aim to illustrate truth without manipulating the scene or the resulting image, and both cover a whole range of subjects from young gymnasts training for the Olympics to the impact of the African AIDS crisis. "I enjoy the time I spend in South America, just shooting on the street, being able to show how the people there really live," says thirty-two-year-old photographer Maki. "Latin countries have a certain energy and their colors are very warm..."

Bradley Wilson of the National Press Photographers Association (www.nppa.org) tells us that as early as the 1800s, photojournalists with huge, hardly portable cameras were making portraits of presidents and documenting the Civil War. By the 1920s, the constant variety, the allure of traveling all over the world, and the possibility of meeting people of all backgrounds attracted more and more budding visual artists to the profession. Today, the majority of documentary photographers and photojournalists work for news outlets (newspapers, magazines, television stations, news websites), either on a full-time or, increasingly, on a freelance/contract basis. Others work for governments, consulting firms, or photography agencies that provide images to the press, publishers, advertising, television, galleries, and museums. For example, Martin, twenty-seven, currently works in the multimedia department at the prestigious Magnum Photos, which supplies documentary-style photographs to sources around the world. "My work appears in a variety of newspapers and magazines and my clients include Canon Europe, Red Bull, *Profil, Falter,* and Contrast Photo Agency," he says. "I've also created a website, Journal of a Photographer, that is dedicated to this long-standing passion." As he gains experience, the documentary photographer may specialize in a certain area (sports, arts, native cultures, and so on), become a photo editor for a media outlet, start a commercial photography studio, or teach at a university or workshop.

A day in the life of a documentary photographer obviously depends on the individual work situation, but the Schools in the USA website (www.schoolsintheusa.com) offers a helpful list of common responsibilities:

- Consult with and discuss work with editors.
- Study assignments to determine the locations and type of equipment needed.
- Rush to locations to take photographs of breaking stories.

- Determine picture composition.
- Adjust cameras for desired focus, exposure, composition, and other settings.
- Choose lenses designed for close-up, medium-range, or distance photography.
- Select the type of film, filters, and lighting equipment.
- Take numerous photographs and choose from the best.
- Write stories for media outlets to accompany photographs.
- Conduct interviews and carry out background research for stories.
- Use airbrush or digital techniques to retouch negatives and prints.

Here, I feel it's important to point out a couple of things. First, some of the documentary photographers I spoke to still use 35mm cameras because they feel that the quality of images from digital cameras is not yet up to par. However, they do leverage technology to make image production faster and more efficient. For instance, most photographers will use scanners to produce digital images from traditional film, and then will electronically edit and send images to news outlets from their laptops. Second, notice that interviewing for and writing stories are listed among the typical responsibilities of a documentary photographer or photojournalist. Indeed, photographers who work full-time for news outlets are expected to be able to communicate stories in a way that journalists can understand, while freelancers are often asked for complete story packages including both a written narrative and images.

Given that most documentary photographers and photojournalists start off working full-time in a media outlet, a college degree will make things a lot easier. You don't necessarily have to have a bachelor's degree in journalism, however. In fact, many editors prefer new photographers to have a broader liberal arts education so that they have a more comprehensive understanding of current events and the subjects they'll be shooting. One thing that news organizations do require is experience. Therefore, before you apply for an entry-level position, you will need to have a newspaper, magazine, or television internship, or a stint of part-time work for a photographer, under your belt.

The best time to do an internship or apprenticeship is while you're still in school, though technically you can do one at any time provided you have enough money saved to offset the low or nonexistent pay. Although media outlets and working photographers are usually grateful for help, opportunities to work with them aren't always advertised. You must go out of your way to make personal contact with them as soon as you decide to pursue this career. E-mail the photo editor at your local newspaper to see if you can shadow a photographer for a day, or better yet, e-mail directly a photographer you respect and see if he would be amenable to meeting for coffee or doing an informational interview over the phone. "While I was still a student, I went to Barnes & Noble and I looked at the magazines I liked," says Maki. "I noted the editors' names and I began to approach them. It was hard to get them on the phone, so sometimes I would just have to drop off a portfolio." If you're successful at arranging an initial get-together, nurture the relationship. Ask potential mentors to look at your photographs, and then make adjustments based on their critiques. Even if they aren't in a position to offer you a job right away, stay in contact, because you never know how they might be able to help you down the line.

If you're out of school and don't have any formal photography training, you might consider taking a classroom or field workshop. Not only will this be a great way to meet people in the industry, but you'll also gain valuable experience and work samples for your résumé and portfolio. You can search for workshops on websites such as Photo.net—just make sure that the one you choose is appropriate for your level of ability, that you have the right equipment, and that you contact a few references to ensure that the course is a wise investment.

A big component of any education or training you'll undertake to become a documentary photographer or photojournalist will be using class assignments and spontaneous photography sessions on your own to compile strong material for your portfolio. According to photojournalist Nancy Ford, your portfolio will give potential employers an idea of your level of talent and creativity, and will show if you understand how to use the camera, have a strong sense of composition, and have the ability to capture a moment. Ford says that a good portfolio also demonstrates how versatile you are as far as shooting different types of assignments, such as spot news, features, picture stories, and sports. Not only should your portfolio showcase a cross section of your work, but it should also include an updated résumé, three to four references, a caption sheet, and if you are mailing it, an SASE. (self-addressed stamped envelope), so an employer can return your work if necessary. Technology now allows photographers to present portfolios using a variety of techniques, such as mounting prints or slides or creating a CD or webpage. Since different employers prefer different ways of receiving portfolios, it may pay to be versatile. No matter what format you choose, however, Ford suggests making your portfolio neat, clean, and effortless to view, and using only top-quality images. Remember that as a new documentary photographer, your portfolio is your principle sales tool, and in looking for your first job, you will want to call on your contacts to help get it in as many hands as possible. As you begin your search, you may also find the following resources useful:

- Canadian Centre for Documentary Photography (www.documentaryphotography.org)
- International Center of Photography (www.icp.org)
- National Press Photographers Association (www.nppa.org)

In his article for the National Press Photographers Association, Bradley Wilson says that the type of adventurer most likely to succeed in this career is naturally curious, highly ethical, both mechanically and artistically gifted, and adaptable to constantly changing circumstances. This last point is especially important. While most documentary photographers enjoy their work, there's no getting around the fact that it can be quite demanding. Even when they work for themselves, their schedules are usually unpredictable and their hours are usually long, and only those who are very well known make a six-figure salary (the average entry-level documentary photographer makes, according to the Schools in the USA website, a paltry $15K). It can also be difficult for busy photographers to focus on long-term projects that require meticulous attention. "I was ambitious about doing a project about elderly people living in retirement homes, and I wanted to photograph a project about the Danube harbor in Vienna," says Martin. "I did research, started to read books, meet with people, maybe even started to take first photographs. But I was never able to continue working on a story."

Finally, the nature of their work means that documentary photographers often find themselves witnessing upsetting situations—from Third World poverty to devastating natural disasters. Still, it's this affective stimulation that draws many adventurous souls to the profession. "I prefer documentary photography to other types because of the special emotions it allows me to feel," says Maki. "I'll form a personal attachment to an event or a scene, and in documenting that moment forever, I'll feel like I'm really doing something new and meaningful."

ESL TEACHER
• • • • • • • • • • • •

> This job has introduced me to a lot of great people here who I would not have met otherwise. I have had several of my students invite my wife and me to their homes and parties. If you decide to teach English overseas, you'll find a lot of like-minded people from all over the world. There are a lot of us, and although all of them got into it for different reasons, there seems to be a good vibe among most of the ones I've run into.
>
> —Geoff, thirty, ESL teacher

PURSUING TEACHING AS A WAY to give back to the community and make a difference in children's lives is not a strange path to today's twenty- and thirtysomethings, but those with an adventurous streak might consider going the distance, so to speak, of teaching English as a second language (ESL). You'd be surprised at how many programs are out there that prepare native speakers to teach in a foreign country, but requirements vary depending on which one you choose.

If you think teaching abroad is for you, the first thing to do is assess your needs. Is there a specific part of the world you'd like to live in? Would you be comfortable in a rural area, or would you feel better living near an industrialized area with access to good medical care and some of the comforts of home? How much of a salary would you need to make? Do you want to teach children or adults, in schools or in businesses? The answers to these questions will help you narrow down the dizzying amount of programs you'll find in a run-of-the-mill Google search. "I chose Shanghai for my first post because I thought teaching there would be a great way to experience the Chinese culture," says Paul, twenty-four, now an ESL teacher for college students in Hainan, China.

To teach in an American school, you must be certified, but overseas, whether certification is necessary is a matter of some debate. It's definitely easier to get a higher-paying post in a more desirable location if you're certified, but if you're willing to put up with some risk and head to remote locations in Asia, Latin America, or Eastern Europe, you might get away with just a bachelor's degree. The SoYouWanna website (www.soyouwanna.com) has a few more tricks up its sleeve when it comes to avoiding certification, including applying to work for the local government, a tutoring facility, or an adult night school.

Assuming you're looking at teaching ESL as a career, however, you're probably going to want to get certified, as nothing is better for developing the skills you'll need to succeed in the classroom. There are hundreds of options for obtaining a TEFL (teaching English as a foreign language) certificate, and whether you want to take a course part-time over the Internet or do an intensive period of study at a physical location, you should be able to find a program that works for you. Most of these courses involve approximately 120 hours of study and cost between $1K and $4K. A good central resource for scouting out programs is the Teach Abroad website (www.teachabroad.com). As you're looking, pay attention to the perks offered with particular courses. Some will provide teaching practice and help place you in a job after you graduate, while others will cover travel-related expenses.

If your certificate program doesn't place you in a teaching position upon graduation, you can either try to get one before you go overseas or try your luck once you arrive. I've heard that teaching jobs that hire on-site pay more, and this option might appeal more to you adventurer types anyway. "I drove around for a day when I moved here and called the first school I saw and asked if they needed an English teacher," says Geoff, thirty, an ESL teacher in Japan. "I went in for an interview and got hired on the spot. I taught my first lesson that day. But from what I understand, this is not the way things usually go. A lot of people come over to a country with a program like AEON or

JET." In the event that you decide to go the first route, you can ask a contact at your certification program to recommend a good teacher-placement firm, or you can check out online job directories on the TEFL Professional Network (www.tefl.com) or Teach Abroad. When choosing a school sight unseen, you might feel better chatting with a few current or former teachers before accepting an offer. Keep in mind that you will likely be asked to sign at least a one-year contract.

How much money you can expect to make depends upon your destination—more desirable locations in Europe will pay less (think $25K to $35K), and will have a higher cost of living attached to them. On the other hand, in the Far East, you'll have a lower cost of living and could make up to $50K if you're willing to settle for being outside a big city. Your school may or may not pick up the cost of your housing, so the type of rental you choose could impact your take-home pay as well.

So what can you expect living abroad as an ESL teacher? Well, for one thing, you'll have to learn the local language as quickly as possible. "Not knowing Chinese has been a big challenge," says Paul. "If I can't translate a word for my students and they don't understand me, I have a real hard time getting my point across. I find that English is filled with so much slang, and sometimes I don't even realize I'm using it." You'll also want to be prepared that teaching your native language is not as cushy a job as it might seem at first. Paul spends hours preparing for each class, and Geoff works at various locations in order to pick up additional compensation. "This job is a full-time one, it doesn't mean you're on vacation in your new country. For some jobs, there's a good deal of lesson planning involved, whereas for others, it's just sitting down and having a conversation with someone in English for an hour or so," Geoff says. "But scheduling can be a problem. It's hard to keep track of where you're supposed to be when you're working at several different places."

Finally, the ESL teachers I talked to mentioned that patience, a sense of humor, and authenticity are useful on-the-job traits. "You have to be yourself, not the person you think is best suited for the job. You'll find that people appreciate your honesty with them," says Paul. Adaptability and optimism, prime characteristics of adventurers, will come in handy when you're living in a foreign country on your own and missing your home, family, and friends. Regardless of the specific teaching situation you choose, you're bound to have an experience you'll remember forever. "This job fulfills my desire to travel and make money at the same time," adds Paul. "And to be honest, I don't know too many twenty-four-year-olds who can say they've done half the things I have in my lifetime."

FOREIGN SERVICE OFFICER

Early in my career I was assigned to monitor the presidential elections in Haiti. I was in charge of a twelve-person team, including Haitian employees, diplomatic security agents, and three U.S. congressional staffers. With thirty-two candidates running for president, I knew it would be interesting. On election day, the voting centers were supposed to open at six A.M., but when we arrived the voting officers were working by candlelight to get things together: assembling ballot boxes and isolation booths, and verifying that the 1,600 ballots per office were clean. By seven-thirty, the crowd outside was growing visibly angry and tension was high. I knew we might be in trouble when the diplomatic security agent said, "Okay, if we have to make a break because they mob the center, jump over that low wall and I'll break the lock off the back gate." Fortunately, at most of the centers, things ended up progressing reasonably well, and it was a great day. Haiti had over 50 percent turnout, the highest ever!

—Liz, twenty-nine, foreign service officer

WHEN MOST OF US HEAR the word *diplomat*, we think of a secretive, high-profile individual who cruises around with special plates on his car, immune to the traffic laws that plague normal citizens. We also typically think of someone with decades of experience under her belt who speaks a half dozen languages. In truth, though, if you've got that adventurous streak and you're a U.S. citizen, you could be eligible to begin a career as a foreign service officer (FSO) today. Let's learn how.

The first step is to read the foreign service material on the U.S. State Department's website (www.state.gov) to see if one of the FSO career tracks is right for you. It's important to review the information about these career tracks carefully, for you will select one at the beginning of the hiring process that you will be tied to for at least the first few years of your employment. The tracks are as follows:

- **Management Affairs.** Responsible for developing personnel, negotiating bilateral work agreements, managing real estate portfolios and financial assets, supervising U.S. embassies, consulates, and other diplomatic posts, and organizing visits between U.S. and host country leadership.

- **Consular Affairs.** Responsible for solving problems for American citizens abroad (including passport, medical, and legal issues), evacuating American citizens in the event of a natural disaster or armed conflict, and screening foreign visa applicants and deciding whether to issue or deny them entry into the United States.

- **Economic Affairs.** Responsible for advancing U.S. economic interests abroad, including developing contacts in foreign organizations, negotiating trade agreements, advising officials on policy developments, coordinating financial assistance in troubled areas, and promoting international cooperation on global environmental and technology issues.

- **Political Affairs.** Responsible for assessing political climates abroad, interpreting events and situations as they relate to U.S. political interests, communicating with foreign governments seeking support for shared goals, and developing and implementing foreign policy.

- **Public Diplomacy.** Responsible for broadening the understanding of American values and concerns in the host country, including leveraging the media to expand awareness; managing creative, cultural, educational, and exchange programs; and effectively communicating U.S. foreign policy.

If you need some help choosing a career track, the recruiting-friendly page on the department's website (www.careers.state.gov) has a quiz that lets you rate how interested you are in performing fifty different FSO activities. "The site is a great place to start if you think you might like the foreign service but don't know too much about the work that we do or what type of work you would personally be interested in," says twenty-nine-year-old FSO Liz. While surfing the site, I also observed that you can sign up for a foreign service e-mail newsletter, which will provide you with inside information and help you keep on top of the application process.

Do you have a bit of financial flexibility? You might also apply for an unpaid State Department internship before undergoing the intense process of becoming an FSO. Liz, for example, served a post at the Bureau of European Affairs during her junior year in college and credits the experience with helping her gain the background knowledge necessary to do well on the FSO entry examinations and enhancing the competitiveness of her application.

In any case, you'll begin the process by going online and filling out an application form that gathers basic personal data, including education and employment history. You'll choose your career track when you register. The online registration also includes the Personal Narrative, in which candidates respond in no more than two hundred words to each of six questions that measure leadership skills, managerial skills, interpersonal skills, communications skills, intellectual skills, and substantive knowledge.

Once this is complete, you'll be authorized to take the Foreign

Service Officer Test. The test, which is entirely computer-based, is given four times a year, each time during a window of eight days, at an authorized, proctored test site. The test includes three multiple-choice sections: job knowledge, English expression, and a biographical information section that asks you to describe your work style, your manner of interacting and communicating with others, and your approach to other cultures. Job knowledge questions cover a broad range of topics, including the structure and workings of the U.S. government, U.S. and world history, U.S. culture, psychology, management theory, finance and economics, and world affairs. In addition, you will be given thirty minutes to write an essay on an assigned topic. You can prepare by ordering the study guide and checking out the reading list on the State Department website. Liz says that you should also "regularly read *The Economist, The New York Times,* and *The Washington Post* to get a better understanding of broad international policy trends."

If you pass the written exam, your application will be considered by a Qualifications Evaluation Panel, which will recommend you for the Foreign Service Oral Assessment, a daylong series of case-study exercises that emphasize problem solving, resource management, and quantitative analysis. For instance, you might be asked how you would respond if you found yourself trapped in the embassy during a severe earthquake. I've heard, however, that it sounds easier than it is, so take your study guide and spend a few afternoons practicing in front of the mirror or a friend.

Once you've finished with the entry examinations, it's time for the fun government stuff. You'll be subjected to a background check and will need to submit forms for security clearance. You'll also have to undergo an intense physical so that the State Department can determine your medical fitness and ability to serve overseas. During this stage, candidates can either help or hinder their chances at acceptance. If you're proficient in one or more foreign languages, for instance, you can take a test over the phone and add points to your score. On the other hand, if you have any history of drug or alcohol abuse, or delinquency in repaying debt, the State Department is much more likely to stick your application at the bottom of the pile.

All clear? You're almost there. Now you'll submit a list of desired assignments and will start a seven-week general orientation class in Washington, D.C. There, you'll receive your first post. What can you expect? Well, during their first two-year assignments, all FSOs perform mostly consular work, which often involves working at an American embassy and awarding visas to immigrants and nonimmigrants. However, as we discussed, many day-to-day responsibilities vary based on your chosen career track. A new political affairs FSO, for example, is responsible for developing relationships with political leaders, journalists, labor leaders, and government officials. One FSO I spoke to scoured the local press for controversial pieces and analyzed the issues for her Washington-based management the same morning.

Newly minted FSOs are also assigned to at least one hardship post, which is an assignment where living conditions (the quality of local health care, crime rate, and so on) are considered more difficult than in the United States. Liz did her hardship post in Haiti and lived in Port-au-Prince for the first two years of her career as an FSO. FSOs serving at hardship posts receive a "hardship" differential of between 5 and 25 percent of salary, depending upon the severity of the hardship. Depending on your first assignment, you'll undergo three to twelve months of specialized training and language courses before heading overseas. And because the State Department is so organized, a formal mentoring process kicks in immediately. You'll have a formal career counselor as well as an assigned mentor from a group of FSO volunteers, both of them willing and available to offer you advice and support unique to this stimulating, but stressful, job.

FSOs are on probation for the first five years of their careers, making a salary that steadily increases from the initial $40K, and are then considered "tenured" with the State Department. This tenure is somewhat like university tenure in that you have more overall job security, though you can still be let go if you underperform over a long period of time. FSOs are reviewed for competitive promotions at fixed intervals, with the goal of securing a position in the high-ranking Senior Foreign Service within fifteen years of the start of their careers. As a senior officer, you can be an embassy ambassador in a small country and make upwards of $100K. The three levels in the Senior Foreign Service—officer counselor, minister counselor, and career minister—generate incomes reaching into the mid-$100Ks.

Compared to most employers and even many federal agencies, the State Department boasts some impressive benefits. In addition to offering top-of-the-line health care and retirement savings programs, the foreign service helps new recruits pay down student loans quickly and provides extended paid vacations for FSOs returning from overseas assignments. As an FSO, you'll also have perks like free housing and air travel, not to mention diplomatic status, which means, among other things, that local police won't bother you and that you're free from annoying things like sales tax and import duties.

If you're an adventurer at heart, it's easy to get caught up in the excitement of applying for and obtaining the seemingly glamorous job of an FSO. The written and oral tests will ensure that you have the impeccable communication, problem-solving, and analytical skills to succeed in the State Department, but before accepting an offer, you should think seriously about whether you could stomach the more difficult aspects of life in the foreign service. The ability to function effectively in a foreign culture is a must, and you'll have to stay composed and professional in the face of unfamiliar or threatening situations. And throughout your career, you'll often have to go without the material comforts of home, and there is a chance you could be subjected to some danger. However, if you're tired of hearing Jon Stewart complain and want to make a difference in how the United States is perceived in foreign nations, and you're adventurous enough to take a leap into a career that will provide unpredictable opportunities to reexperience the world every day, the foreign service could be exactly what you're looking for.

NEWS CORRESPONDENT

While I was in college, I had interned at several stations and networks, but when it came time to look for a job, I didn't really call on any of those contacts. I subscribed to an online listing of journalism jobs and sent out lots and lots of videotapes. I mean, I must have mailed more than a hundred tapes to television stations all over the country. I got to know the clerks at the post office personally. I even brought them brownies when I finally landed a job!

—Jamie, thirty, news correspondent

WHEN I WAS A KID, I used to dream about being a newswoman. I had always thought that being on camera, reporting on events like the *Challenger* space shuttle disaster or the fall of the Berlin Wall, was the most glamorous career a girl could have. And when I got to school at Northwestern, I met a lot of people with the same idea. By then I had decided I wanted to be a psychologist or a writer, but many of my schoolmates, enrolled in Northwestern's famed Medill School of Journalism, were already on the path to future news stardom. You'll hear from two of them, Jamie and Peter, in this section.

Broadcast journalism is an interesting field in that there's not a lot written about it—online or otherwise. When I asked news correspondents how they found out how the business works, most said they learned from professors in college or industry mentors shortly thereafter. The U.S. Bureau of Labor Statistics' *Occupational Outlook*

Handbook (*OOH*), however, does offer a comprehensive job description, part of which I will share with you here. The *OOH* tells us that news correspondents gather information, prepare stories, and make broadcasts that inform about local, state, national, and international events and present points of view on current issues. In covering a story, they investigate leads and news tips, look at documents, observe events at the scene, and interview people. If they aren't reporting live from a scene, they may go back to the office to determine the emphasis of the story, write it, and edit accompanying video. The type of material a news correspondent covers and how much control they exert over their stories depends on the individual. For example, Peter, thirty, focuses on breaking news stories as a national correspondent for NBC and often receives specific assignments from a producer, while Jamie, thirty, is a news correspondent for a local network in Tennessee and reports on general interest, Nashville-related stories of her choosing. "My typical day involves arriving at work, calling my contacts, surfing the Internet, and reading as many local papers as I can," Jamie says. "I then pitch my story ideas to producers, set up interviews, and leave with a photographer to shoot. We either return to the station to edit, or a live truck meets us in the field where we put the story together. Basically, it takes nine hours to produce a ninety-second story."

Broadcast employers prefer correspondents to obtain a bachelor's degree in journalism or mass communications, for which you would study subjects such as copy editing, basic reporting, journalism ethics, and television production. However, even more important is relevant on-the-job experience. For this reason, if you're new to the field, you may be better off first pursuing an internship or freelance position at a local station or other news organization. A major advantage of undergraduate journalism programs is that they usually help students secure these types of opportunities. If you didn't attend a journalism school, you're going to have to rely on old-fashioned networking to get your foot in the door. "You have to go out there and show that you're bright and willing to work, and that they should take a chance on you," says Peter, who got his first on-air position in Lexington, Kentucky, at the age of twenty-one. "It'll take awhile, but you'll need to build relationships with people who are in a position to mentor you."

Remember that the larger and more prestigious the network or station, the more competitive the jobs will be, so for your first job, be realistic and set your sights on a smaller outlet. Resources you might find helpful in your search include:

- Broadcast Education Association (www.beaweb.org)
- National Alliance of State Broadcasters Associations (www.careerpage.org)
- National Association of Broadcast Employees and Technicians (www.nabetcwa.org)
- National Association of Broadcasters (www.nab.org)
- The Rundown (www.tvrundown.com)
- TV Jobs (www.tvjobs.com)

When you attract the interest of an employer, you will be asked to submit your résumé and a video montage showcasing your reporting skills. You will have to interview in person, of course, and may have to do an on-camera test as well. "News directors will be looking for someone who reflects the community in which the broadcast airs," says Peter. "But not only do you have to look and act the part, but you really have to know what you're talking about as well." Your first job will likely be as a general assignment correspondent, and then after a few years of experience, you will be qualified to specialize in a particular area (health, technology, foreign policy, et cetera) or move to a larger media outlet. Depending on the specific direction of your career, it may be helpful to eventually earn a master's or Ph.D. in journalism.

A day in the life of a news correspondent is an adventurer's dream, because each one is different, and each one involves being right in the middle of the action. "I don't know what I'll be doing, or where I'll be going, until I get to the office in the morning," says Peter. "I've covered the war in Israel and the tsunami in Indonesia. I've interviewed Fidel Castro and Shamu the killer whale. I've had the opportunity to witness the economic explosion in China firsthand—tasting the pollution and seeing the cars edge out the bicycles. It's only when you physically step into a new culture that you can really understand how the people live, work, and interact. It's exhilarating and exhausting."

To that point, while a career as a news correspondent does offer its share of excitement, it does not lend itself well to a balanced life. Work hours are long, irregular, and hectic, and there is always a new deadline to apply a new dose of pressure. Like other adventurers, news correspondents sometimes find themselves in harm's way. In the initial years of the Iraq War, for example, ABC correspondent Bob Woodruff was severely injured in an explosion and *Christian Science Monitor* reporter Jill Carroll was kidnapped while on assignment. In terms of salary, entry-level, full-time positions start low (think $18K to $25K). "Starting salaries are embarrassing," says Jamie. "As a new reporter, I would cover contract disputes for teachers and labor strikes for firefighters, and they were all earning considerably more money than I was." But, says Peter, "at the beginning of your career, it's not about the money. You want to be in a position to make mistakes while no one is watching." However, although the field is generally not a lucrative one, it's not out of the realm of possibility for top local and national correspondents and anchors to exceed six figures annually.

And what exactly does it take to be in the elite company of the well-known folks we watch on the news every day? The *OOH* cites persistence, initiative, resourcefulness, a commitment to accuracy, a good memory, physical stamina, and emotional stability. "An innate curiosity and some skepticism are important," says Peter. "And since you're the one who's responsible for delivering information to people, you have to bring your best effort to every story. You also have to be willing to learn, from the people whose stories you're sharing as well as other correspondents. Even now that I'm at a network, I still consider myself a student of journalism."

If you're going to be working on air, it makes sense that you have to be comfortable on camera, with an easy-on-the-eyes appearance and a strong speaking voice. Finally, getting started now means you will need to keep your finger on the pulse. Technology is rapidly changing the journalism industry, and in the coming years, some of the most lucrative news correspondent opportunities may be in the digital realm. And most of all, you should be prepared to go wherever your career takes you. "I haven't really had a plan, I've gone where the jobs have taken me," says Jamie. "Because of that, I've lived and worked in Tallahassee, Nashville, and soon, Minneapolis. In each city, I've spent time out in the community meeting an amazing variety of people, and talking to them about the issues that matter most in their lives. I can't imagine an office job offering opportunities like that!"

OCEANOGRAPHER

When we are doing field research on a ship, every day is an adventure. We refer to this type of trip as a "cruise," but it is anything but a relaxing vacation. On an oceanographic cruise, where ship time is on the order of thousands of dollars per day, every second counts. The team typically works twenty-four hours a day, with three groups of people, or "watches," working four hours on, eight hours off. There are always new challenges to face when we discover something new and have to change the science plan, or when something goes wrong with an ROV [remotely operated vehicle] and it needs to be fixed, or when we have to wait for a storm to blow over, or when last week's hamburgers are being served as sloppy joes for dinner. You never know what trials you are going to wake up to every day, and it certainly keeps you on your toes.

—Katy, twenty-eight, oceanographer

OCEANOGRAPHY IS THE STUDY of the biological, chemical, geological, optical, and physical characteristics of oceans and estuaries. According to the Office of Naval Research, it's a relatively young discipline. Although oceans represent more than 70 percent of the earth's surface, as few as fifty years ago 98 percent of the floor remained unexplored. But thanks to oceanographers, we have recently gotten our first glimpses of the deepest ocean trenches and what the water portion of our planet looks like from outer space, have confirmed the theories of plate tectonics and continental drift, and have discovered creatures that don't depend on light to survive. An oceanographer's goal is to understand ocean systems and their relationship to other parts of the earth—such as the atmosphere, solid landmasses, and living organisms—as well as the consequences of human activities on the ocean environment.

The field of oceanography includes a few subspecialties outlined by the Office of Naval Research. Biological oceanographers typically study what controls the numbers and kinds of plants and animals in the marine environment. They are interested in how marine organisms develop, relate to one another, adapt to their environment, and interact with it. Chemical oceanographers study the composition of seawater, its processes and cycles, and the chemical interaction of seawater with the atmosphere and sea floor. Geological oceanographers explore the ocean floor and the processes that form its mountains, canyons, and valleys. Physical oceanographers study the physical conditions and processes within the ocean such as waves, currents, eddies, gyres, and tides, the transport of sand on and off beaches, coastal erosion, and the interactions of the atmosphere and the ocean. There's even such a thing as archaeological oceanography, which integrates archaeological and oceanographic research and involves site mapping, protection of deep sea remains, and artifact conservation. That's twenty-eight-year-old Katy's area of expertise, and the projects she has completed while working for the Scripps Institution of Oceanography and the National Oceanic and Atmospheric Administration (NOAA) recently led her to receive National Geographic's Emerging Explorer award. "I've been involved with a number of diverse projects around the world," she says. "All of these experiences have enhanced my skills in remote survey operations, engineering, navigation, and scuba-diver-based oceanographic and archaeological research."

Oceanographers in all subdisciplines are employed in educational and research institutions, federal government agencies including NOAA and the U.S. Geological Survey, and independent consulting firms. Why do they require an adventurous personality? Well, most oceanographers are hands-on researchers, often traveling around the world and spending months at a time at sea collecting data. The work that follows a scientific cruise, analyzing and interpreting results in the lab using specialized computers and other instruments, can in fact be tedious when compared to the excitement of making a new discovery in the field. Many oceanographers prefer their phantom sea legs to their real legs, and bide their time putting together research and grant proposals, teaching, writing papers for academic and scientific journals, and fine-tuning their equipment—all the while looking forward to their next adventure. Does this sound like your dream job? Here's how you get it.

Oceanography is one of the few scientific careers that do not require an advanced degree for entry. You can get a job as a laboratory technician or an entry-level researcher with any bachelor's degree, although you'll be far more competitive if you majored in one of the basic science disciplines (biology, chemistry, or geology) and can show proficiency in mathematics, writing, computers, data management, and statistics. Before going after a full-time opportunity, however, you should assess whether oceanography is a smart career choice for you. Ideally, your exploration would incorporate an internship or part-time job that allows you to get a flavor for real research. "My first research cruise was the nail in the coffin when it came to deciding on a career path," says Katy. "I joined Dr. Robert Ballard's team from the Institute for Exploration, MIT, the Woods Hole Oceanographic Institution, and other universities and research institutions to search for the ancient Black Sea coastline and potentially well-preserved shipwrecks in the Black Sea's deep, anoxic waters. Those three weeks were a crash course in oceanographic and archaeological research that has inspired me to this day."

Many academic institutions with graduate-level oceanography programs offer summer research opportunities, or you could volunteer to work in the lab for an aquatic scientist in your area. "People are surprised at how easy it is to get involved in research," says Jim, twenty-five, who is working as a research assistant at Oregon State University while he pursues his master's degree in chemical oceanography. "If you are interested in a certain topic, look up what is happening in a relevant scientific journal, see who is publishing on that issue, and contact him or her." Additional sources you might check out for internships and fellowships include:

- American Association for the Advancement of Science (fellowships.aaas.org)

- The Environmental Careers Organization (www.eco.org)
- National Oceanic and Atmospheric Administration (www.rdc.noaa.gov)
- National Sea Grant College Program (www.seagrant.noaa.org)
- Naval Research Enterprise Intern Program (www.onr.navy.mil)

Before or in concert with your hands-on experience, the American Society of Limnology and Oceanography (ASLO, www.aslo.org) recommends reading about whichever ocean environment particularly interests you, as well as about weather and the water cycle. You should also peruse issues of well-known oceanography-related periodicals such as *Nature, Oceanus,* and *Sea Frontiers.* Finally, it will help to become affiliated with ASLO, as well as with the Oceanography Society (www.tos.org). Attending events and seminars sponsored by these organizations will provide you with terrific networking and learning opportunities, as most experienced oceanographers use them to keep up with the latest advances in the field.

Speaking of advancement, if you're diligent, independent, willing to work hard, and a good problem solver, the sky is the limit with an oceanography career. "You can achieve a high degree of success if you have the ability to provide valuable answers to important scientific questions, and also to communicate those answers to scientists, politicians, and people in the general public who care," says Jim. But chances are, you will have to put in some serious time in order to reach the top levels of the profession. Senior scientists and full university professors usually make over six figures and enjoy a fair amount of prestige, but they all have Ph.D. degrees in oceanography that require an additional four to eight years of schooling on top of your undergraduate education. With just a bachelor's, your salary will likely top out around the mid–five figures, so if you're ambitious, you might look to secure funding for graduate study. ASLO tells us that graduate students in oceanography are generally supported financially (that is, with paid tuition and a stipend to cover living, research, and travel expenses) by a variety of methods. These include teaching assistant-ships through one's department or university, graduate research assistantships, and fellowships from a number of agencies including the National Science Foundation (www.fastlane.nsf.gov), the Environmental Protection Agency (www.epa.gov), and the Smithsonian Institution (www.si.edu).

Currently, Jim is working on optimizing the chemistry that allows us to measure copper. He just finished a research project in the Gulf of Aqaba in Israel, in which he measured iron, and is preparing to travel to Monterey Bay to deploy a new copper instrument. "Working at sea is both fun and monotonous," he says. "In my experience, even the largest of ships become quite small after a few months of being trapped on them with the same people. We work long hours, and sometimes the work is repetitive and mundane—like pipetting fluid into multiple bottles for hours on end—but it's worth it because I'm always learning." Indeed, most oceanographers possess a high degree of job satisfaction. "I love my job," says Katy. "At any given moment, it can be exciting, challenging, exhilarating, tiring, amusing, stressful, fast-paced . . . and the list goes on. I am privileged to work with a talented team of scientists and engineers who both work well and play well together. I look forward to going to sea every year with this group because we always have a good time while getting the job done."

OUTDOOR ADVENTURE GUIDE

I grew up kayaking, and when I first came to Washington, I ran into some rafters on the Sauk River and asked them where I should go for guide training. They pointed me in the right direction, and after training, I ended up getting work first on the Skagit River in the winter doing Bald Eagle floats, and then I got hired by a larger company that has permits on eleven different rivers here in the North Cascades. I was really busy the next seven summers running all over the state playing on all the rivers and loving it. People are always telling me to get a real job, and I look around and say, "How do you get any more real than this?"

—Jeff, thirty-four, outdoor adventure guide

MY FRIENDS AND I HAVE ALWAYS enjoyed traveling to exotic destinations, even before ecotourism was as hot as it is now. I've been scuba diving in Tahiti, white-water rafting in New Zealand, and zip-lining in Costa Rica. I'm not the most intrepid of adventurers, however, so I always take a guided trip. While the group is learning how not to get killed in the wild, the conversation inevitably strays to the leader's line of work. Outdoor adventure guides think they have the coolest jobs in the world, and many of us would agree. Is this something that you could actually do for a career, though? Let's find out.

Outdoor adventure guides organize and lead expeditions around the globe. According to Monster, a guide is responsible for making all travel arrangements, including reserving lodging and dining, scheduling excursions, assembling equipment and supplies, and arranging for visas. During trips, the guide educates participants on cultural customs and the natural surroundings, coaching individuals on the basics of activities and overseeing the group's safety.

Although you can now hire an outdoor guide to do just about anything anywhere (ascend Mount Fuji, chill with the penguins in Antarctica, et cetera), the majority of those employed in this field provide guidance for the more common adventure fare, such as hiking, rock climbing, diving, kayaking, sailing, rafting, camping, skiing, biking, and horseback riding. They typically work for tour companies, resorts, and parks. It is usually the more seasoned guides who have their own businesses, for it takes a lot of knowledge about the market for your particular activity and your area's tourism market in general in order to be successful. Also, the management and administrative aspects of running an entrepreneurial venture often don't appeal to adventurers who would rather be at the center of the action.

Depending on the specific situation, customers may be run-of-the-mill tourists who need lots of hand-holding, or may be physically fit, experienced connoisseurs of nature who can give the guide himself a run for his money. "Every day on the river is different for me—different lines through the white-water rapids and different guests along for the ride," says Jeff, thirty-four, an outdoor adventure guide in Washington. "As the trip leader, I'm responsible for everyone on the raft, and that's fun. I get to be the primary entertainer, which includes giving the intro and the paddle briefing before the trip, but I also talk to my guests about the places we're going so that they can help preserve and protect them."

An up-and-coming specialty in the outdoor adventure field is experiential education. Experiential educators include instructors, camp counselors, and mental health professionals who teach through direct experience. Many of these individuals use outdoor recreation activities to help people overcome emotional and behavioral disorders. "I work an eight-day-on, six-day-off schedule with a group of approximately eight to twelve teenagers. The wilderness is used as a therapeutic intervention for kids facing challenges in their lives," says Karyn, thirty-one, an experiential educator in Georgia. "We sleep under tarps, hike frequently, hold groups, and work one-on-one with the students. I love my job as it gives me a chance to work with kids at a point when they are really struggling with their identities."

As you can imagine, one thing most outdoor adventure guides have in common is an irregular schedule. In North America especially, adventure guiding tends to be seasonal, meaning that you either work during the warm or the cold months. And even during the period that you're supposedly on, you might go days or even weeks without working. "If you're a summer guide, seasonal work can be hard," says Jeff. "But it can work out well if you have a ski area close by to work at during the winter. Besides, it prevents burnout when you can end a long season of doing what you love by changing things up a bit, and doing something else that you love."

Educational requirements for becoming an outdoor adventure guide vary. Most travel companies require only a high school diploma, provided you have significant training and/or certification in the sport or activity you'll be leading. Not everyone who likes vacationing in the mountains is qualified to lead a snowshoeing expedition, for example, and your potential employer will expect you to be able to perform your activity of choice at a substantially higher level than the average customer. Chances are, you will need to be certified in first aid and CPR as well. In the coming years, experiential educators will likely be required to have an additional accreditation from the Association for Experiential Education (www.aee.org).

The bottom line is, you'll want to make sure you have the right qualifications before you go out and apply to be an adventure guide. You can find out by searching for job advertisements describing the type of guide position you're interested in. For instance, as a result of my research for this section, I learned that an outdoor guide in Dobbs Ferry, New York, must come to the table with ropes certification and two years of experience leading outdoor recreation programs, and a hiking guide in Salt Lake City, Utah, must have wilderness first-responder certification, a basic understanding of bike mechanics, and extensive knowledge of the region. Nearly all tour companies I reviewed also required new guides to attend at least a few days of orientation and training prior to their first assignment. As you're getting acquainted with the field, here are some places to scout out:

- Backdoor Jobs (www.backdoorjobs.com)
- CoolWorks (www.coolworks.com)

- Environmental Career Opportunities (www.ecojobs.com)
- GORP (gorp.away.com)
- JobMonkey (www.jobmonkey.com)
- Looking for Adventure (www.lookingforadventure.com)
- Outdoor Adventure Professional Network (www.oapn.net)
- *Outside* magazine (outside.away.com)

What else should potential outdoor adventure guides be prepared for? Well, as you have no doubt guessed, these positions are physically demanding. While on the job, you may be living fairly primitively, and you'll have to keep a cool head during the emergency situations that will inevitably arise. Also, like other adventurer careers, some amount of risk comes with the territory. "You could get hurt, of course," says Peter Voyt, in his Monster article on adventure careers. "But there's also risk and ambiguity in trying to find an adventure job in the first place, keeping that job once you've got it, and making enough money to take care of yourself."

Speaking of salary, it probably won't come as a surprise that people who get to spend all day outdoors doing what they love generally don't make a whole lot of money. There's no industry standard for what guides get paid, but I've been told that they can make anywhere from $18K to $40K a year, or $75 to $300 a day. Fortunately, benefits are usually included with jobs that are considered full-time. "Most companies include health care, and mine has a 401(k) package and quarterly bonuses," says Karyn. "Plus, you are not able to spend any money while you're working in the woods, so smaller dollars go a little farther."

Successful outdoor guides are the consummate adventurers. Not only do they cope with uncertainty well and respond effectively to adversity, but they also love sharing their enthusiasm for nature and sport with others. Reliable and patient, they sweat the big stuff (like giving accurate directions to a hiking group or leading a raft full of tourists out of dangerous white water), but are more apt to let small setbacks go. Those who are also great teachers and communicators will be most likely to win the choicest positions as the demand for eco-tourism services continues to increase. "If you're outgoing, support-ive, and a good listener, you'll find that this profession is pretty open to people with various skill sets and interests," says Karyn. "And while sometimes I get stressed out when we have lots of kids or my staff is demanding, I cannot imagine a job I would rather have."

TRAVEL JOURNALIST

My stories are based on horses and travel, two things you can't always control, so having an adventurous spirit is important. In Spain, I rode the horse that the queen rides when she visits Doñana National Park on the southern coast, and the plan was for me to canter over this large set of dunes on the way to the ocean. A member of my staff was hang-ing out of a jeep in front of me, as I rode behind. Well, Figo, the horse that I was riding, thought that we were racing the jeep, so as the jeep accelerated, so did Figo. I was motioning for them to slow the jeep down, and of course, they thought I wanted to speed up, so we were flying over these dunes. I ended up just sitting back and smiling. Sometimes you just have to let go.

—Darley, twenty-seven, travel journalist

IN MY SURVEY RANKING the most desirable jobs for twenty- and thirtysomethings, travel journalist was number one—by a landslide. It's easy to see why. Who wouldn't want to get paid to fly to exotic loca-tions, poke around all the coolest places, and then write about their impressions and opinions? Breaking into this highly sought after field is not as difficult as you might think. In his *Travel Writer's Guide,* Gordon Burgett claims that nothing is easier to sell in the writing world than travel, and it's estimated that around a million articles are published each year. "It was a risk, moving away from a regular salary and betting that I could make it as a freelance writer," says Darley, twenty-seven, a travel journalist and the producer of the PBS travel series *Equitrekking.* "But if you can find a niche in the marketplace and convey your passion, then you have a good chance of succeeding." In this section, we'll look primarily at two forms of income-generating travel journalism—writing for newspapers and magazines, and authoring travel guides.

Let's start with newspapers and magazines. Obviously, the best gig you can have is to be on the editorial staff of a publication that regularly runs travel pieces, but these jobs are exceptionally competitive, and chances are you won't get one without a great deal of experience doing freelance work first. In other words, you'll have to start small, perhaps with local newspapers. Travel editors at these publications are most receptive to freelancers because it costs a lot less to buy a story and photos from an individual than to pay to send a reporter to a far-off destination. According to L. Peat O'Neil, author of *Travel Writing: See the World, Sell the Story,* the preferred method of selling to newspaper editors is to e-mail the complete story (800 to 1,000 words), including a short sidebar on where to stay and eat, and photos. This means that not only will you have had to do some traveling on your own dime first, but you'll also have to research the demographic markets your story will appeal to most, the travel story format of the newspapers that cater to those markets, and the current lifestyle and leisure trends your story can hook into. Note that 900 words do not give you a lot of space to play around with, so you'll have to practice writing tightly. O'Neil suggests that a great way to break in is to think regional. Editors at your local newspaper will be hard pressed to turn down a story by a native that offers an insider's perspective of an attractive vacation destination.

Gordon Burgett tells us that consumer magazines (*Travel & Leisure, National Geographic Traveler, Condé Nast Traveler,* et cetera) and specialty/trade magazines (*American Bicyclist, AAA Going Places,* United Airlines' *Hemispheres,* et cetera) are a travel writer's best market. Unlike most newspaper editors, magazine editors will commission an article before you take a trip, so Burgett says that you should start by researching the magazines in which you'd like to appear and determining the type and style of stories that occupy their pages. For example, you might decide that you want to publish a story in Southwest Airlines' *Spirit* magazine. After reviewing the publication, you'd note that *Spirit* targets educated travelers and frequently prints anecdotal, in-depth feature stories about destinations in the western United States where the airline flies. The articles include provocative photography and are written in a witty and enthusiastic tone. Based on this information, you'd have a good shot at pitching a first-person account of your adventures as a business traveler exploring New Mexico. If the editor says yes, you're on your way. You'll probably have to pay the majority of your own expenses, but at least you'll be going with a bona fide assignment in hand. Now you'll actually have to write your magazine article. Here are some tips for making that part of your journey a success:

- Research your location so that you have a working knowledge of the place before you get there.
- Take a photography class so that you can visually document your travels with skill.
- Get more bang (and stories) for your buck by using one trip to visit a variety of interesting places in geographic proximity to one another.
- Keep a journal of observations that are uniquely yours and offer a fresh perspective. Tell your destination's story in a way that it hasn't been told before.
- Use sensory details to make people and places come alive for your readers.

- Don't fall into a boring narrative pattern of "first I did this, then I did that." Choose a compelling theme for your piece, and create a story line around it.
- Be vigilant about accuracy: check your facts and make sure you have names and titles spelled correctly.

It will undoubtedly take some time to become established in the freelance travel journalism world. The most important thing you can do in the beginning is to build a body of published work, which in the beginning may mean writing for any outlet that will have you, including your alumni newsletter or a mom-and-pop website. "Even if you're taking unpaid jobs and writing for free, it all adds to your clip collection and establishes more credibility for later on," says Darley. I also heard from several journalists that you can jump-start your career by selling each story idea to multiple, noncompeting publications, but this can be tricky, so make sure you know the rules pertaining to your situation. Last, but certainly not least, remember your humility. "I can't tell you how many people try to do the whole freelancing thing and act like prima donnas," says Matt, thirty-one, a travel journalist based in Northern California. "Every assignment is something worth gratitude. Every editing session is an opportunity to learn something about the craft. Editors appreciate a modest approach." Lots of help is available for newbie newspaper and magazine travel journalists—you might check out the American Society of Journalists and Authors (www.asja.org), the Society of Professional Journalists (www.spj.org), or online resources such as Travelwriters.com (www.travelwriters .com), goTravelNews.com (www.gotravelnews.com), and the Travel Writer's Life (www.thetravelwriterslife.com).

Another option for those who want to be travel writers is to author guidebooks for organizations such as Lonely Planet, Frommer's, and Let's Go. These publishers generally hire a different person for each title, and base their evaluation of candidates on the requirements of the destination. Unlike other writing-related jobs, formal education isn't mandatory so long as you have excellent writing and language skills, extensive travel experience, a good understanding of the destination's culture, the ability to work under fixed deadlines, and, of course, a sense of adventure. You should be prepared for the fact that guidebook writing isn't as easy and glamorous as it sounds, and may at times be repetitive, stressful, and even dangerous. Guidebook authors are expected to write tens of thousands of words and work impossibly long hours. And while researching this section, I read a *New York Times* story about a thirty-year-old Lonely Planet writer who got attacked and pistol-whipped when he walked out of a bar in Caracas, Venezuela. This type of experience is not all that unusual. Fortunately, guidebook publishers do their part to make sure new authors are up to the task. Before going on assignment, they're given twenty hours of training in subjects like self-defense, cartography, and driving, and sometimes do a dry run in the United States before leaving for foreign soil.

Travel journalism has its share of tough realities, and you have to be a particular type of adventurer in order to make it work for you. "My job is different every day, and sometimes I have no structure," says Matt. "But I still have to have a near-anal sense of organization, and the discipline to go out and get stories on my own, because the work isn't just going to fall in my lap. I always have to be motivated to push myself." Everyone in the field, though, agrees that there are significant advantages to committing to a career as a travel journalist. "There are so many interesting characters around the world, and I enjoy exploring a place with the locals and seeing life through their eyes, even if it is only for a few days," says Darley. "With my job, you are constantly reminded of other people's perspectives." And contrary to what you may have heard, it's even possible to make a decent living. While you won't be able to support yourself writing newspaper stories, which generally pay just a few hundred dollars each, magazine and guidebook assignments are more lucrative. It's not unheard of for an established magazine writer to get high four figures for a single piece, and guidebooks pay anywhere from low four figures to low six figures, depending on the length of the journey and the resulting material. One thing's for sure: it's a big world out there, and if you're a competent writer and you want to get a well-rounded view of everything the earth has to offer, there's no better way to do it than to be a travel journalist.

The Creator

Acting appeals tremendously to the creative side. I love telling stories, and it's immensely fulfilling to be able to do that for my life's work. There's always a lot of autonomy when creating a character (good directors generally look for a collaborative process), but, for me, my favorite acting challenge is when I get to perform in a new play. Creating a character from scratch, working with a playwright as well as a director, and getting in on the ground level of a story is something that I find very rewarding.

—Kyle, twenty-eight, actor

WHEN I TALK TO PEOPLE ABOUT THEIR DREAM JOBS, most mention at least one career that allows them to express their inner creativity. For these individuals, creativity equals fulfillment, and the highest value is placed upon it. But what is creativity exactly, and what makes a creator? The famous psychologist Carl Rogers described creativity as the emergence of a novel, relational product that grows out of the uniqueness of the individual. Henry Miller, the author of classics *The Tropic of Cancer* and *The Tropic of Capricorn,* said it is the occurrence of a composition that is both new and valuable. Renowned creativity expert Roger von Oech identified a creator as one who imagines familiar things in a new light.

Whatever the official definition, personality experts agree that creative types find satisfaction in developing products such as art, music, or physical spaces that allow them to express themselves and their distinctive worldviews. "I love playing around with colors and creating natural, beautiful cosmetics that I myself want to wear," says Kristin, twenty-nine, a makeup designer. Ryan, a twenty-six-year-old chef, feels the same way when it comes to food. "It's wonderful to find inspiration in everyday life," he says. "One of the most rewarding parts of my job is discovering a brand-new flavor that I can incorporate into my signature dishes." Similarly, creators enjoy the challenge of turning a vision into a practical reality. "As an artist, the single most daunting test you'll face is figuring out how to make a concept work, how to achieve a look while maintaining a budget," says Peter, twenty-five, a video game designer.

Emotional and imaginative, the creator intuitively sees beauty and feeling, or the potential of beauty and feeling, in an empty space. "At the very beginning of a project, I'll go and just stand in the location," says Jaime, twenty-four, a landscape architect. "I'll spend a lot of time thinking about how it's going to feel when we're done." Laurel, a twenty-eight-year-old book author, told me that how she feels and what she writes go hand in hand. "Writing is actually a very personal experience," she says. "My letters to loved ones will often elicit tears, and I'll scribble journal entries when I'm depressed." And while creators certainly need to draw on their inner resources to craft a tour de force, they don't discount the importance of communicating openly with the people they work with and for. "Maintaining our standard as

> I dream of being a fashion designer. I'm a small size and I can never find nice-fitting business clothes, and when I do, I have to buy them right away and miss out on the sale events. I've always imagined starting a fashion line for petite, chic, and urban girls so they wouldn't have a hard time shopping for anything, and my friend and I have talked about opening up a clothing shop that combines her Indian heritage and my Latina heritage.
>
> —*Maria, twenty-four*

a premier label is all about communication with our vendors," confirms Emily, twenty-five, a fashion designer. Thirty-nine-year-old Bryan, an interior designer, adds: "The ability to listen to what a client is really saying is incredibly important in realizing her vision for her home."

More than any other passion profile, the creator prefers a flexible work environment that encourages originality and the freedom to do his own thing. Chris, a twenty-nine-year-old video game designer, has what he considers a perfect situation. "I never have to set my alarm," he says. "And as for dress code, there isn't one. I could go in naked if I wanted to, as long as I didn't mind the awkward stares and the chafing from the chair I sit in all day." Andrew, a thirty-one-year-old professional musician, likes that his career choice supports his wandering tendencies. "I've moved around the country a lot," he says. "I find that the change in setting keeps me inspired." Not surprisingly, many creators dislike conformity and are prone to making impulsive decisions in pursuit of their goals. "I once snuck into a big agency party in Hollywood," says Jon, thirty-two, a screenwriter. "My friend and I were joking around in loud Boston accents, which caught the attention of a junior studio executive standing nearby. It was risky, but I ended up becoming friends with this guy, and that's what jump-started my career." When he was fresh out of culinary school, twenty-six-year-old Phil spontaneously applied to work at a gourmet food store in one of the wealthiest towns in the country. "When I had to cook for the head chef, I almost choked," says Phil. "But he called me and said the food was great, and I got the job!"

Creators want to be considered important contributors in any and all tasks. "I love that I have a high degree of input into our projects," says Chris. "If I want to pitch a new game idea, I simply turn around in my chair and yell it out to the owner of my company." They also thrive on praise for their work. "I remember people's reactions to my first performance in front of an audience,"

> The screenwriter and musician jobs both provide a high degree of creative expression. It goes without saying that movies and music often have a lasting impact on their audiences, so I see that these jobs would be incredibly fulfilling.
>
> —*Marc, twenty-nine*

says Kyle. "The laughter was really loud, and there was so much more of it than I expected—and it felt good." Sharon, a thirty-seven-year-old book author, agrees. "It's so much fun to hear from couples who got married, thanking me for the ideas I sent them or telling me that my advice saved their day." On the other hand, though, creators don't necessarily need praise to feel good about themselves, for there is a certain amount of ego involved in having a successful creative career. I think it's only natural given that many creators endure constant rejection and have only their own self-worth to rely on. "You have to be confident in yourself, accepting that even if you're in the lucky working minority, you'll still hear a hundred no's for every yes," says Ryan, thirty, an actor. Indeed, confidence was a theme that came up again and again in my conversations with creators. "You have to be secure in what you're doing because you can't write trying to anticipate the market's flavor of the day," advises Ben, thirty-four, a movie screenwriter. And sometimes, confidence means having the courage to break free from what you were taught. "The truth is, what your teacher told you to do might not be right for you," says Paul, twenty-eight, a professional musician. "You have to be true to yourself, in what you play and how you play it." Jaime expressed a similar sentiment. "You have to be an advocate for your own vision, because it might be different from what your employer is expecting."

As people who see the big picture, creators may sometimes forget how a whole is the sum of its parts. Step-by-step project execution and an endless stream of details can get them down. "I dislike the coordination of the business side," admits Emily. Chad, a thirty-one-year-old interior designer, feels the same way. "Artists should never be allowed to have checkbooks," he says. "Early on, I realized I am not good with money, so I hired someone to handle the finances." But for many creators, the lack of rigid organization leads to a sort of frenetic efficiency. "My schedule as an author varies from having a string of ten appearances in ten days in ten cities to sitting at home writing from the moment I wake up to the moment I fall asleep," says Laurel. "For an ADD person like me, this is the ideal job!"

> Being an interior designer shows that you have an eye for style and are extremely creative. With the advent of shows like *While You Were Out* on TLC and *My Celebrity Home* on the Style Network, who wouldn't want to have this job?
>
> —*Schnelle, twenty-two*

The creator jobs in this chapter—actor, book author, fashion designer, interior designer, landscape architect, movie screenwriter, performance musician, restaurant chef, and video game designer—were selected as some of the most popular occupations in my survey. They are the careers that people tend to desire, envy, and compete for the most. However, as you'll see by reading about the incredible individuals in this chapter, finding employment in a creative field is definitely possible with a little ingenuity and a lot of passion. Let's see how it's done.

ACTOR
• • • • • • • •

> The first time I was ever on a real film set, I did a commercial standing on a bus, singing to a group of kids about cell phones. After a full day in which everything that could have gone wrong did, I realized that my earpiece was gone. I had to stop the shoot—a big faux pas—to explain what was wrong. The whole crew sighed as if to say, "You're keeping me from having dinner with my family, kid." Well, all my professionalism went out the window and I burst into tears. That day, I learned that my main job as an actor is to handle the inevitable pressure, give the director what he wants, and not mess up. That day had nothing to do with "acting." It was about juggling, balance, confidence. As an actor, you'll never be in the same situation twice. The game is to be comfortable without knowing what's going to happen.
>
> —Ryan, thirty, actor

THOUGH I WASN'T SURPRISED when acting came in near the top of my surveyed list of dream careers, I hesitated to include it in this book. Because while I do personally believe that acting is one of the most intriguing professions out there, I don't think that most people sit down and consciously, as they do with many of the other jobs in this book, weigh the pros and cons. Indeed, the creative people I interviewed said that they became actors because they couldn't do anything else, because it's the only thing that fulfills them emotionally. They live with the knowledge that their odds of success are very low, and that finding work doesn't get easier—and they persevere. In case you are among this passionate, dedicated group, and know you want to be an actor no matter what, read on. Hopefully this section will have some news you can use!

Acting is one of the few careers in which formal training is de-emphasized. Some would-be actors study in college, and even fewer pursue a master of fine arts in acting. Good actors are always learning, however, so most find studio or even community acting classes and workshops to be helpful in mastering the craft and shaping their careers. "I suggest finding a studio and treating it like a gym," says Ryan, thirty, an actor in Los Angeles. "Go to work out your acting and to hook up with a community of motivated actors who understand the realities of the business and are working on their careers daily." Word on the street is that the best acting schools include the Actors Center (www.theactorscenter.org), the T. Schreiber Studio (www.tschreiber.org), and the Stella Adler Studio (www.stellaadler.com)—not just for the quality of the education, but because of the invaluable industry contacts you'll make there.

Basic acting classes will teach you essentials such as how to develop a character, how to work with a script, how to use your voice, and how to move on stage and on camera. You may also learn different techniques of acting, such as Stanislavski, Meisner, and Adler. If you can only afford a few classes, choose carefully those that fulfill your needs, zero in on what you need to work on, and help you improve the qualities that make you special. Just make sure you ask a trusted professional for a recommendation before opening your wallet. The Internet in particular is notorious for serving up shady services for actors. Getting your career off the ground will be tough enough without being burned by a scam.

Whether you decide to invest in training or not, prospective actors should always be performing—for free if necessary. Katherine Mayfield, author of *Acting A to Z,* suggests getting started by auditioning for community theater or college productions in your area. The more experience you can get, the better off you'll be, and you'll build your résumé as you go. Local theater will also connect you with other actors, who are the best source of information about viable opportunities. You can also learn the ropes by acting in student films, which you can find out about by calling your local college's film or media arts program, or low budget independent films, which sometimes offer open casting calls advertised in local newspapers. Finally, if you contact your local film commission to find out about studio movies scheduled to be filmed in your area, there's a chance you could get work as an extra.

Once you have some expertise under your belt, your goal will be to join the ranks of "working" actors. Working actors, you should note, make an average of $5K a year and have day jobs to support themselves financially. "If you're doing this job for the money, find something else," says Kyle, twenty-nine, an actor in New York. "Unless you're really, *really* lucky, you're not going to get rich acting." Working actors usually reside in the entertainment industry hubs of New York and Los Angeles, and they are constantly on the road. "I'd say about 90 percent of my time as an actor is split between preparing for auditions, driving to auditions, waiting in hallways to audition, and then actually auditioning," says Ryan. "Another 7 percent of my time is dedicated to marketing and representation issues, and if I'm lucky, 3 percent of the time I get to be on a set actually filming something."

Working actors read trade newspapers like *Back Stage, Drama-Logue,* and *Variety* and websites like the ActorSite (www.actorsite.com) and Actingbiz (www.actingbiz.com) regularly, and constantly have their noses on the trail of what's being cast, where, and by whom. In order to become one of them, you'll want to have a headshot, or an eight-by-ten professional photograph of yourself, taken. The best headshots are natural and actually look like you—or so I've heard. On the back of the headshot, you can print your résumé, or a roster of your recent acting jobs and experiences. Although many working actors periodically send their headshots, résumés, or current achievements to casting directors via postcards or e-mail blasts, securing auditions is most efficient when you're represented by a talent agent who lines up opportunities and negotiates jobs for you.

According to the Screen Actors Guild (SAG, www.sag.org), agents are much more receptive when someone they know introduces you to them. Obtain referrals by networking with people you meet in the business: for example, if a casting director likes your audition, ask him if he knows any agents. If you do attempt to contact an agent without a referral, keep your marketing materials simple—a headshot and résumé will do. In your cover letter, highlight any recent awards or reviews, and invite the agent to see you in any current performances that showcase your talent. And before you sign, make sure the agent is a member of the Association of Talent Agents (www.agentassociation.com) and is endorsed by the Screen Actors Guild and/or the Actor's Equity Association. Reputable talent agents should not charge you anything until you work, at which time they are entitled to 10 percent of your earnings as a performer. "At the start of your career, be prepared to fight for representation," says Ryan. "There are at least ten people who look just like you and are just as talented as you, and your challenge is to show agents why you'll be easier to sell than the look-alikes."

As a working actor, auditions will be a staple of everyday life, and you'll need to know the lay of the land. While some auditions are open call, which means anyone can show up, most are by invitation only, which is why an agent comes in handy. Once you receive your sides—or a couple of script pages you'll be expected to read—study the character and learn your lines. On the day of the audition, dress in something the character might wear, but don't let your "costume" overshadow your performance. Arrive a few minutes early so that you can warm up your vocal cords and rehearse your lines one last time. As you're auditioning for the casting director, try to perform the role as you would in the actual production. If the casting director likes you, you'll be "called back" to audition again. This time, there will be fewer actors competing for the role, and more people present in the audition, such as producers and studio executives. Repeat your original performance as closely as possible, and don't freak out if they ask you for a different take on the scene. They're probably just testing how well you can take direction. Still, you may not get the part. "You face rejection constantly," says Kyle. "For how you look, what you sound like, the way you move, et cetera. The key is to realize that while you as an *actor* may be rejected, no one can reject you *as a person*. You have to maintain a separate sense of self-worth."

The Screen Actors Guild tells us that to most people in the entertainment world, "professional" actor means "union" actor. Unions negotiate and enforce collective bargaining agreements that establish equitable levels of compensation, benefits, and working conditions for performers. Film actors need to join the Screen Actors Guild if they want to work on most Hollywood movies or commercials. To work in network or cable television, actors should join the American Federation of Television and Radio Artists (AFTRA, www.aftra.org), and to work on Broadway and in larger theaters, you will probably need to be a member of the Actor's Equity Association (www.actorsequity.org). You're typically eligible to join these unions after you've worked on a few affiliated productions, but specific requirements vary by the organization.

Union membership is another step forward in your acting career, but you still have a long way to go. SAG reports that most performers need several income streams to earn enough money to sustain performing as a full-time career. For instance, one year they might have SAG earnings of $7K, AFTRA earnings of $12K, and Equity earnings of $13K. "There's a natural ebb and flow to this business," says Kyle. "Some months you'll be the hottest thing walking with more work than you can shake a stick at. But there will be times when no one remembers who you are. You just have to ride it out. Things in this industry can happen *so* quickly, and you have to be ready to grab that next opportunity."

BOOK AUTHOR
• • • • • • • • • • • •

I can write while at the coffee shop, on vacation, on a train—inspiration comes out of nowhere. I get to be creative with the things that happen in my life. For instance, once I made a bunch of football-related bets with someone I was dating. The guy didn't last, but I took that concept and turned it into a book about how couples can play and enjoy sports together. I love that I can take a simple idea and transform it into content that will be useful and meaningful for people.

—Sharon, thirty-seven, book author

LOTS OF PEOPLE DREAM of writing books. How many times have you heard a friend talk about writing the Great American Novel, or maybe his fabulous idea for a humor book? Although the popular saying goes "Every person has a book in him," writing is one of those careers that many think of as shrouded in mystery and virtually unattainable. As an insider, I can tell you that becoming a professional author is every bit as possible as breaking into many of the other jobs in this book. Success doesn't necessarily require a master's degree in creative writing, or any other type of official education. However, like the individuals in other competitive careers, you will need a systematic approach and a great deal of persistence and determination to make your dream a reality. Let's look at some specifics.

In this section, we'll talk about two types of books: fiction and nonfiction. If you want to become an author, the first thing you will need is another job. As a fiction writer, you'll have to pay the bills while you take writing workshops, draft and edit your novel for publication, and send it out for professional review. Though you can receive upwards of five figures for a first novel, you won't see a penny until a publishing house buys it, and this won't happen until you have a polished final product. The nonfiction market is a bit different. You can sell a book on the basis of a proposal and receive a four- or five-figure advance to write it, but publishers will want to see that you have the right knowledge and experience to be a credible author. Your other job—the one that supports you financially—may very well provide that expertise. Twenty-eight-year-old Laurel, for example, had several years under her belt as a magazine fitness and beauty editor when she sold her first nonfiction self-help book, *The Gurus' Guide to Serenity*. Laurel's situation is not uncommon. Working journalists have the easiest time selling books because they have a built-in audience, have niche subjects they know inside and out, and have proven writing ability. The point, though, is that it's usually not practical to quit your day job right away, and in fact you may have to work in another field for several years as you strive to get your writing career off the ground.

Whether you set out to write fiction or nonfiction, you'll want to do some research before getting started. Look in Barnes & Noble or on Amazon for books similar to the one you want to write, and note how they are structured, sold, and marketed. If you're a chef or a psychologist who wants to get into the nonfiction book business, read as many culinary or self-help books as you can get your hands on. Similarly, novelists should be well versed and competent in their genre of choice. Test your marketability and skill level by submitting short pieces to writing contests and literary journals such as *Glimmer Train, McSweeney's,* and *Zoetrope: All-Story*. And if you want to write for teenagers, for instance, familiarize yourself with the titles featured on top children's book websites such as the American Library Association (www.ala.org) and School Library Journal (www.schoollibrary journal.com).

Online forums such as WritersNet (www.writers.net) and Absolute Write (www.absolutewrite.com), and trade magazines like *Writer's Digest, The Writer,* and *Publishers Weekly,* provide valuable information for all writers. Networking with other authors, of course, is a great way to find out what's out there and to keep tabs on industry trends. Joining associations such as the Society of Children's Book Writers and Illustrators (SCBWI, www.scbwi.org) or the American Society of Journalists and Authors (ASJA, www.asja.org), forming online or in-person critique groups, and attending local or national writers' conferences serve the additional purposes of helping you fine-tune your writing, locate people who are interested in your work, and find a sense of community. "Being around intriguing people awakens my own enthusiasm," says Laurel. "Passion breeds passion."

Once research has informed the strategy for your novel or nonfiction proposal, you're ready to write! Ironically, for some new book authors this is the most difficult part. "Writing books for a living can be challenging because your day lacks structure," says Shari, thirty, a novelist. Laurel agrees and adds: "You have to be a self-starter, because no one is going to get you up in the morning to start writing. You are wholly responsible for whether you finish or not, so you have to be disciplined." Your nonfiction proposal, or a thorough outline of your book idea, should include a summary of the topics you'll cover, a description of the market and target audiences, a brief analysis of the competition, how you'll conduct your research (primary sources, interviews, and so on), your professional biography and credentials, a proposed table of contents, and a few sample chapters. Your completed fiction novel should be around 85,000 to 100,000 words (young-adult books can be a bit shorter) and should fit into an existing genre category such as literary fiction, women's fiction, romance, or science fiction. Countless books exist on how to write and edit a great novel, and I advise you to consult the experts as you develop your theme, plot, and characters. The authors I interviewed cited several favorite resources, including E. M. Forster's *Aspects of the Novel,* Browne and King's *Self-Editing for Fiction Writers,* Sol Stein's *Stein on Writing,* and Strunk and White's *The Elements of Style.*

When your novel or proposal is ready for prime time, you'll need to turn your attention to the task of finding a literary agent. While some smaller and independent publishers do accept submissions directly from authors, agents are the channel through which the majority of books are published. If an agent decides that your book has potential, she will use her connections to get the project sold to a reputable publishing house in exchange for 15 percent of your earnings. Because agents are busy and their reputations are on the line, they are extremely selective in signing unpublished authors as new clients. Your first step should be to target agents who represent your type of book. If you can get an author to refer you directly to his agent, this is the best way to proceed. Otherwise, thumb through popular guides such as the *Literary Marketplace, Writer's Market,* and *Jeff Herman's Guide to Book Publishers, Editors, and Literary Agents,* and locate agent names in the acknowledgments sections of favorite books in your genre. In making a list of twenty to twenty-five agents who you believe would be the best fit for your material, make sure your targets are members of the Association of Authors' Representatives (AAR), have solid sales records, and charge absolutely no fees besides the standard 15 percent commission. It's unfortunate, but there are incompetent and unethical agents out there who run scams capitalizing on the publishing hopes of naïve new authors. You should make initial contact with each agent via a query letter, or an attention-grabbing teaser, no longer than a few paragraphs, that stimulates interest in your book. Although most queries are sent by e-mail these days, there are still agents who insist on the traditional approach of a snail-mail letter accompanied by a self-addressed stamped envelope (SASE) for their reply. For more specifics on writing a query that will stand out from the hundreds agents get every day, check out *How to Write Irresistible Query Letters* by Lisa Collier Cool.

You've delivered a compelling, creative product, so logic says you should sign with an agent and have your first book published within a few years. However, most new authors are unprepared for the enormous amount of rejection that comes with the territory. "You have to have a very thick skin," says Sharon, thirty-seven, a wedding book writer and novelist. "You have to keep pushing forward when you're getting all no's. Some editors will say horrific things about your writing, but if it's constructive, you have to be able to accept it." However, if despite your best efforts, your attempts to secure agent representation don't bear fruit, you could consider an alternative medium such as self-publishing, online print on demand (POD), or e-book publishing. Self-publishing requires the author to bear the entire cost of publication and to handle all marketing and distribution. POD is digital printing technology that allows a book to be printed and bound in minutes, and authors pay on a per-sale basis. E-book publishing, which is still largely unused by the mainstream but has a good amount of potential, delivers books and other content to readers electronically, using open e-book standard software and handheld readers. Top services including iUniverse (www.iuniverse.com) and Lulu (www.lulu.com) offer authors a combination of these alternative publication vehicles. Keep in mind, though, that these mediums still lack the prestige of commercial publishing, and if your goal is a long-term, profitable writing career, you're still better off going the traditional route—even if it means selling your book to a small, independent press.

All published authors will tell you that the work doesn't stop once you have a book contract. Over the following year or so, you will work with editors, art designers, sales representatives, and publicity staff to prepare for the publication date. During this time, you will want to take a crash course in book marketing so that you will have tools at your disposal to ensure your own success. And don't forget to use your newly published book to capitalize on other income-generating opportunities such as keynote speaking, magazine feature writing, and corporate blogging. In *The Savvy Author's Guide to Book Publicity,* Lissa Warren suggests working with the in-house PR staff to develop press materials; send advance copies out for review; pitch to appropriate print, radio, TV, and online media; arrange bookstore visits; excerpt content for publication elsewhere; and develop an author website. "You cannot be afraid to promote and sell yourself," says Laurel. "You have to put yourself out there and convince everyone of how great you are, because unless you can afford a personal publicist, no one is going to do it for you."

Profitable book authors are not just good writers, they're good businesspeople too. And once you've figured out the formula—create something that will sell, sell it, and then repeat—you'll join the ranks of those who get paid to do what they love. Just don't forget to be patient. "You can't expect the moon right away," says Sharon. "What's meant to happen will happen when the time is right, so for now, enjoy working on whatever project is in front of you. The big opportunity is coming."

FASHION DESIGNER

I have been obsessed with fashion since I was a little girl. My mom still has my first collection of line sheets called Emily's Exclusives, which I made when I was about seven years old. I co-founded my first line, Primp, based on a very simple concept—splattered bleach! In 2004, I co-founded my second successful line, emilynoelle, with my partner Noelle. We were really struggling waiting for our first significant break, and one day I was at home watching TV when I saw Jessica Simpson wearing our design on her hot show *Newlyweds*! From that point on, we could not make our hoodies fast enough. They were suddenly on girls from Portland to Paducah.

—Emily, twenty-five, fashion designer

IN MOVIES AND ON TV, the life of a fashion designer looks ultra-glamorous—dressing up gorgeous models and actresses, mingling at swanky parties and shows, and seeing your work splashed across the pages of *Vogue* and *W*. But while some fashion designers are as famous as the Hollywood A-listers they work with, behind the scenes, they're not just clothes horses but workhorses. According to Fashion-Schools.org (www.fashion-schools.org), their responsibilities include creating new designs, analyzing fashion trends, and working with production, sales, and marketing departments to produce a finished, ready-to-wear, salable product for apparel manufacturers, stores, and individual clients. Fashion designers usually specialize in a specific area of clothing (sportswear, kids, bridal, et cetera) or accessories. Collections may be either haute couture—items that are designed and custom-fitted for private customers—or ready-to-wear—items that are produced in large quantities and available in retail stores. (Note that some consider makeup design to be part of the fashion industry as well.)

As you can imagine, the fashion industry is pretty competitive, so it may be a relief to learn that there are a variety of ways in. Fashion juggernaut Ralph Lauren started learning the business as a child and bought men's suits with his allowance. Top wedding designer Vera Wang, on the other hand, came to the profession later in life, after she got engaged at thirty-nine and couldn't find a decent gown for a bride her age. Most agree, however, that attending a prestigious design school such as the Parsons New School for Design or the Pratt Institute will provide the best foundation for a successful career. The best schools are selective, of course, and application usually involves sending a portfolio of design drawings that demonstrates a unique vision and an understanding of modern fashion sensibilities.

In school, you'll study hand drawing, CAD (computer-aided design), color composition and form, pattern making, draping, and cutting techniques, and the business and marketing aspects of fashion. But Fashion.Net (www.fashion.net) tells us that one of the most important advantages of design schools is how closely they work with the industry. Parsons, for example, has "designer critic projects," where world-class designers like Donna Karan and Michael Kors work directly with undergraduates. Ambitious students can also show off their work via awards and grants.

In addition to or in lieu of a fashion degree, an internship is an excellent way to get hands-on experience and exposure that will prepare you for a career as an in-house or independent designer. The Fashion Group International suggests contacting individual designer showrooms or fashion houses to get information on their programs, scanning *Women's Wear Daily* for contacts and help-wanted ads, and applying directly to the group's headquarters in New York City. Other internship and job search resources that might prove helpful include the Fashion Tool (www.thefashiontool.com), Fashion Net (www.fashion.net), and FashionJobsCentral.com (www.fashionjobscentral.com). Since there's a good chance your internship will be unpaid, use your time there to get to know as many influential people as you can, for the right connections will help you ascend the fashion career ladder much more swiftly.

The internship is typically a huge feather in your cap when, portfolio and photos of your finished products in hand, you apply for your first industry job. Most new designers begin as assistant designers, sample makers, or sketchers in top houses such as Bebe or Chanel, while others go to work for mass-market manufacturers or innovative new brands. "Even if you're interested in starting your own company, you should first try working for a start-up in your area of expertise," recommends Kristin, twenty-nine, founder of the natural cosmetics brand Afterglow, who works on the makeup side of the profession. "Witness the passion, the dedication, challenges, and growth that come with starting one's own business." After a few years in an entry-level position, you might become a full-fledged designer in a particular group (dresses, denim, et cetera), or even a design director, who is the steward of the brand and provides direction to a team of designers.

Although most new designers first work for someone else in order to establish their reputations, others, like Kristin and twenty-five-year-old Emily, co-founder of the celebrity-friendly leisurewear line emilynoelle, launch their own labels right away. Many who succeed do so by identifying an open niche in a particular market, while others create lines that appeal to a broad spectrum of people. "My skin is pretty sensitive to makeup, and after I realized that everything at Nordstrom's cosmetic counters included loads of artificial ingredients, I saw that there was an opportunity to create a gentle line that was free of the chemicals included in major brand cosmetics but at the same time offered a great, fashionable palette," says Kristin.

In any case, advance planning for your fledgling business is critical. Whether you're creating mass-market tees or haute couture shoes, you must know the mechanics of your industry; how you'll manufacture, distribute, and merchandise your product; and what employees you'll need to hire. Since you'll need enough money to keep your line afloat for a full year without generating profits, save in advance, take out a loan, and cut expenses by operating your business from home in the beginning. It helps to live close to or in the major fashion capitals of New York City and Los Angeles, because it's easier to meet contacts and attract national distributors. "Don't move to Alaska!" advises Emily. "You need to be close to the action, so it's L.A. or bust for me as a newcomer in this industry." Additionally, you might want to check out *The Apparel Strategist* (www.apparelstrategist.com), a monthly newsletter that helps people run fashion-oriented businesses and offers useful tips on organizing promotional events and getting samples reviewed by the fashion press.

Needless to say, there is a definite entrepreneurial streak in this creator. Fashion designers in all areas of the profession should know how to negotiate contracts, choose partners, license products, and develop marketing campaigns. Fashion is driven more by large corporations than you might think, and so in the midst of the inventive, visionary thinking that sets you apart from scores of other designers, you must be able to focus on hard-core business realities. "While I can't imagine anything more boring and frustrating than filing, invoicing, dealing with suppliers, and collecting money, it's all part of the job," says Emily. "I'm involved in all elements of emilynoelle, from the designing and marketing to the shipping, logistics coordination, and financial management." Fashion designers have to be superb communicators as well, because often it's your speaking and writing skills that will persuade skeptical customers of your work's value. "I found that a great way to communicate about the Afterglow brand was via the Web," says Kristin. "The Internet is increasingly about communities of like-minded people, and it gave me instant access to my ideal customers—women with sensitive skin and women who are concerned about their overall health."

Unfortunately, you will also pay a premium for a place in this highly desirable industry. Most of the designers I spoke with said that jobs are high in stress and low in pay, although the Princeton Review reports the average annual salary after five years as a respectable $51K. As long as you're prepared to deal with fashion's lengthy hours, slow career progression, and often superficial culture, you can be one of the privileged few who make their homes in one of the most stimulating industries in the world. "It's really fun and exciting, and it's a wholly creative career," says Kristin. "I can be visually creative in an aesthetic sense, and strategically creative in a business-planning and problem-solving sense. I can't imagine another job like it!"

INTERIOR DESIGNER

Having designed interiors for very-high-profile clients in the entertainment business, I have come across some monumental egos. This is particularly the case in Hollywood where people don't understand the meaning of the word *no*. The ability to compromise, and to persuade, has really helped my business. A subtle suggestion can go a long way, especially if you can make the client think the great idea was hers.

—Bryan, thirty-nine, interior designer

WHEN YOU ARE IN A PHYSICAL SPACE, do you notice details about your surroundings and dream up ways to improve their appearance? Have you thought about ways to redesign your home, your office, or your favorite store or restaurant? It's possible you could be an interior designer. While interior design really is one of the most creative careers out there, it tends to be misunderstood. Interior design is not the same as interior decorating, which involves working mainly with colors and fabrics. Interior design, on the other hand, is a multispecialty discipline concerned with enhancing the function, safety, and aesthetics of commercial and residential properties.

According to the American Society of Interior Designers (ASID), the interior designer knows how to plan a space and how to render that plan visually. He's knowledgeable about the materials to use, and how texture, color, and lighting interact to give a space its look and feel. He understands structural requirements, safety issues, building codes, and other technical aspects. The successful interior designer is imaginative and artistic, but he's also a pragmatic businessman and a master communicator. "The ability to listen to what a client is really saying is important in realizing his vision for a design scheme," says Bryan, thirty-nine, an interior designer and the owner of the L.A.-based firm Bryan Wark Designs. "Many designers have a reputation for being flamboyant and temperamental, but I think a more low-key approach has served me well." At the helm of a team of architects, contractors, and other building specialists, the interior designer organizes and oversees projects so that the final product is aesthetically appealing and meets clients' needs.

Interior designers come to the field with a variety of life experiences. "I grew up in my father's design studio, where he and his brother designed and built custom homes," says Bryan. "I spent much of my childhood entertaining myself with colored pencils, drafting supplies, and interior design magazines. Later, I studied sculpture and furniture design at UCLA, eventually blending the two disciplines to create 'functional art.'" Chad, thirty-one, is an interior designer and the owner of DeWitt Design Studios in San Francisco. "At California College of the Arts, I auditioned for HGTV's *Designer Finals* show," he says. "I was selected, and so I set out to raise the bar for home-redecoration reality shows. I proved what I was capable of, and pretty soon I had my first client."

Do you think you have something special to bring to the profession? Completing an associate or bachelor's degree is now almost a necessity for breaking into interior design. In many states, to call yourself an interior designer you must complete a training program accredited by the Foundation for Interior Design Education Research (FIDER) and pass a licensing exam given by the National Council for Interior Design Qualification (NCIDQ). ASID recommends that you first explore all of the educational options in your geographic location, from general two- and four-year programs at large universities to more specialized art and design schools. Before you jump into a program, talk to faculty to make sure the institution you choose will meet your needs. In particular, you'll want to be reassured that the school will do everything in its power to help you land a job in an industry where entry-level opportunities can be few and far between.

Speaking of which, you won't want to wait until you have your degree to start preparing to be out on your own. As you complete your courses, take photos of finished projects and save work samples for the portfolio you will create in online and DVD formats. It's wise to get involved with ASID (www.asid.org), as well as with the Interior Design Educators Council (IDEC, www.idec.org) and the International Interior Design Association (IIDA, www.iida.org) at the student level. In addition to networking benefits, these associations offer competitions in which you'll be able to test your design skills and earn early recognition. Interior designers agree that having professional affiliations and awards on your résumé will make you, as a new graduate, more attractive to potential employers. While you're still in school, you should do your best to secure an internship with a reputable interior design firm, where you will have the opportunity to work one-on-one with a certified professional. Even if you have to work for free, you'll get invaluable expertise watching projects develop from soup to nuts and learning how theory is put into practice in the real world. Best of all, if the firm loves you, they might very well hire you after you're finished with your education!

Once you've overcome the hurdle of the degree, you'll turn your attention to finding an entry-level job in the field. Association job banks at the sites mentioned in the previous paragraph are an excellent start. You might also think about becoming an in-house designer for a furniture store or auction house, or hooking up with the NCIDQ Interior Design Experience Program, which provides supervised work experience and mentor services to new designers. Since most interior designers are self-employed, finding job opportunities in the big firms might be a bit of a challenge. If this is the case, use your school and association connections to contact sole proprietors about the possibility of an apprenticeship. "Shoot for the top, even if it means relocating to get the job," suggests Bryan. "As you're looking, pay attention to design trends in all areas—home, fashion, garden, jewelry, et cetera—and read any and all publications related to the field."

The Dezignaré Interior Design Collective also suggests breaking in with contract or part-time work. Many design firms hire this way for temporary workload crunches and often, after seeing your capabilities, will consider you for a permanent position. This approach can get you into places where you might not otherwise have a chance, and you'll be able to learn by example. During your first few years of on-the-job training, you probably won't earn much more than $25K. But you'll have the chance to become familiar with resources and vendors, find out how designers secure and charge for projects, market their services to the public, and supply products to their clients—all with the eventual goal of becoming a supervisor in a large design firm or, even better, the owner of your own studio. "I think having your own business is key," says Chad. "Your income tops out around $80K working for someone else, but working for yourself, you can earn six figures." Bryan agrees. "I love being self-employed," he says. "But there are ups and downs. Building a client base takes a long time, as 90 percent of new business is referred. Promotion is critical. Once I started getting projects published and hired a PR firm, things really picked up. Now I can accomplish a huge amount of work sitting at my desk in the morning with a cup of coffee, listening to some music. I have a job that fuels my creativity and clients who are good friends." What more could you ask for in a career?

LANDSCAPE ARCHITECT

If I think about it, I've been working toward this job my whole life. I loved art in school, of course, and I was always rearranging the furniture in my room, making forts out of the living room cushions, and building tree houses in the backyard. I can see something special in an empty space—a world of possibilities.

—Jaime, twenty-four, landscape architect

WHY DOES YOUR COMMUNITY look the way it does? Who designed the grounds of the college campus where you take classes, the park where you take your nephew to play, or the garden in front of your office building? In most cases, it was probably a landscape architect, a person responsible for the analysis, planning, design, management, and stewardship of outdoor spaces. Landscape architecture as a formal profession has existed since the mid-1800s, when Frederick Law Olmsted and Calvert Vaux designed New York's Central Park to appeal specifically to the recreation needs of the public. If you're interested in a career that uniquely combines art and science with an appreciation of natural resources and the environment, landscape architecture could be your calling. Let's take a look at what these people do and how you might become one of them.

As described in the U.S. Bureau of Labor Statistics' *Occupational Outlook Handbook,* landscape architects most commonly design residential areas, recreational and industrial parks, shopping centers, and golf courses so that they are not only functional but also beautiful, and compatible with the natural environment. Landscape architects work for many types of organizations—from real estate development firms starting new projects to municipalities constructing airports or parks. In planning a site, landscape architects analyze natural elements such as the climate, soil, slope of the land, drainage, vegetation, and even where sunlight falls at different times. Then they collaborate with architects, surveyors, and engineers to determine the best arrangement of roads and buildings, and with environmental scientists and foresters to find the best way to conserve or restore natural resources.

Once these decisions are made, landscape architects create detailed plans indicating new topography, vegetation, walkways, and other landscaping details, such as fountains and decorative features. "My favorite project involved designing a courtyard for a Head Start preschool," says Jaime, twenty-four, a landscape architect at Green-Works in Portland. "We thought about how three-year-olds were going to use the space. We wanted an educational element and an environmental element, so we ended up channeling rainwater into depressed spaces in the pavement. We envisioned these little kids interacting with natural processes, learning about the physics of water, asking their teachers, 'Where does the water go and how does it get there?' "

While it may sound like landscape architects spend a lot of time outside, most of their project work actually takes place in the office doing research, building plans and models using computer-aided design (CAD), and generating lists of construction materials and cost estimates. Even when designs are approved, landscape architects spend a lot of time making edits and adjustments and giving presentations to clients and other professionals working on the project. According to The Princeton Review, while some supervise the installation of their designs, others hand off projects to separate contractors. Landscape architects specialize in areas such as residential development, parks and playgrounds, and historical restoration. Although most of them work for landscape architecture firms or government agencies, at least 20 percent are self-employed.

As you've no doubt gathered by now, landscape architecture involves so much more than making a space look pretty. In addition to the obvious creativity and understanding of the arts required, landscape architects must have a working knowledge of the environment and must be able to analyze design and engineering problems. "You have to be a translator," says Jaime. "Your clients might know the area well, but won't know the right design to meet their needs. You have to be able to listen, and think critically about the big-picture theme and how you could carry out a vision technically. I go to sleep thinking about this stuff. It's like counting sheep for me."

It's not quite as easy as counting sheep, though, and that's why some advanced education is necessary, either at the undergraduate or graduate level. Four- or five-year undergraduate programs usually combine design and construction study with common college coursework in art, history, and the natural and social sciences, and result in either a bachelor of landscape architecture (B.L.A.) or a bachelor of science in landscape architecture (B.S.L.A.). However, in the event that you'd like to enter this field and have already completed an undergraduate degree in another discipline, you can obtain a master of landscape architecture (M.L.A.) and become a full-time practitioner within three years. "While it is possible to break into the field as a draftsperson or a residential landscape designer, your job options will be pretty limited if you don't have a B.L.A. or an M.L.A.," says Craig, thirty-two, a landscape architect in Maryland.

With this amount of education ahead of you, the decision to become a landscape architect is not one you should make lightly. Take the time to explore the information available on the American Society of Landscape Architects' website (www.asla.org) and read several issues of industry publications such as *Landscape Architecture, Landscape Journal,* and *Landscape and Urban Planning.* Make sure all of the schools you are considering are accredited by the Landscape Architectural Accreditation Board, and if you need more inspiration, check out Design-Intelligence's *America's Best Architecture and Design Schools,* which now has nationwide rankings of landscape architecture programs.

While you're working toward your degree, you should already be looking ahead to your future career. Take advantage of your school's resources to land a summer internship at a landscape architecture firm or government organization, because this position could be your way in once you graduate. "My school helped me get an internship with the Vancouver Parks Department," says Jaime. "While I was there, I worked with people at many of the top design firms, including GreenWorks. I kept in touch with them, and once I was on the job market I was already a step ahead."

When it comes to shopping for or preparing for an internship, the American Society for Landscape Architects' website won't disappoint, providing everything from an online directory of landscape architects and JobLink employment listings to professional development offerings such as specialty practice information, business tools, and research services. Joining the organization as a student affiliate member is a smart idea because the networking activities will connect you with experienced landscape architects who may be in a position to offer you an apprenticeship. And before you strike out on your own, you'll need one of those. In order to become a certified landscape architect, you have to spend a few years working for someone else, obtain a strong reference, and sit for a three-day, multipart licensure exam. "The informational interview is a great way to seek out apprentice opportunities," says Craig. "I made a list of the firms in the area. I called a partner at each one and asked to see some designs. I was just hoping to get some good advice and maybe a few leads, but it turned out better than that. I got offered a part-time position and have been here ever since."

This career requires a lot of preparation, that's for sure. But landscape architects are rewarded for their dedication. Within a landscape architecture firm or even a government agency, there are substantial opportunities for advancement through the ranks of project management, and those who are self-employed can do extremely well. While entry-level landscape architects earn an average annual salary of $35K, the median for all levels of the profession is around $70K, and it's not unusual for firm owners to break $100K. And according to the U.S. Bureau of Labor Statistics' *Occupational Outlook Handbook,* this is a good time to be entering the field. A growing population, rising land costs, and new environmental regulations are rapidly increasing the demand for landscape architects' expertise. By 2014, this will be one of the hottest professions out there, so you're just in time!

MOVIE SCREENWRITER

I was a mechanical engineering major in college. One semester, I studied abroad in Florence and went to the Uffizi museum. Until then, I hadn't thought much about art, but seeing Botticelli's painting of Venus was a defining moment in my life. I would sit in front of that painting for hours, just admiring it. It moved me so much, and I realized I wanted to make people feel like that too. And that was when I decided I wanted to write movies.

—Ben, thirty-four, movie screenwriter

SOME SAY THERE ARE AS MANY screenwriters in Los Angeles as there are actors. Why? Well, like acting, screenwriting is an art that many dream of conquering, and becoming fabulously wealthy and famous as a result. Dreaming is a good thing, but if you're thinking about devoting your career to professional movie screenwriting, you should also be exposed to a healthy dose of reality before you hop on the next bus to Hollywood. First, you must learn the mechanics of how screenwriters turn their muse for the creative into paying jobs, and what it will take to make it happen for you.

Keeping it simple, there are two basic paths to making a living as a professional screenwriter. The first, and the one people commonly picture when they think of a screenwriter, is writing "on spec." A spec screenplay is written "on speculation," which means that the writer just went ahead and completed it without any guarantee that the script would ever be produced. The spec script involves the most amount of risk for the writer, because regardless of how much time and energy he invests in his work, he may never receive financial compensation. However, considering industry estimates that 80,000 original spec scripts are written each year, screenwriters don't seem to be daunted by this proposition.

In order to join the ranks of spec script writers, you must begin with a compelling, marketable idea and a strong outline that confirms that your story can be sustained through a hundred-plus-page screenplay. Understand your niche, or the genre you feel most passionate writing in, and use free Internet sites like Simply Scripts (www.simplyscripts.com) to read every successful original screenplay you can get your hands on. Young screenwriter Eli Roth, for example, was well versed in horror classics like *The Texas Chain Saw Massacre, Audition,* and *The Thing* before he made it big with his first spec script, *Cabin Fever,* in 2002.

The brilliant idea that would make a terrific movie doesn't necessarily have to be your own. As a writer just getting started, you probably don't have the cash to purchase the options to a novel, for instance, but you could investigate whether film rights are available for a particular short story or foreign piece by contacting the publisher's rights department. If you're able to secure the rights, you'll have the freedom to adapt the material in an original screenplay. While this might sound like a far-fetched approach, it has been known to work for young screenwriters. "Awhile back, I purchased the rights to an obscure Malaysian film for $7K," says Ben, thirty-four, a screenwriter. "I adapted the script for American audiences and caught the attention of Bruce Willis, who just signed on to produce it."

If there's one thing you've probably heard already, it's that the market for original screenplays is fiercely competitive, so your product must be provocative and of the highest quality, and you must know how to sell it. Lenore Wright, the author of a syndicated column called "The Screenwriter's Web" and the e-mail newsletter *Script Market News* says that an original script needs memorable well-drawn characters, a story that plays out visually, and a hook of some kind that will make it promotable. If it does not have these three qualities, you do not have a movie. Smart market research is another critical aspect of writing and selling an original screenplay. Among the need-to-knows: what films in your genre have been made already, what films are shooting or awaiting release, and what scripts have been bought and by whom. To research this, check out resources like Done Deal Professional (www.donedealpro.com) and *Variety*'s Film Production Chart.

Once you've edited, formatted, and had your finished script critiqued, the real adventure begins. Given the glutted status of the market, you'll have to be creative and persistent in attracting an industry representative who can ensure that your script is read by the right people. The more traditional route involves signing with a literary agent in Los Angeles or New York who will submit your script to his contacts in exchange for 15 percent of your earnings when the project sells—a decent chunk of change when you consider that first-time spec scripts reportedly garner an average of $100K to $200K. Scout out potential agents in annual directories such as the *Writer's Market* and the *Guide to Literary Agents* and target those who represent your type of work. Hundreds of resources out there provide copious details on the best way to write a query, or introductory letter, but suffice it to say that your initial communication with an agent should present your spec script in its most intriguing light and demonstrate why you have the potential to make money for him over the long term.

As a new writer, getting an agent is a difficult proposition, and you should be prepared to weather lots of rejection and keep querying and submitting even when it seems like the odds are against you. Participating in prestigious screenwriting competitions often helps. Two top competitions are UCLA's Diane Thomas Screenwriting Award and the Nicholl Fellowships, the latter of which is sponsored by the Academy of Motion Picture Arts and Sciences (i.e., the Oscar people). Literary agents have a way of finding the talented screenwriters who win these contests and helping them to get their scripts in shape for the market.

Despite your best efforts, you may not attract professional interest in your spec script. In this case, one option is to apply for a job as a coveragist at a film studio. A coveragist reads scripts that are sent to the studio and helps determine if they're worth producing. Similarly, while you're trying to pay the bills, you might take a job with a Hollywood talent agency or production company. "I broke into the business by working as an assistant for a big-time producer and a manager who had a lot of A-list celebrities as clients," says Ben. "I thought it was an excellent way to learn more about the business and craft of screenwriting and network with industry insiders." Another option is to pursue jobs that need screenwriters—otherwise known as writing on assignment—using your completed spec script as sample writing material. The major studios all have lists of open writing assignments, which are projects based on ideas from the executives, books, and purchased scripts, that need revising. Writing on assignment has many advantages over writing spec scripts. You know you will get paid for your work (anywhere from a few thousand dollars total to $200K per week), your script is more likely to make it to the screen because the project is already in development, and you have the opportunity to work with talented individuals who can open doors for you. While you don't necessarily need a completed spec script to apply for assignments, you should prepare a repertoire of sample material that demonstrates your command of the craft. Of course, as a new writer, it's not easy to get assignment jobs either, especially high-profile ones. However, if you don't try, there's no chance you'll get anywhere, right? Resources to check out include:

- Done Deal Professional (www.donedealpro.com)
- InkTip (www.inktip.com)
- MovieBytes (www.moviebytes.com)
- ShowBiz Data (www.showbizdata.com)

Aspiring screenwriters sometimes consider going to film school. At the prominent ones, which include UCLA, the University of Southern California, NYU, and the American Film Institute, you'll meet industry contacts that may be able to jump-start your career. However, as you know from spending four years in college, education is pricey, and it's debatable whether the script-writing practice you'll do in class will serve you any better than what you could do for free on your laptop at home.

This section should leave little doubt that becoming a professional movie screenwriter is quite an undertaking. You need a bellyful of passion that drives you to write in the absence of financial incentives, but on the other side of the spectrum, you must also have a steady supply of practicality and professionalism. Because show business is above all a business, you'll have to recognize the futility of taking rudeness or rejection personally, and know how to play your politics when necessary. You'll need to learn to multitask—for most writers spend their days simultaneously working on new projects, trying to sell finished projects, promoting the projects already out there, and doing other work that brings in a paycheck. However, when I asked veterans about the most important characteristic of an aspiring screenwriter, the quality I heard most often was "persistence" or "commitment." The path to success in this business is long and full of roadblocks, but by tirelessly practicing your craft and putting a new log on the fire every time one burns out, you'll be competing with the best of them. Remember that there's a reason why showbiz legend Eddie Cantor said, "It takes twenty years to become an overnight success." So be patient, be confident, and above all—keep working at it!

PERFORMANCE MUSICIAN

> I've played piano everywhere, under all kinds of circumstances. Right now, I'm working on a Broadway show that's a "twist" on *Oliver Twist*. But I've played at Caroline's Comedy Club in New York City, as a drag queen who popped out of a cake while Joan Rivers was on stage. I've worked at a dueling piano bar in Raleigh, North Carolina, playing "God Bless America" for a mother whose son was in Iraq. My journey in the music business is a bunch of dots, and it's sometimes hard to see how they're all connected. My goal is to find the path, and then follow it without digressing.
>
> —Andrew, thirty-one, performance musician

THERE'S SOMETHING ABOUT MUSIC. Everyone can appreciate it on some level, and millions of elementary school students learn to play the violin, the trumpet, or the piano every year. Of the kids who spend months mastering medleys and practicing scales, however, only a select few go on to performance careers. For this section, I chatted with some young musicians who are making a living with their instruments, and found out just what it takes to make it in the highly competitive music world.

Musicians, like many creators, enjoy the process of expressing themselves through a cultural medium. They thrive on performing in front of a crowd, entertaining and engaging the community. "Because no one ever wants to hear the same thing played the same way, I have to figure out what about the piece inspires me," says Paul, twenty-eight, a trombone player with the Gaudete Brass, a professional quintet in Chicago that plays eight to ten concerts a month all over the country. "This way, I'll be able to communicate the message of the music clearly, even though I can't use words." Andrew, thirty-one, a New York–based studio and floor pianist who has recorded with the Scissor Sisters, agrees. "Performance musicians usually have to play what other people want to hear, but they also have to differentiate themselves and make pieces their own. That takes creativity."

Talented and successful musicians learn certain skills, usually from a young age, including music reading, keyboard playing, the ability to recognize musical sounds including intervals and chords (also known as aural skills), singing in tune, and harmonization. Most students have natural prowess in these areas that is "fine-tuned" through private lessons and experience with a band, choir, or orchestra. While the professional musicians I interviewed felt that a university education was helpful in providing opportunities to increase technical proficiency on an instrument, they also thought it was possible for a gifted and conscientious musician to self-train. "The college experience in and of itself is not necessary for a career in music," says Paul. "It simply provides a forum to hone your skills so that you can perform at the level of your competition, network with other musicians, and expose yourself to different styles—and there's no real reason you can't do those things on your own."

While the term *starving artist* has definitely been liberally applied to performance musicians, they can generate income in a surprising number of ways, including as a recording artist, an instrumental soloist, a studio musician, a private function musician, an orchestra or band member, a hotel or restaurant floor musician, and a theater musician. However, despite the variety of positions available, you'll need to work hard if you wish to earn your living as a musician—and this goes beyond perfecting your craft. "First of all, depending on what you're trying to do, you have to understand the business of music from that perspective," says Paul. "For example, in my career, I've needed to learn how to license rights to use other people's music, how to copyright a piece, and how to go about recording a CD for commercial distribution." You also have to be able to aggressively promote yourself and your expertise. "The field is very subjective, and because a lot of people don't understand the difference between amateurs and professionals, you have to be persuasive in convincing employers of your value," says Paul. "One thing is for sure, you can't sit around and wait for the phone to ring. You have to create your own opportunities."

If, like Paul, you're looking to establish yourself as an independent act, Christopher Knab, the author of *Music Is Your Business,* offers these additional tips:

- Prove to the industry that ordinary fans in your city love your music. Give away sample CDs of your music on the street and/or put songs on websites that allow people to download new music.

- Play often and play for free. Offer your services to nonprofits, charities, and religious groups, and hang out at clubs and venues where musicians can play. As you establish yourself and more and more people show up at your shows, the paid gigs will increase.

- Make your promotional materials as compelling and informative as possible. Inventory any accomplishments, positive reviews, training and awards, past sales, and live appearance highlights, and organize them into professional handouts. Customize each kit for the music business gatekeeper you're sending it to.

- Research the labels and music publishers you hope to be signed to. Find out about their stability as businesses, their reputations in the industry, and the executives' background and experience.

- Before you sign a contract, choose a reputable and ethical entertainment attorney with lots of deal-making experience within the music industry.
- Be an effective self-manager at the start by securing your own gigs, generating your own publicity, planning tours, dealing with personal issues that arise, and schmoozing with music business personnel. Once you've had some success, select a well-connected and well-respected manager who can handle the day-to-day for you, and, more important, get you recording and publishing contracts.

As a studio and floor pianist, Andrew is always on the hunt for jobs with existing groups or organizations. "I read the musician boards on Craigslist [www.craigslist.com] every day, I take advantage of the alumni and career resources at the school where I trained, and I don't hesitate to walk into a venue and introduce myself," he says. "All in all, I try to surround myself with people in the business. It helps to live in a big city, in a cutting-edge neighborhood, where you can soak up different influences." Through my research, I identified some additional resources that might be useful as you scope out gigs, including *The Musician's Atlas* (www.musiciansatlas.com), which provides information on 20,000 music businesses and key industry contacts in twenty-five categories; *The Music Phone Book* (www.musicphonebook.com), which lists contacts for 10,000 live music venues across the United States; and music job portals such as EntertainmentCareers.Net (www.entertainmentcareers.net), MyMusicJob.com (www.mymusicjob.com), and Showbizjobs.com (www.showbizjobs.com).

Securing gainful employment is one thing, but if you're trying to make it as a professional musician, you will need to be prepared for what many describe as a harried and unpredictable lifestyle. "I spend the majority of my day practicing my trombone and networking, because I have to continue to progress on my instrument while searching for that next paycheck," says Paul. "When we have gigs, the commutes often take a long time, and punctuality is everything in the music business." The social interactions with other musicians can be stressful as well. "Personalities can be challenging," says Paul. "Everyone has an idea of how things should be done, so you have to know how to compromise and resolve conflicts effectively. And because human error is a factor in this business, you have to be patient too."

I'll conclude our look at professional musicians with a topic that's usually at the top of people's minds: what kind of money they can make. According to the National Association for Music Education, orchestra musicians can make up to the mid–five figures, while small ensemble musicians and floor musicians typically average a few hundred dollars per performance. The lack of a standardized pay scale or career trajectory frustrates many musicians. "The money you receive for a gig doesn't correlate to where you're located or how good you are," says Andrew. "You're not in this to get rich, but because you get to spend your days in the company of music: listening to it, reading it, writing it, rehearsing it, and collaborating on it." Paul adds: "Music is not a well-compensated field. When you're able to piece together a comfortable living doing what you love to do, that's the pinnacle of success."

RESTAURANT CHEF

I consider myself an artist. I have an appreciation for art, but unfortunately I have no ability in painting, drawing, or building. I can, however, make food. I love to use food with vibrant colors and aromas, and to think of my canvas as an empty plate waiting to be made up. In cooking, you use all of your senses—tasting, touching, smelling, hearing, seeing—and when you start a new dish it's like you're a little kid in Disney World for the first time.

—Phil, twenty-six, restaurant chef

WHAT ARE THE SECRETS behind restaurant food? Why is it that the entrées we order out always taste a million times better than anything we could make at home? Even for those of us who like to mess around in our kitchens a bit, there's something awe-inspiring about watching the waiter arrive at your table with a dish that looks like it belongs in a museum. And at one time or another, most people who have a natural talent for throwing random ingredients into a bowl and arriving at a delectable masterpiece wonder what it would be like to turn their passion into a career as a restaurant chef.

Although it might seem like restaurant chefs spend their lives thinking about and preparing food, they are actually some of the most well-rounded people you'll meet. According to CookingSchools.com, the most successful chefs share a variety of qualities, including a high level of creativity, a willingness to try new things and refine techniques, a keen business sense that marries quality with cost efficiency, and the ability to work well as part of a team. Phil, twenty-six, a chef at La Mie in Des Moines, Iowa, and Ryan, twenty-six, a chef at Cafe Myth in San Francisco, echo these sentiments. "If you're not organized, you're going to lose the game," says Phil. "Either your food will be cold, it won't be ready to serve, or you'll be out of it completely." Ryan adds: "Good chefs want to better themselves. I'm always looking for opportunities to stage cook [cook for free as a guest] in other restaurants so I can learn what others are doing."

The specific job responsibilities of a chef also include more than you might think, and vary depending on where you work and in what capacity. In addition to preparing, seasoning, cooking, and arranging dishes, though, many chefs also create and price menus, buy food supplies and equipment, ensure kitchen cleanliness and safety, and oversee kitchen staff. "I'm in charge of dinner at La Mie," says Phil. "I do all the prep work, run the line at night, and make sure my customers enjoy what they're eating. As far as menu planning goes, we're just a couple of guys in the basement, sharing a cold beer and our best ideas for new things to serve."

Even if they're talented, restaurant chefs usually have to work their way up within the kitchen's hierarchy, beginning as line cooks, who are responsible for a certain part of the menu or type of food. Line cooks who learn new skills, take on extra responsibility, and show initiative may be promoted to departmental specialists, who manage the production of groups of foods such as cheeses, salads, or desserts. From departmental specialist, it's possible to become a sous chef, the second in command who directs the preparation, cooking, and storage of food and is responsible for behind-the-scenes kitchen management tasks such as forecasting food requirements, adhering to apportionment regulations, maintaining records, and conducting inspections. Finally, the head of the complex operation known as the restaurant kitchen is the executive chef. Some executive chefs still do their share of cooking, but many spend a great deal of their time directing the kitchen staff, strategizing with partners and investors, and serving as the public face of the restaurant. "I teach classes too," says Ryan. "And I don't like having days off, so I'll do a private party at someone's house where I'll show the group how to make mojitos. It's great fun."

Sound good to you? Well, before you can get started, you'll need the proper training. Conventional wisdom says that prospective chefs should start by attending an independent cooking school, such as the Culinary Institute of America (www.ciachef.edu); a vocational institute, such as Johnson and Wales University (www.jwu.edu); or a two-to-four-year college degree program in hospitality or culinary arts, such as the New School's culinary arts program (www.newschool.edu). CookingSchools.com, an excellent resource for researching training options, says that cooking schools vary greatly in both the time it takes to complete the program and in what you'll get (certificate, diploma, degree, et cetera) when you graduate. In most cases, a shorter program will be more intensive or will require that you specialize in a particular area (such as pastry).

Application procedures also depend on the institution, but you will typically need to provide evidence of your high school education, test scores, and personal references. Some schools will ask you to come in for an interview, write an essay, or do some other task that illustrates what kind of person you are and what potential you might have as a chef. It is recommended that you select a school that is accredited by the American Culinary Federation (ACF, www.acfchefs.org). In a culinary school or program, you will spend most of your time in the kitchen mastering basic cooking skills (chopping, sautéing, et cetera), and learning to use equipment, handle and store food safely, prepare nutritious meals, plan menus, and minimize waste. Many institutions place students in internships or volunteer positions with local restaurants and hotels as part of their programs, and this type of assignment may provide enough experience so that you can skip over the entry level in your first official restaurant job.

Useful as culinary school can be, there are those who don't believe it's necessary and suggest working as an apprentice for an already-established restaurant chef instead. The American Culinary Federation has an apprenticeship program (www.acfchefs.org) that relatively inexperienced students are eligible for, or you could check out culinary and hospitality job sites such as ChefJobsNetwork.com (www.chefjobs network.com), Chef2Chef (www.chef2chef.net), and Foodservice.com (www.foodservice.com). Both Phil and Ryan suggest doing an apprenticeship abroad if you can swing it. "Travel to the places whose food you love to eat," says Phil. "Your experiences with chefs there will give you a whole new appreciation and respect for the culinary arts." And if you really want to get ahead quickly, there's no substitute for going out to eat constantly and introducing yourself to people. "In San Francisco, my favorite restaurant was Gary Danko," says Ryan. "I called the sous chef every Sunday for twelve weeks to ask if there was a stage position available. He kept turning me down, but I got to know the crew, and as soon as something opened up, I was in and working with one of the best chefs on the West Coast."

Even once you have a job, the life of a restaurant chef is not an easy one. Most chefs with fewer than ten years of experience make less than $40K a year, and the more prestigious the restaurant, the harder you'll have to work. Good executive chefs can surpass six figures, but even at the highest levels of achievement, this is not a profession that guarantees a lucrative income. "I'm not going to be a line cook at a high-end chain even though that might pay more," says Phil. "I would much rather have a lower-paying gig in a great work environment with food I really want to make." And while the market for good chefs is only getting better as people start caring more about what they eat, the gratifying nature of the work does make it continually competitive. There's one thing that professional chefs all agree on, though: you'll have a much better chance at success if you're willing to do whatever it takes to learn the ropes, which might include working as a dishwasher or moving to a remote location. And it's advisable to get rid of that ego. "You hear about the bad-tempered, mean chefs," says Ryan. "But it's usually the good-natured people who get ahead."

VIDEO GAME DESIGNER
· ·

> As lead world artist, I'm responsible for supervising the construction of any piece of environment art you see in the game. This can be anything from a giant tower reaching toward the clouds to a mound of Orc poo, steaming in the morning sun. I love my job because I get to create entire worlds no one has ever seen before. It's rewarding because I know people will be playing the game I make to escape from reality for a while and just relax from the everyday stresses.
>
> —Peter, twenty-five, video game designer

WHEN I WAS GROWING UP IN THE EIGHTIES, video games were looked upon as kids' stuff. Babysitters would roll their eyes when my brother and I spent hours glued to the TV, controls locked in our sweaty hands. At the time of this book's writing, however, the video game industry was taking in more than $8 billion a year, and the launches of new Xbox, PlayStation, and Nintendo consoles were making international headlines. If you're a creator who has always dreamed of making games for a living, there may be no better time. Let's see how it's done.

If you talk to video game designers, the first thing they'll tell you is that video game design is not a solo art. Production usually involves storyboard artists, character artists, level designers, texture artists, programmers, interface designers, audio technicians, and professional testers. At smaller developers, however, designers may be responsible for a variety of these functions. For example, Chris, twenty-nine, is the resident 3-D artist at the thirteen-person Wideload Games in Chicago. "I create in-game assets, like environments (the interior of a pirate ship), scenery objects (the chest full of gold in the pirate ship), and visual effects (the cigarette smoke from a pirate's cigar)," explains Chris. "I also animate characters and objects within the scene."

Another thing video game designers will tell you is that people who want to enter the field should really love games, play them constantly, and know inherently what makes a good and bad game. But that's not all. Video game designers also need advanced technical training in graphic design and computer animation in order to have the skills to create the extremely sophisticated, three-dimensional worlds of today's games. "Autodesk's 3ds Max and Adobe's Photoshop are the bread-and-butter programs of the industry, and you have to know them well," says Peter, twenty-five, a video game designer in New York. "Knowledge of architecture is big too, because the arrangement of objects in space can be used in very creative ways to imprint emotions on people and set moods for different environments."

For most game design hopefuls, these skill requirements mean obtaining a digital design degree, or at least attending a few video game design courses, where you'll learn how to use relevant hardware and software, and read and write in basic computer languages. Your video design "boot camp" will also include training in storyboarding, characterization, animation, modeling, and editing, and if you're a prospective sound designer, you can expect to learn music basics, digital recording, and sound mixing, effects, and sequencing. There are several strong programs with multilocation or online options, including DeVry's Game and Simulation Programming degree (www.devry.edu), ITT's Digital Entertainment and Game Design degree (www.itt-tech.edu), and the Art Institute Online's Game Art and Design degree (www.the-art-institute-online.com).

There is, however, such a thing as being self-taught. If you have raw talent in the areas described above, Phil Marley, author of the *Fab-Job Guide to Become a Video Game Designer,* recommends you put it to work by using a level editor to create add-on levels for games like Quake, by working on a MUD (multiuser dungeon, or an online game played by groups of people through a network), or by designing a conversion of an existing game or an entirely new game. Lorne, twenty-six, a video game designer in Seattle, agrees. "If a game comes with level or map editors, play with them," he says. "Put your levels or MODs [modifications of existing games] on the Internet, let people mess around, and listen to the criticism and suggestions. This will give you great experience, but also a sense of what life as a game designer is like."

It's also a good idea to enter the contests the big studios hold occasionally. Winning a competition such as Xbox and Rare's "Kameo Design Your Skin" or BioWare's "Neverwinter Nights Story Module" could very well be your way in the door to the highly desirable gaming industry. All of these projects should provide you with fodder for your portfolio, or an online and offline collection of your most creative and accomplished game designs, software, and/or demo reels.

Once you have the required skill set and a portfolio that's ready to go, what's the next step? An unpaid or low-paid internship in a game studio is an obvious choice, but this may require some digging on your part. Apply to as many places as you can, even if they're not advertising internships, and ideally start your search a year before you need the job. If you'd prefer to jump directly into the entry level, interviewing to be a game tester might be your best option. In order to do this job, you have to be a consummate player who can master multiple games at every level, and have a good working knowledge of Microsoft Windows and other frequently used operating systems. "I'd read that being a game tester was the best way to break in, so I spent a summer doing just that: playing games, riding around on scooters, and drinking soda," says Peter. "When I heard the studio was looking for level designers, I marched into my boss's office and told him I had been developing MODs for years. The next thing I knew, someone sat me down in the artist pit and put me to work."

Whether you're hunting for an internship or entry-level job, making the right contacts is the name of the game. Start by asking your family and friends if they know anyone who works in a game studio and might be willing to talk to you about the industry. Expand your network by checking out websites such as Gamasutra (www.gamasutra.com), CreativeHeads.net (www.creativeheads.net), *Game Developer* (www.gdmag.com), and GameDev.net (www.gamedev.net) and looking up contacts at game developers, studios, and even employment agencies. The online forum at the International Game Developers Association website (www.igda.org) is a good place to hang out and network with gaming professionals, as are the major gaming trade shows: E3 (www.e3expo.com), SIGGRAPH (www.siggraph.org), and the Game Developers Conference (www.gdconf.com). Take advantage of every opportunity to meet contacts in person, and don't forget to follow up immediately. Craft your materials (résumé, portfolio, et cetera) to match the creative vision of your contact's studio, and remember to be professional even if his company seems ultracasual. For the interview itself, Phil Marley says that you should be prepared to answer questions about current game-related events and where you think the industry is going. You may also be expected to sell an imaginary game concept to the interviewer or perform similar creative-minded tasks.

If all goes well, you will eventually secure employment with a game developer or studio, and you'll want to know what to expect. Well, while most developer atmospheres are fun and at least a little lighthearted, they are incredibly fast-paced as well. "We're artists as well as tech nerds, so we wear a lot of hats," says Lorne. "Not only do we have to make things look impressive, but we have to make sure they work too. We have to collaborate with programming teams, executives, sales and marketing, and then we have to sell our vision to the press." Your hours will be long, many of your projects won't ever make it to the stores, and you may have to move where the jobs are (California, Washington, New York, et cetera).

The good news is, once your career gets going, you'll not only be doing the job of your dreams, but you'll be decently compensated for it too. Animation Arena (www.animationarena.com) cites the average annual salary for a video game designer with three years or less of experience as more than $44K. Mid-level designers top $67K, and top-level ones sometimes surpass six figures! "Where you go with your career, and how fast you move up in it, is entirely up to individual choice, discipline, and goals . . . just like any other job," says Peter. "But video game design really is one of the most creative, fun jobs there is. You wear a baseball cap and shorts to work every day, and you get to see something you worked on displayed on store shelves throughout the world."

The Data Head

My parents always encouraged me to go after whatever I wanted, with hard work and determination. When I see something I want to do, it never occurs to me that I might fail at it. What I love most about my job now is the analytical aspect—it drew me to engineering in the first place. The best part is delving into a project and trying to attack it from as many different angles as possible. You have to figure out the best solution while trying to foresee and combat any potential problems that might occur before the "project" is built or goes into operation.

—Peachie, twenty-five, environmental engineer

MARIE CURIE. STEPHEN HAWKING. Sally Ride. Bill Gates. Bill Murray's character in *Ghostbusters*. They're some of the more memorable data heads we've known, and we respect their keen intellect and ingenious problem-solving ability immensely, even as we might poke fun at them for being occasionally, or not so occasionally, nerdy. When we think of the data head, the picture that comes immediately to mind is of someone who excels at math and the sciences and prefers to collaborate with machines over human beings. But in fact, data heads are a diverse lot, and if you get the chance to chat with a few, they'll no doubt surprise you.

One of the defining characteristics of the data head is a gift for gathering and organizing information, and then synthesizing it into meaningful components. "In my job, you have to be able to take highly technical information, digest it, interpret it, determine what the best option is, and then explain it to your client in a very basic, easily understood manner," says Kim, twenty-eight, a financial adviser. "We examine other people's servers and network environments and find their mistakes," adds Gary, thirty-two, an information security specialist. "Sometimes, you have to look deep, and that can mean extrapolating the inner workings of systems whose inner workings are hidden by design. We have to make a lot of educated guesses and infer how things work based on whatever behaviors we can observe." In large part due to their rational, methodical mind-sets, data heads deplore bureaucracy and prefer to work on their own if that means that tasks will get accomplished more effectively. "Research programs can be run inefficiently, which really frustrates me sometimes," admits Matt, twenty-eight, a pharmaceutical scientist. Evan, thirty-seven, a meteorologist, shares some of the same sentiments. "Private-sector meteorology is in some ways more gratifying because I have more direct control over my own success and the freedom to make things happen," he says.

The data head is the most even-tempered of the passion profiles in this book, and she tends to believe that common sense is king. "The personality trait that has served me best is my levelheadedness," says twenty-five-year-old Peachie, an environmental engineer. "I'm always able to think things through before taking action, and so I'm able to perform my tasks with minimal mistakes even in

> A pharmaceutical researcher relies on deductive reasoning, and the job uses technology to function at higher and more efficient levels. I feel like I'd be using my love of science to actually help people.
>
> *—Kristen, thirty-eight*

stressful situations." Data heads are happiest when they have the opportunity to integrate new and existing information to achieve concrete and consequential goals. Says Michael, a twenty-nine-year-old urban planner: "Adjusting ideas and applying them to a new project—like improving transit access or decreasing our reliance on private automobiles—is the most challenging and rewarding part of planning." Laurie, also a twenty-nine-year-old urban planner, agrees. "I'm intrigued by how things function, by the forces that shape them," she says. "We don't always have the option of developing the perfect solution, but part of what makes the job interesting is having to find a workable one that accomplishes the same objectives."

Always practical and thorough, the data head is known for his high performance standards, and he'll settle for nothing less than the best final product. "It's important to me to get tangible results in every project I take on, whether I'm trying to lead a product development team, recruit the best new engineers, or improve the collaboration between product development and our supply base," says Beth, thirty-one, a pharmaceutical scientist. As a result, the complexity of their work sometimes causes them a bit of anxiety. "Accurate forecasting is a combination of mathematics, physics, and experience. Knowing what will happen is not always easy, and when you've spent a lot of time trying to get it right and you're not, that's frustrating," says Kevin, thirty, a meteorologist.

A financial adviser is hopefully knowledgeable enough to make the right financial decisions, and is therefore already secure. One's free time can be used to help others achieve financial success!

—*Ken, twenty-eight*

The data head's skills may make him a strong candidate for leadership positions, but a lack of social skills and/or political savvy may get in the way of his career growth. "Honestly, the hardest thing for me has been figuring out how to interact with different people on the job," says Peachie. "In order to be successful, it's vital that you learn how to put your emotions aside and be able to relate effectively to your co-workers on a daily basis." Adds Gary: "I'm an introvert, and so management, and the things that come with it, just don't sound very appealing to me." Data heads hate to be micromanaged, and may, consciously or unconsciously, stubbornly pursue their own agendas in the face of disagreement. "Quality control will sometimes get infuriated with me because I'm producing a report the way I want, not the way they want," says Matt. "I've been known to have to submit it three times." Nevertheless, you can earn a data head's respect by appealing to her finely tuned sense of reason.

Data heads work in thousands of different careers, but this chapter will focus on several jobs—including computational linguist, environmental engineer, financial adviser, information security specialist, meteorologist, pharmaceutical scientist, and urban planner—which allow these talented individuals to leverage their natural analytical abilities for the purposes of advancing human knowledge and improving public welfare.

> I think urban planning is a cool job because the ergonomics and aesthetics of city design and public spaces is important to me, and I think it affects everyone who comes into contact with it. The modernist, purely functional architecture of the seventies and eighties was horrible, and it would be enjoyable and gratifying to help make cities and public spaces pleasingly livable for future residents.
>
> —*Ellis, twenty-four*

COMPUTATIONAL LINGUIST
• •

> My supervisor at Stanford contacted me to see if I was interested in joining a start-up he was involved in. This company, YY Technologies, was using the English grammar we had developed to create a range of applications, including automated customer service, and they wanted to branch out into Japanese. I speak Japanese, and as one of approximately two people in the world who both spoke Japanese and were trained in the style of grammar engineering used by the company, I could basically name my price. It was a delightful job, essentially teaching Japanese to a computer, and it gave me the credentials and connections I needed to land the job I have now.
>
> —Emily, thirty-three, computational linguist

A LOT OF PEOPLE ASSOCIATE linguistics, which is the scientific study of language, with an academic career. Others think of a linguist as someone who is fluent in several languages and travels the world as a translator. One of the coolest careers I've heard about in years, computational linguistics, involves a slightly different take on this interesting field. In general, linguists investigate how knowledge of language is acquired, how it interacts with other mental processes, and how it varies depending on the person or the region. They study how the structure of language (such as sounds or phrases) can be represented, and how different components of language (such as intonation and meaning) interact with one another. According to Wikipedia (www.wikipedia.org), computational linguistics is an interdisciplinary field dealing with the statistical and logical modeling of natural language. This career originated in the 1950s, when people first tried to use computers to translate foreign-language texts into English and sought to develop algorithms and software for intelligently processing language data.

In 2000, *The Wall Street Journal* published a high-profile article on the explosion of the computational linguistics field. The immense opportunity of the Internet was leading established and start-up technology companies to hire linguists in droves. These linguists, who had completed various levels of education and had computer science expertise as well, helped companies use natural language processing to respond meaningfully to requests for help or information. What were some of the initial applications? The *Journal* provided the example of how an online customer asking about shaving products might be automatically asked whether he also needed razors, blades, or shaving cream.

In the years that followed, as the Internet became even more commercially viable, hundreds of companies sprang up around the development of fast and user-friendly products that leveraged linguistic phenomena to get customers the right data in the fastest, most efficient manner possible. Today, a computational linguist working within a technology company or research institution might be responsible for building or testing natural language processing systems, or engineering linguistic applications (sometimes known as lingware) or related software. Or, her role might involve making it easier for people to access critical knowledge resources, as is the case with thirty-two-year-old Helen, a computational linguist in Colorado. "My job entails describing the variation of language and devising ways for programs to deal effectively with that variation," she says. "On a daily basis, this translates to activities such as searching bodies of text for specific grammatical structures or conceptual constructs, describing the features of variation, and then programming automatic concept recognizers and text processors to deal with the variation."

Some computational linguists are helping to develop future

technologies. "I recently had a meeting with some folks from a local start-up company, VoiceBox, which builds conversational speech–based interfaces for a variety of gadgets, including satellite radio, in-dash navigation systems, and other sources of information you might find inside a car," says Emily, thirty-three, a computational linguist in Seattle. "Their technology allows you to control these via natural spoken commands and requests, to which the car can reply via a synthesized voice. While KITT from *Knight Rider* and HAL from *2001* are still a long way off, it's thrilling to be involved in bringing such fantasies one step closer to reality."

If all this sounds as intriguing to you as it does to me, you're probably wondering how you can score a gig in the field. The good news is, there are several ways in. Your best bet is to complete a bachelor's, master's, or doctoral degree program in computational linguistics, which will teach programming languages such as C++ or Perl and will offer coursework in natural language processing, artificial intelligence, machine translation, and text mining. Those who have obtained a bachelor's degree in linguistics, and have therefore mastered basics such as phonetics (the study of sounds), morphology (the study of words), syntax (the study of sentences), and semantics (the study of meaning) are pretty marketable too. However, due to the shortage of private-sector candidates with computational linguistics experience, many enter the field purely on the strength of their computer science or computer engineering skills. "What I hear from hiring managers at human language technology companies is that it is rare to find people who are trained in both computer science and linguistics, so they typically end up taking people who are trained in computer science and giving them some linguistics and computational linguistics training on the job," says Emily.

The contacts you'll be exposed to by doing a formal degree program in computational linguistics may make finding your first job in the field relatively easy. But those data heads entering from the computer science side of things will likely need a little more assistance. The experts I spoke with recommended getting involved with the Linguistic Society of America (www.lsadc.org), the Association for Computational Linguistics (www.aclweb.org), and the North American chapter of the Association of Computational Linguistics (www.cs .cornell.edu/home/llee/naacl). All of these organizations will point you in the direction of valuable learning resources, networking opportunities, and employment options. You can also make headway by attending their industry conferences. "These events act as venues for the cutting-edge work in natural-language processing," says Helen. "There are usually student rates, and some conferences accept volunteer work at the event in exchange for registration fees." In addition to your networking activities, you should scout openings advertised by the top companies in the field (Microsoft at www.microsoft.com, IBM at www.ibm.com, Cymfony at www.cymfony.com, Google at www.google.com, AOL at www.aol.com, and so on), or by checking out the following websites:

- ComputerJobs (www.computerjobs.com)
- Dice (www.dice.com)
- Jobs for Programmers (www.prgjobs.com)
- Linguist Careers (www.linguistcareers.com)
- The Linguist List (www.linguistlist.org)
- Technology Recruiter (www.technologyrecruiter.com)

Finally, be patient, because there is a lot to learn before you'll be able to be an effective member of a computational linguistics team. "Even if you haven't landed that job yet, find projects to keep yourself busy so you have more hands-on experience with challenges common to the field," says Helen. "Teach yourself new programming languages and new software engineering practices, practice with existing natural language processing tools that are out there, and stay up to date with

current linguistic research and innovation by reading tech journals."
Suggests Emily: "If you live near a university, find out if they have computational linguistics or natural language processing research going
on. Colloquia and other research presentations are usually open to the
public, and there are typically e-mail lists that you can join."

It's a rare individual who is blessed with equally strong language
interpretation, analytical, and critical-thinking skills, and for this
reason gifted computational linguists tend to be well compensated.
According to Robert Half International, starting salaries for software
engineers range from $63,250 to $92,750, and those with a background in computational linguistics often hit six-figure salaries in just
a few years. It's far from an easy road, though. Computational linguists are required to develop products in a pressure-filled environment, under tight time frames and budgets, and their success often
depends on the strength of the technologies they're working with.
"Everything is done on the computer, and so if a server goes down or
a hard drive acts up, my work completely halts," says Helen.

Nevertheless, the future for computational linguistics is certainly bright. "I fell in love with linguistics during my second semester
in college, but I felt like I had to make my peace with studying something that I saw as having little practical application," says Emily.
"There's still that perception, and now people are starting to say that
computer science isn't a profitable field to go into because so many
jobs are being outsourced overseas. But, in fact, U.S. industries are
hungry for graduates trained in human language technology."

ENVIRONMENTAL ENGINEER

I had the opportunity to build a highway utilizing a very large spectrum of employee skills. One particular employee was a recent graduate of high school. I realized at some point that he did not know standard units of length (inch, foot, et cetera), and I considered how I might convey this information to make him functional for our project. My solution was to cut blocks of wood at various lengths and to have him carry them around. So when I needed something about a foot long, I would ask him to measure for me. I found that the key to measurement is getting the mental picture of a few units and then everything seems to fall in place. As for the individual, it would seem that I was teasing him, but he received my suggestion well and carried his blocks around with him for a few months, generally proud of his position of value in the group.

—Stacey, thirty-six, environmental engineer

WHEN I WAS DOING RESEARCH for this section, I came across a bunch of cool environmental engineering projects on a website called A Sightseer's Guide to Engineering. One of them was the Theodore Roosevelt Dam, which, when construction was finished in 1911, was the world's largest all-masonry dam. It recently underwent a nine-year, $430 million renovation project, adding 444,000 cubic yards of concrete to the dam and 6.7 million pounds of reinforced steel (849 miles long if placed end to end).

According to JETS, the leading nonprofit educational organization dedicated to promoting engineering and technology careers, environmental engineers protect public health and safety and ensure that nature's ecosystems are not adversely affected as they are employed to benefit humankind. Assignments include the development of long-range community, regional, or facility plans to serve the public and protect the environment.

Environmental engineers are the ones behind the scenes, working every day to keep our planet from deteriorating more than it already has. They're involved in water and air pollution control, recycling, and waste management, and they use their skills in biology and chemistry to study and find solutions to major environmental problems such as acid rain, gas emissions, ozone depletion, wildlife extinction, and global warming. For example, twenty-five-year-old Peachie is in her first job engineering water filtration systems. "The main part of my job is to take the operating parameters of an application and put together a proposal for the best water filtration system," says Peachie. "This process includes evaluating the parameters individually and as a whole, sizing the filter system to accommodate the water that will be passing through it, looking for parameters that will be problematic and then coming up with solutions."

Stacey, thirty-six, is a little further along in his environmental engineering career—he's the president and senior engineer at Richardson Smith Gardner & Associates in North Carolina. "My job consists of various solid waste design and consulting activities," Stacey says. "In general, we help our clients obtain various local zoning and environmental permits for development of solid waste facilities, which may involve land, air, or water quality. I have always enjoyed this job as it allows me to use my mind, to be practical, theoretical, and to spend time outside a little bit each week."

As you might imagine, environmental engineers, who according to the U.S. Bureau of Labor Statistics make up approximately 30 percent of the engineering population, require a significant amount of science education before becoming eligible to enter the field. The bureau's *Occupational Outlook Handbook* tells us that environmental engineering usually requires a bachelor's degree in some type of engineering, with coursework in mathematics and the physical and life sciences. Some colleges also offer two- or four-year degree programs in engineering technology, which include hands-on laboratory classes that focus on current issues in the application of engineering principles and prepare students for practical design and production work. If you majored in another scientific discipline such as math, physics, or chemistry, you may be able to secure an entry-level job because environmental engineering is a specialty in relatively high demand.

Like other scientific careers, getting your first job in environmental engineering requires making good use of the contacts you've established through your educational experiences. The best way in is to get an internship while you're still in school, either through the career center or on the recommendation of professors, alumni, or other experienced professionals in your life. "When I was at NC State, my cousin worked for a woman at the pollution prevention department with the state and her husband needed a young engineering student to work part-time with his start-up engineering consulting company," Stacey says. "When my cousin told me about the position and said that the company did landfill design, I commented that working with landfills sounded like a horrible job, but I called anyway and got the job. Here I am running the company fifteen years later."

If you've missed the internship boat, however, try getting involved with industry organizations such as the National Society of Professional Engineers (www.nspe.org) and the American Academy of Environmental Engineers (www.aaee.net). These associations offer great resources for helping aspiring environmental engineers break into the profession, including networking opportunities, job openings, and background reading. "Engineering groups related to my field have been extremely useful in my postcollege life," says Peachie. "I suggest looking for groups in your area of interest—environmental remediation, for instance—because these can offer focused training that can be used on the job and for growth in your field."

Although graduate study is not necessary unless you plan to join a university faculty or research and development organization, you will need to get certified as a professional engineer in order to move your career forward. According to the National Society of Professional Engineers, licensure laws vary from state to state. Generally, though, the requirements are graduation from an accredited engineering curriculum followed by approximately four years of engineering experience, and finally the successful completion of a written exam. Most state laws provide for a prelicensure certificate for new grads who don't yet have the four years of experience under their belts. To find out about your state's licensure requirements as well as how to prepare for and take the exams, you can contact your state's licensure board via the National Council of Examiners for Engineering and Surveying website (www.ncees.org).

And what can you expect once you're finally on the job? The U.S. Bureau of Labor Statistics' *Occupational Outlook Handbook* says that beginning engineering graduates usually work under the supervision of experienced engineers and, in large companies, also may receive formal classroom or seminar-type training. As new engineers gain knowledge and experience, they are assigned more difficult projects with greater independence to develop designs, solve problems, and make decisions. Engineers may advance to become technical specialists or to supervise a staff or team of engineers and technicians. "From an entry-level engineering position, the paths you can take are numerous," says Peachie. "Once you find a niche that you are interested in, you can enter into any of the fields that are a step in getting a project completed: research and development, engineering design, specification writing, manufacturing, installation, or project management. Your growth and direction will depend on your specialization and what area you like best: the conceptual realm or the physical-production realm."

In order to advance in the profession, you'll need to be highly analytical, detail-oriented, and a strong problem solver and communicator. You'll need to have the ability to manage multiple projects simultaneously and see them all through to satisfactory conclusions. And there will inevitably be challenges. "My company's main focus is in the solid waste industry, which, at times, is not the most appreciated," says Stacey. "The NIMBY [Not in My Back Yard] sentiment can enrage a community."

Fortunately, due to increasing environmental concerns, the job market for engineers in this specialty is projected to be excellent through 2014. As a group, engineers earn some of the highest starting salaries among those with bachelor's degrees, and a recent survey by the National Association of Colleges and Employers indicated that new environmental engineers make nearly $50K annually. And for many, the money's just the icing on the cake. Says Peachie: "This career path offers a lot of forward thinking and breakthrough ideas that you can be a part of, and your mind is constantly at play."

FINANCIAL ADVISER

I needed to transfer to San Diego since my fiancé and I were planning to relocate there after our wedding. While I was attending a conference in Orlando, I found out that there were only two asset management firms in San Diego. Furthermore, there was a client relationship manager from one of the firms in attendance. When I realized that she was heading into the restrooms after one of the sessions, I positioned myself next to her to wash my hands. After initiating a conversation with her regarding the conference, she gave me her business card and we sat next to each other at the next session. As my career has progressed, most of my big breaks have come from building a network of contacts who referred me to opportunities that weren't listed anywhere.

—Quan, twenty-nine, financial adviser

DO YOU REMEMBER that Morgan Stanley wedding commercial from a few years ago where this older guy, who you think is the bride's father, stands up and gives this heartfelt toast? At the end of the toast, he says something like, "And I feel privileged to be her financial adviser." The point of the commercial is, of course, that Morgan Stanley advisers treat their clients like family and are invested in all of their most critical life moments. It's a rather nice sentiment, if you ask me.

A job in finance can mean many different things depending on who you are and what you're looking for in a career. For instance, financial analysts work for banks, securities firms, and mutual and pension funds to assess the economic performance of companies and industries for firms and institutions with money to invest, while financial advisers generally assess the financial needs and prospects of individuals. For the purposes of this section, we'll focus on the financial adviser, also known as the financial planner, role. According to the Princeton Review, personal financial advisers determine how their clients can meet lifelong financial goals through smart resource management. They examine past and current performance of their clients' monetary assets and suggest steps clients should take to meet long-term goals such as sending a child to college or supporting themselves in retirement.

The U.S. Bureau of Labor Statistics' *Occupational Outlook Handbook* tells us that the financial adviser's work begins with an information-gathering consultation with the client. The adviser then develops a comprehensive financial plan that identifies problem areas, makes recommendations for improvement, and selects appropriate investments compatible with the client's goals, attitude toward risk, and expectation for a return on the investment. Advisers usually meet with established clients at least once a year to update them on potential investments and to determine whether the clients have been through any life changes—such as marriage or disability—that might affect financial goals. Some financial advisers spend all of their time working for one client. "I evaluate investment opportunities for a high-net-worth family," says Quan, twenty-nine, a financial adviser now in Grand Rapids, Michigan. "I visit companies and speak with management, evaluate whether their marketplace position is defensible, and close deals on behalf of the client."

Most financial advisers begin their careers working for banks, mutual fund companies, or investment firms. Such firms typically require candidates to have a bachelor's degree, preferably in business administration, finance, economics, or accounting. While a master's degree in business administration certainly helps, it's not necessary at the entry level. And unlike many of the jobs profiled in this book, getting that first job is not the most challenging step you'll take as you initiate your new career as a financial adviser. "I was offered an opportunity to interview at every firm I contacted and I received several offers," says Kim, twenty-eight, a financial adviser in Long Beach, New York. "It's not a difficult field to break into unless there is a hiring freeze, but it *is* paramount that you carefully research the firm and the environment that you will be working in. What is their ideal clientele? What is their mission? Does this overlap with your own personal values?"

Once you're on the job, though, things get a whole lot tougher. In addition to learning the trade and performing long hours of research for clients and superiors, you will be immediately responsible for building your own client base. "This career comes with a distinct right of passage that could only be compared to that of a resident doctor," says Kim. "During your first few years you can easily work seven days a week, giving up most or all of your own personal time for the sake of surviving the hurdles (the quotas, the training requirements, et cetera) that your particular firm enforces."

Most newbie financial advisers are required to pass a comprehensive two-day, ten-hour Certified Financial Planner (CFP) examination that covers the financial planning process, tax planning, employee benefits, retirement planning, estate planning, investment management, and insurance. Fortunately, in addition to the support you'll receive from your employer, there are some great third-party organizations that are ready and willing to guide you through the process of establishing yourself in the profession, including the Financial Planning Association (www.fpanet.org), the American Academy of Financial Management (www.financialanalyst.org), and the American Financial Services Association (www.afsaonline.org).

Financial advisers who get ahead quickly will be true data heads, with a little networker mixed in. They are experts at gathering and analyzing information, number crunching, and using their economic, mathematical, computer, and deductive-reasoning skills to solve problems and achieve goals. However, because a substantial part of the job involves attracting and retaining clients, financial advisers must also have excellent interpersonal prowess and sales ability. They will have the communication chops to educate clients about complex financial concepts in an easily digestible manner, and they will have the self-discipline necessary to manage their workload independently. "Hard work and a good attitude help to bridge the gap of being young and not having any relationships or experience to bring to the table," says Quan.

It's also essential to be tenacious and to have a thick skin in the face of frequent rejection. "The overwhelming majority of people coming into this profession start from scratch with various levels of knowledge in finance (twenty-two-year-old communications majors versus experienced equities traders) and various-size Rolodexes (people with zero contacts versus those who know the Trumps)," says Kim. "Interestingly, where you start on the totem pole doesn't really correlate with how high you're able to eventually get. Persistence is the common trait that all established advisers have."

If this sounds right up your alley, you're in luck, for the financial services field is booming. The U.S. Bureau of Labor Statistics reports that employment for personal financial advisers is expected to increase faster than average for all occupations through 2014, as baby boomers enter retirement and a better-educated and wealthier population requires investment advice. Other promising factors include industry deregulation, the rapid expansion of self-directed retirement plans, and a rise in the number and complexity of potential client investments. It's a well-compensated career path too. The median annual earnings of financial advisers hover around $65K, and bonuses and commissions can easily put an experienced adviser into the six-figure bracket.

As your career progresses, you will likely establish some long-term client relationships that will be the bread and butter of your practice. You may be promoted into a management position in a financial services or investment firm, or you may choose to start your own planning business. "Now that I'm a little farther along, I find that the opportunity to educate, the opportunity to reap the rewards of building my own business, and the opportunity to be my own boss are all major attributes of being a financial adviser," says Kim. "And when I sit across the table from a client I know I have helped, nothing feels more gratifying."

INFORMATION SECURITY SPECIALIST

> Once, we were working for a bank, which happened to be the national bank for a country (fortunately, not my country). They wanted to introduce some online banking features for their customers. Our job was to try to break into the Web server before it was introduced to the public. We noticed that if you went to a particular link, you could see people's account numbers, usernames, and passwords. Although we documented this in our report, someone along the line decided to leave it. About a year later, I was cleaning out my bookmarks, and I accessed a link, and as it turns out, they had never fixed the problem. Every once in a while you come across something huge that nobody wants to deal with. It's really quite breathtaking.
>
> —Gary, thirty-two, information security specialist

SOME SAY THAT the information security field sprang up around the activities of hackers, those devious guys who break into private computer systems and dump in their malicious code. Regardless of how it got started, however, today information security is big business. Crimes involving the destruction of whole networks and the theft of identities and other assets are no longer limited to a select group of individuals, and widespread security measures are necessary to protect the mission-critical operations of every company and business in the world today—from your local dentist's patient records to Citibank's billions of online transactions.

According to the Virginia Alliance for Secure Computing and Networking, information security specialists find and solve security problems in computer systems. They pinpoint issues like insecure passwords, poorly configured networks, and computer-related policies that employees aren't following correctly; plan for viruses and system crashes; set up applications that secure information from unauthorized access; and train people to follow these procedures. "My group is responsible for responding to computer security incidents which could include managing the incident response process, augmenting the incident response team, or providing advice regarding incident response planning and new vulnerabilities," says Nathan, thirty-three, an information security specialist in New York.

One of the information security specialist's most intriguing responsibilities is tracking the latest threats and responding to them with innovative strategies, which may involve breaking into their own systems and finding weaknesses before hackers do. "Currently, I am doing penetration testing," says Gary, thirty-two, an information security specialist in Chicago. "This means I attempt to break into clients' computers in order to find the vulnerabilities and assess the overall security posture. The first part of any test involves a reconnaissance phase where I thoroughly explore the environment. It's important to get inside the minds of the administrators and figure out what mistakes they might make."

As information security is a relatively new field, certifications and on-the-job experience are often valued above formal education, though employers ideally prefer candidates to have a bachelor's degree in computer science or information technology. There are numerous entry-level, vendor-neutral information security certifications available, and the most popular will likely have changed again by the time this book goes to press (tops at the moment are (ISC)^2 and SSCP). However, experts recommend that you obtain at least one of these before you begin your job search, and if you're interested in specializing in a particular platform, you may want to investigate vendor-specific credentials as well. Most certification programs include classroom and computer-based training and at least one formal exam. You should also keep in mind that security specialists employed by companies doing work for the federal government often need to go through the process of government security clearance.

Even with the right technical knowledge and background, getting your first job in information security can be a tough proposition, because security tends to be a more competitive area of systems management than, let's say, data storage. For this reason, Ed Tittel, in an article for *Certification Magazine,* says that many aspiring information security specialists initially accept jobs as systems administrators, network administrators, help desk managers, or tech support professionals. "Don't be discouraged if you have to start out doing menial tasks," says Nathan. "Most of the time, even the most talented and brilliant student can not survive alone on an engagement that carries the type of pressure associated with computer security incidents. On-the-job training is critical to your success, because allowing a person to get right into this type of work without any practical experience would be setting them up for failure."

The information security community is where the experts suggest recent grads sniff around for work. "At the beginning of my career, I became involved in various groups related to computer security," says Gary. "Some of them were primarily online, and some of them involved face-to-face contact. I met some really intelligent people, many of whom were crucial in providing direction and leads. The guidance of a community was very helpful in charting a course through it all." Some organizations that may be helpful to you as you wade into the waters of information security include:

- AFCEA International (www.afcea.org)
- American Council for Technology (www.actgov.org)
- Association for Computing Machinery (www.acm.org)
- The Center for Internet Security (www.cisecurity.org)
- Cyber Security Industry Alliance (www.csialliance.org)

- Information Resources Management Association (www.irma-international.org)
- Information Systems Security Association (www.issa.org)
- Information Technology Association of America (www.itaa.org)
- International Security, Trust, and Privacy Alliance (www.istpa.org)
- (ISC)² (www.isc2.org)
- SANS Institute (www.sans.org)
- Security Industry Association (www.siaonline.org)

According to the *(ISC)² Career Guide: Decoding the Information Security Profession,* typical organizations that hire information security specialists, and computer specialists in general, include professional services firms, governments, telecommunications firms, and banks, but as I mentioned earlier, all types of businesses are discovering a need for this type of expertise. Sought-after skills include knowledge of network systems, security policies, protocols, and software, and an understanding of the best practices for developing a sound security infrastructure. The best information security professionals have the analytical and problem-solving chops to synthesize and derive important information from huge amounts of data, and are able to understand the interplay between the various components of a system. "I think you have to be naturally curious, and have the ability to teach yourself and adhere to self-imposed deadlines," says Gary. "It really is a challenge to be the 'security guy' in your company. You've got to be prepared to have your most reasonable, modest, and necessary suggestions ignored. People will come up with really horrible justifications for their reckless behavior, and these justifications will be accepted by your superiors and people who should know better."

Information security specialists also need to be comfortable with the high degree of personal accountability and risk that's inherent to this career choice. As the frontline bodyguards for the entire organization, however, they never have to worry that their job is not critical to the bottom line or that they're not making enough of a difference. "This job requires the ability to troubleshoot just about anything, and quickly, because every case is different and the specific technology, platforms, and applications are all diverse," says Nathan. "You never know what to expect. Even if the situation is described to you ahead of time, it will always be different once you arrive. Things almost never go as planned."

Information security specialists who do well in their jobs are well positioned to take on increasing levels of leadership within a company. The $(ISC)^2$ *Career Guide*'s typical career path involves approximately one year as a security administrator, four plus years as an information security analyst or engineer, seven plus years as an information security manager, and nine plus years as a director of information security or chief security officer. Reaching higher levels of the profession requires more general business and management skills and a bevy of additional IT certifications, but the significant pay increases may be worth the extra effort. $(ISC)^2$ tells us that an entry-level IT administrator can expect to make around $50K, eventually progressing to just over $100K as an information security manager. It's not unusual for chief information security officers or other IT professionals at the executive level to earn several hundred thousand dollars a year.

The U.S. Bureau of Labor Statistics predicts that the demand for computer security specialists will continue to grow as businesses and government invest heavily in cyber security, placing a high priority on safeguarding their data and protecting vital systems and electronic infrastructures from attack. "I have to say that I've been lucky," says Nathan. "My interest and talent has been recognized and I have had the opportunity to train under some incredibly talented and well-respected folks in the industry. Right now, I'm in the best job situation I've ever had."

METEOROLOGIST

When I was in the seventh grade and president of a 4-H club, I invited John Belski, the local meteorologist from WAVE TV, to come and speak to our group. I kept in touch with John and on numerous occasions solicited advice concerning college, jobs, and television. Once I finished my internship and began working at my first paying job, I would bring tapes home with me and stop by to have John critique them. Time after time, I would take them back with a few items to work on . . . "Try interacting more with the anchors" or "Don't be scared to ask a question back at them." I will never forget the time I stopped by to have a tape critiqued and after viewing it there was silence. There was no advice, nothing to be worked on. John said, "I don't have anything to add." Eventually, just as I graduated, a weekend position had opened at WAVE. I applied, and with the help of a good word from John, I got the job.

—Kevin, thirty, meteorologist

THE SCIENCE OF METEOROLOGY has been around since the time of the Greeks, when Aristotle and his contemporaries tried to understand how winds and rain would affect the society's agricultural and navigational operations. The field as we know it has been around since the mid-1800s, and today, meteorologists, also called atmospheric scientists, study how the atmosphere's physical characteristics affect our environment on a daily basis. Meteorologists predict the weather, of course, but they also do work to interpret climate trends and control the effects of pollution. In this section, we'll focus primarily on two of the most popular branches of meteorology: weather forecasting and television weathercasting.

Weather forecasters collect data on air pressure, temperature, humidity, and wind velocity from satellites, radars, and sensors—using mathematical calculations to make both short- and long-term forecasts for the public and private sectors. Many weather forecasters in the United States work for the National Weather Service, but thousands of others are gaining traction in weather service companies that provide custom predictions to utility, agricultural, shipping, and disaster management clients whose business operations are sensitive to weather conditions. For instance, thirty-seven-year-old Evan works as a private consultant in Miami, Florida. "A typical job for me might involve providing up-to-the-minute forecasts for a client who needs to know if he will need additional equipment in the event of a hurricane."

Television weathercasting employs the high-profile meteorologists we know and love. This very competitive career track involves researching and producing weather forecasts as segments of larger news broadcasts, and delivering predictions on air and online through the use of specialized graphics. "My day is spent coming up with a creative and unique way to present a forecast and then delivering it to our television audience," says Kevin, thirty, a television weathercaster in Louisville, Kentucky. "Depending on the weather, sometimes I may spend the most time coming up with a creative graphic to illustrate a point. I also prepare and deliver live weather reports over the radio every fifteen minutes from four to seven P.M., in addition to Internet updates."

Although most experts will tell you that meteorology is tough to break into because it's such a small field, the educational barriers to entry are rather low when compared with many other scientific professions. Entry-level weather forecasters working for the federal government, for example, must have just a bachelor's degree. While you will need coursework in atmospheric science and other subjects such as mathematics, physics, engineering, and computer science, a major in meteorology is not essential. As a television weathercaster, you might not even need to get a bachelor's, provided you perform well on camera and know how to get the information that results in accurate forecasts. The majority of meteorologists with master's or doctoral degrees pursue academic careers in research and teaching.

Your strategy for launching a career in meteorology will depend on whether you're interested in weather forecasting or television weathercasting. For the former, it's best to start while you're still in school. The American Meteorological Society's *Career Guide for the Atmospheric Sciences* recommends checking out the organization's summer internship resources on their website (www.ametsoc.org) and investigating federal government initiatives such as the Student Career Enhancement Program and the Student Temporary Employment Program (both at www.weather.gov). The guide also suggests participating and networking at AMS events, and getting involved with other third-party associations such as the National Weather Association (www.nwas.org) as well. Evan recommends staying in regular contact with the people you meet who are currently working in the industry. "Read the meteorology trade magazines, and get to know people who have jobs in the environment you want to be in. If you're lucky, they'll let you know ahead of time when someone is leaving."

When it comes to scoring a gig as a television weathercaster, you'll probably need to volunteer or intern at a news station in a small market in order to learn the ropes. "I applied for my first paying job when I was sophomore in college," says Kevin. "There was a weekend position open for the six and eleven P.M. newscasts. I think I would have paid them to do it. Some of the best advice I received was to put myself ahead of everyone else, so when I graduated I would stand out." If you are able to get a position like Kevin's, try to get as much on-camera time as you can. News directors will require not only a résumé but also a DVD of you presenting the weather. Once you have some experience to speak of, you might sign on with a talent agency that represents meteorologists. "These firms will package your materials and present them to their news director clients when they're looking for someone specific to fill a position," Evan tells us.

The experience of your first job will vary greatly based on the road you choose. According to the U.S. Bureau of Labor Statistics' *Occupational Outlook Handbook,* entry-level weather forecasters in the National Weather Service, for instance, must complete a period of training before moving on to their core daily responsibilities, which include routine data collection, computation and analysis, and basic forecasting. Those who do well have a strong grasp of scientific and mathematical principles, as well as the analytical ability to extract key data to solve problems. "I've found computer modeling to be an invaluable skill," says Evan. "I write my own programs that allow me to put in raw data and come out with a forecast that highlights the information that's critical to that particular client."

New television weathercasters can expect long, irregular hours as they cope with never-ending forecast deadlines and periodic weather emergencies. Their first years on the job will likely be spent in less desirable locations, for positions in the larger media markets are über-competitive and require significant experience. "You have to be prepared to relocate often, especially in the beginning," says Evan. For these reasons, it's imperative that television weathercasters be flexible, organized, open-minded, and able to put together a complex forecast that can be communicated in an easily digestible manner. "Despite what some people may think, I don't get the forecast from somewhere else," says Kevin. "A lot of time and energy goes into making an accurate forecast, which is especially true when it comes to snow and severe storms."

Advancement in the field may include getting certified by AMS, which, for forecasters, requires a minimum of five years' experience and involves passing an examination to demonstrate thorough meteorological knowledge. AMS also offers a professional certification for broadcast meteorologists. Progressing in your career, you can expect your job opportunities and earning potential to increase. As previously mentioned, private weather consulting firms are booming, and you have the potential to top six figures if you decide to go that route. Weather forecasters in the federal government start low (around $30K), but they too earn a respectable average salary of $81K once they reach the supervisory level. But more important than the compensation is the job satisfaction meteorologists derive through their passion for weather. "In high school, people used to call me to see if school would be canceled due to snow," says Evan. "I compared the information on the Weather Channel to conditions outside and gave them my forecast. I've been involved in meteorology ever since, and with advances on the Internet, the field is only getting more and more exciting."

PHARMACEUTICAL SCIENTIST

I was the design engineer for the next generation Mammotome EX, a minimally invasive breast biopsy product. While waiting in line at Panera, I initiated some small talk with the woman standing next to me. As we spoke, the woman mentioned that she had had a rough time over the past few months; she had been diagnosed with breast cancer. She shared some specifics about the experience, and I realized that she recently had a Mammotome breast biopsy. Although the diagnosis was cancer, her experience with the Mammotome procedure was very positive. I was touched that my product line had helped to deliver an accurate diagnosis in the least invasive way possible. This happenstance conversation demonstrated the impact that I can have on millions of people without ever meeting them.

—Beth, thirty-one, pharmaceutical scientist

TALK ABOUT A CAREER with intriguing possibilities. People entering the pharmaceutical research field today may be the ones discovering the cure for cancer or Parkinson's disease tomorrow. Although the U.S. pharmaceutical companies sometimes get a bad rap, they routinely make astounding advances that save lives, and, from what I hear, aren't bad places to work either. If you're a data head who wants to use your scientific background for the greater good, you might consider becoming a pharmaceutical scientist. Here's some detail about what breaking into the field entails.

According to the American Association of Pharmaceutical Scientists, the pharmaceutical sciences combine a broad range of scientific disciplines that are critical to the discovery and development of new drugs, therapies, and medical devices. Some of the more common specializations include drug discovery and design, which deals with the design and synthesis of new drug molecules and includes medicinal chemistry, combinatorial chemistry, and biotechnology; drug delivery, which is concerned with the design of dosage forms—such as tablets, injections, or patches—that deliver the drug to the site of action within a patient; drug action, which examines how the drug works in a living system; clinical pharmacology, which is concerned with the use of drugs in the treatment of diseases and leverages human clinical trials to determine efficacy, adverse effects, and drug-to-drug interaction; and drug analysis, which involves separating, identifying, and quantifying the components of a sample.

Twenty-eight-year-old Matt, a senior research associate at Novartis, spends his days engaged in both drug action and drug analysis for the company's wide range of prescription medications for ailments such as heart disease, high blood pressure, and diabetes. He's responsible for testing animal organ and plasma samples to determine if a drug is working the way it's supposed to. "It's my job to quantify the drug's efficacy in the body, to gather early support as it moves through the process of getting approved by the Food and Drug Administration," he says.

While the majority of pharmaceutical scientists are employed by private-sector pharmaceutical companies, others work as researchers and professors at universities, as regulatory scientists for government agencies like the Food and Drug Administration (FDA), or as researchers at national laboratories such as the National Institutes of Health (NIH). An undergraduate degree in chemistry, biology, pharmacy, or engineering is a prerequisite for the entry-level position of research assistant. The research assistant, who receives a broad-based introduction to the pharmaceutical world, records, stores, and summarizes information and data, prepares technical reports, and develops laboratory skills and familiarity with equipment. "You should expect that your first job will be low-level and the work very routine," says Matt. "You won't have much of a chance to be creative or innovative, and you have to be tolerant of that at the beginning of your career." Adds Beth, thirty-one, an R & D project director at a top pharmaceutical company in the Northeast: "Make the most of each opportunity, no matter how small. Success with smaller projects will directly lead to greater responsibility and rapid professional growth. Focus both on delivering results and on how you deliver the results: for example, through strong teamwork or a rigorous research approach."

Recent college grads looking for research assistant jobs may want to start by educating themselves about the pharmaceutical industry in general. The Pharmaceutical Research and Manufacturers of America website (www.phrma.org) and the American Association of Pharmaceutical Scientists website (www.aapspharmaceutica.com) are great places to check out relevant publications, networking events, and internship and employment listings. Specific job opportunities can also be found on industry job portals including BioSpace (www.biospace.com), hireRx (www.hirerx.com), and MedZilla (www.medzilla.com), and you might also take advantage of openings advertised through your college's career center. "My first paying job was an internship at a medical device company," says Beth. "I made the original contact at an MIT career fair and then interviewed on campus with the company's recruiting team. I shared my passion for medical device engineering and my solid academic background and was hired after my sophomore year."

Matt also suggests that you might get in the door by connecting with a temporary employment firm specializing in pharmaceuticals. "I signed on with Kelly Scientific right out of school," he says. "Almost immediately, I got contract work doing clinical research studies that eventually resulted in a full-time job." Women may find that they're especially marketable, as the pharmaceutical industry is still predominantly male and most organizations are striving to even things out.

The typical pharmaceutical research career has ample room for growth. From the position of research assistant, you can progress to a research associate, an associate scientist, a scientist, a senior scientist, and a principal scientist. After you've reached a certain level, you may also have the option of taking on a cross-functional role in research management, regulatory affairs, pharmacoeconomics, or communications. At the moment, most people who reach the top levels of the profession get a Ph.D. along the way, but many say that's changing and that experience in the lab is increasingly worth more than formal education. You'll be happy to learn that compared to other industries, compensation is quite generous. According to a recent American Association for the Advancement of Science salary survey, pharmaceutical research assistants make more than $65K with just a bachelor's degree, and six-figure incomes are standard after a few years.

Like other data heads, pharmaceutical scientists are highly analytical and have had the math and science coursework to back up their natural talent. "You have to be anal about the details, because one small error can mess up a whole batch of samples," says Matt. A cool-headed approach to troubleshooting is critical as well. "Development setbacks occur frequently," says Beth. "When something goes wrong, my first step is to pull the team together to diagnose the situation. I do not try to lay blame but want to ensure that we learn and do not repeat the mistake or ignore the issue as we move forward." Additionally, pharmaceutical research environments can be political and difficult to navigate at times. "Drug research isn't always run like a well-oiled machine and loyalty to the company doesn't always work in your favor," says Matt. "You have to have a good sense of what you're worth and what you have to offer."

If you think pharmaceutical research might be for you, now's a great time to test-drive it as a career. A special supplement on hiring trends in the pharmaceutical field published in *The Scientist* reported that the number of people employed in the U.S. industry is expected to grow from 413,700 to 536,000 over the next decade, and that research and development spending, which exploded in 2004, is still steadily increasing. "I love my job because I have the opportunity to impact patients with my daily work, collaborating with my fellow team members to solve complex problems," says Beth. "And I feel very fortunate to work at a company where my personal values align very closely with the corporate culture."

URBAN PLANNER

The biggest challenge that I have faced as a young planner is my desire to learn, do, and accomplish great and meaningful results immediately. Why can't we transform the world in a day? I have worked on some great projects in the year that I have been a planner, but I have had to learn to be much more patient and persistent. When working with nationally renowned planners, it's hard to find the right balance between asserting myself, sharing my ideas, and listening and learning to individuals who have thirty years of experience and an encyclopedic knowledge of planning practices.

—Michael, twenty-nine, urban planner

OUT AND ABOUT IN OUR NEIGHBORHOODS, we see their work everywhere. They're the ones who decide how traffic will flow through a new suburban intersection, or whether a park would increase tourism to a downtown area. If you take the time to look around outside and wonder how every aspect of your community came to be, you'd marvel at the skills of the urban planners who made it all possible. Urban planning, also known as regional planning, is a low-key profession that tends to exist under the radar of dream careers, but it's ideal for data-head personalities who are interested in creating public systems and places that improve the welfare of their fellow citizens.

At its core, urban planning is working with members of the community to develop a broad vision for a project that will satisfy a predetermined goal. According to the American Planning Association's (APA) excellent website (www.planning.org), this vision takes the form of recommendations that address economic, environmental, regulatory, and accessibility concerns. Most urban planners specialize in one or several areas, such as community development, urban design, land use and code enforcement, transportation planning, housing, and natural resources planning. "As a transportation planner, I work on a wide range of projects," says Michael, twenty-nine, an urban planner at a private consulting firm in Washington, D.C. "The balance between creative thinking and engineering-based transportation analyses is great. One day I'll address accessibility and mobility issues on a regional scale, envisioning opportunities for a more efficient and sustainable transportation network using maps, graphics, and written examples, and the next I'll analyze the traffic impact of a small residential development on local intersections using engineering software and statistical analyses."

Like Michael, most urban planners analyze research and gather data using tools like electronic mapping and scenario visualization. And, as you may have already guessed, urban planning is a team effort, and planners spend their days collaborating with public officials, engineers, architects, and health professionals, among others. "My job is to strategize how I can bring about change given the realities of how the city administration works," says Laurie, twenty-nine, an urban planner for the Boston Redevelopment Authority. "For instance, the water and sewer department is planning to redo the sewer in a street that we planned to redesign. We need to work with the commission so that their reconstruction effort advances our design goals, coordinating the whole process so that it's most efficient and effective." Planners like Laurie are also responsible for keeping up with government legislation related to their area, and in facilitating public participation in their projects.

Information on the amount of education required for entry-level urban planning jobs is mixed. The U.S. Bureau of Labor Statistics' *Occupational Outlook Handbook* suggests that in order to be truly competitive, you follow your bachelor's degree with a master's degree in urban planning, architecture, or civil engineering from a program certified by the Planning Accreditation Board (PAB). Along the way, it'll also be handy to pick up a working knowledge of data-head staples like statistics and computer modeling. "I gained credibility by having a master's degree and the general and applied knowledge I developed during the program," says Michael. "I also think it is good to continue one's education by reading and pursuing training programs that update or enhance existing skills. Planning practices and tools, especially modeling software programs, are constantly shifting, which makes it important to stay informed and up-to-date."

Urban planning jobs are plentiful within federal, state, and local governments, and also within the private sector in real estate development companies, nonprofit organizations, and consulting firms. The master's degree will definitely grease the wheels when it comes to finding entry-level employment—having only a bachelor's will require a bit more ingenuity on your part. "While I was getting my B.A., I applied for the New York City Urban Fellowship, a program that grooms twenty promising college grads for public administration," says Laurie. "The experience helped immensely in applying for my current job and in getting into grad school."

Both Laurie and Michael cited persistent networking as a major factor in getting plum positions in the planning world. "At one point, I did about sixty informational interviews and volunteered on a bunch of committees for the Society of Architects," says Laurie. "I sent out postcards to everyone I met updating them on my career, and three years later people still comment on them." Adds Michael: "Just start writing and calling people who do what you want to do. It can be a long process and you may not get the exact job you want, but it will create opportunities that are unexpected and rewarding." Joining APA as a student or associate member and attending the career sessions at the annual conference are thought to be useful as well. Below are some resources to check out as you're learning about the profession and/or looking for work:

Books

- *A Career Worth Planning: Starting Out and Moving Ahead in the Planning Profession* (Jones and Macris)
- *A Guide to Careers in Community Development* (Brophy and Shabecoff)
- *The Job of the Practicing Planner* (Solnit)
- *What Planners Do: Power, Politics, and Persuasion* (Hoch)

Websites

- Architecture Job Bank (www.architecturejobbank.com)
- Careers in Government (www.careersingovernment.com)
- City Limits (www.citylimits.org)
- Cyburbia (www.cyburbia.org)
- Planetizen (www.planetizen.com)
- University of Michigan, Taubman College of Architecture and Urban Planning (sitemaker.umich.edu/urpjobs/home)
- USAJOBS (www.usajobs.opm.gov)

And what can you expect once you secure that first opportunity? Well, for one thing, you'll be constantly balancing the data-head and networker sides of your personality. The U.S. Bureau of Labor Statistics' *Occupational Outlook Handbook* tells us that successful planners are able to think in terms of spatial relationships and visualize the effects of their plans and designs, all while reconciling different viewpoints and communicating constructive policy recommendations. "The built environment is constantly shifting and the forces at work are complex and overlapping. Often different stakeholders have competing visions or altogether destructive visions of how to address complex problems," says Michael. "Good planners know how to leverage the sharing of ideas and opinions to produce better results." Adds Laurie: "Planners sometimes have a reputation as being city wreckers, and so we constantly have to regain the confidence of our communities, but uninformed people who care about their neighborhoods can be pretty vocal, and it's a challenge when our professional opinions aren't valued."

After a few years of work experience, you'll need to get certified by the American Institute of Certified Planners (AICP), the professional institute of the APA. The process involves taking an exam offered twice a year. After this, your career will be poised for takeoff. In the public sector, for example, you'll receive increasing amounts of managerial responsibility in larger jurisdictions, and may be promoted to highly visible positions such as community planning director or city manager. In the consulting world, you may advance from senior planner to director and possibly to chief planner. "There is substantial room for growth, though who you work for is very important in how quickly your career will progress," says Laurie.

The urban planning profession will continue to grow as populations expand and innovative community systems are needed to keep pace with technological and security concerns. In 2006, the APA reported the median annual salary of urban planners as $64K, but compensation may be significantly higher for experienced planners working in the private sector. Says Michael: "I make a good living, but more importantly, I make a difference, which makes for a good life. I am compensated for being an active participant in shaping communities and thinking about what we can do better to improve opportunities, quality of life, and other pressing concerns that affect us all."

The Entrepreneur

> When I was just getting started and had little professional experience planning events, I talked to prospective clients about every party and wedding that I had ever been to as if I had planned them single-handedly. I tried to remember everything about these events (name of the band, construction of the centerpieces, et cetera) so I could speak about them with a fair amount of confidence. I would also take notes on the events that I attended and follow up with vendors that I saw there so that I could use these events as jumping-off points in my own career.
>
> —Lindsay, twenty-nine, event planner

WHO WOULDN'T ENVY THE ENTREPRENEUR, a person with the courage to stand on a high board and dive into the pool below without a moment's hesitation? Starting a business in today's world is never easy, and successful entrepreneurs like Lindsay have to have the smarts—and the guts—to make it happen despite the obstacles of inexperience, money, and competition. The number of Americans taking their careers and their futures into their own hands, though, is currently higher than at any time in the last decade. As I write this book, more than 23 million people (or almost 12 percent of all Americans) are in the process of starting a new business or are managing one that is less than four years old.

Though entrepreneurs come in all shapes and sizes, they are

united by their ability to push past fear and take leaps of faith in the pursuit of a vision. "A true entrepreneur isn't deterred by risks, but stimulated by them," says Lindsay, the owner of Lindsay Landman Events. "There is no ceiling for us, because we push the envelope every time to achieve something that hasn't been done before." Julia, thirty, the co-owner of the bridal boutique Hitched, agrees. "It's a rush to chart unknown territory and create something tangible of which we can be proud. Every day presents a new challenge, and every day has small, and sometimes even big, rewards."

> **I can't think of a job more portable and convenient than Internet-based business owner. It would allow me to do business anywhere in the world, and on my own terms. I also like the casual nature of this career, and being able to work from home and set my own schedule.**
>
> **—Christa, twenty-two**

The risk-taking nature of the entrepreneur, however, is accompanied by an ability to observe the world around him and uncover needs that he can meet. "I'm always on the lookout for annoying, everyday problems that are just aching for solutions," says Brian, thirty-two, an inventor. Many of them can trace the origins of this talent to their childhoods. "When I was growing up, tourists used to come out to our area to pick apples," says Kori, thirty-two, the owner of Kori Elizabeth Events. "I was just in second grade, but I saw an opportunity. I built a lemonade stand—not just any stand, but a yellow one with brightly striped curtains. Under my supervision, my friends sold drinks, cookies, and candy to the hungry apple pickers."

At the same time, though, the smartest entrepreneurs accept that they don't know everything, especially when just starting out. They are skilled in seeking out expertise and using the learnings and opinions of others to their own advantage. "I've worked with reputable trainers from all over the world," says Lisa, thirty-nine, the owner of Studio Elle Pilates. "I aim to get to them before they retire so that I can soak up all their knowledge." Steve, thirty-six, the founder of the popular blog Micro Persuasion, uses an RSS reader to keep tabs on what dozens of marketing and business experts are saying every day. "I have to be an information junkie," he says. "To do my job well, I always need to have a sense of what others consider important, and what I should be blogging about."

The entrepreneurs I met were full of energy and even somewhat frenetic, which is probably an evolutionary response to the active, harried lifestyle they must lead. "One moment I'll be working with a customer and the next I'll be rushing to a strategy meeting with my partner," says Carin, thirty-one, Julia's co-owner in Hitched. "There's never a dull moment and we are busy from morning until night . . . and then some." Most entrepreneurs wouldn't trade the craziness for anything, though—they aren't the type of people to be happy sitting at a desk from nine to five or dealing with the bureaucracy or routine of traditional business environments. "When I put in a good day's work, I get to see the results immediately," says Beth, thirty-three, a professional organizer. "I set my own hours in order to be the most effective, instead of languishing in an office in corporate America on someone else's watch." Will, thirty, the founder of sports blog Deadspin, is right there with her. "Business meetings, and other such things, are the antithesis of productivity," he says. "I love being able to work when I want, the way I want."

The endless amount of difficult tasks involved in launching a new company—from drafting a business plan and securing financing to attracting customers and marketing your offering—require an

> Being a bed-and-breakfast innkeeper would be the best job for me, because I love to cook and entertain. How amazing would it be to create this great house and invite people to come and stay there while you cook for them? They would be coming for a vacation, so they would be grateful and happy, and meanwhile I would be doing what I love.
>
> —*Renee, twenty-four*

upbeat, optimistic outlook and a streak of resourcefulness. "Inevitably, your plans won't cover everything," says Terry, thirty-five, who had to open his bed-and-breakfast, Artists Inn Residence, a year late after unforeseen circumstances delayed the renovation. "You have to trust that you'll find a way to make it happen, even in the face of big setbacks." And whether her business is still in the incubation stage or is fully hatched, the entrepreneur never stops coming up with new ideas. "I try to keep myself from thinking about product launches and feature articles when I'm enjoying dinner with my girlfriend, but I often find my personal to-do list popping into my head at the most inappropriate of times," says Jonah, twenty-four, the owner of Rival-fish, an online sports apparel business.

As you can imagine, most entrepreneurs encounter their share of naysayers. "When I first started out, a business coach told me I was making the worst decision focusing on technology marketing," says Alyah, thirty, the owner of the Internet-based marketing firm Active-Nation. "Thank God I didn't listen to him, because this niche has actually been a major reason for our success. It makes me laugh every time I remember this guy telling me how I was going to fail." Jenna, twenty-five, the owner and president of Model Challenge USA, had a similar experience during her firm's infancy. "There were a lot of venue owners who didn't take us seriously in the beginning," she says. "I love getting phone calls from owners who hung up on us a few years ago. Now that we've made a name for ourselves, they want in." Entrepreneurs who don't have thick skins have to grow them quickly, for if they let difficult people, including clients, stand in their way, they won't last very long. "I can't take what clients say personally," says Gina, the owner of It's an Organized Life. "Some people question me through the whole process, as if they don't believe what I'm telling them. I have to remember that it's not about me, and that I can only help those who want to be helped."

But entrepreneurs, incredible as they may be, aren't perfect. They do have the tendency to jump into situations without thinking them through, and to skip over critical details as they struggle to move a business forward. "Back in high school, I had a crush on this guy, and so I decided to plan this huge Sadie Hawkins dance just so I had an excuse to ask him on a date!" says Lindsay. Lisa shares a story about a time when a situation at her fitness center got too hot to handle. "I had to take some time off after 9/11, but one of the teachers who covered for me was mediocre and didn't bother to charge anyone," she says. "My clients held on and waited for me to come back, but they weren't happy. I almost went out of business." Fortunately, though, the best entrepreneurs usually land on their feet. "It was out of the ordinary to start a business in which we had no experience," says Julia. "But by taking our time and doing significant research, we were able to insert ourselves into the market."

> My dream job is to start a business as a professional organizer. I actually like creating filing systems and methods that make living and working easier and more efficient. Plus, I do this for my friends and family for free already and it would be wonderful to use my natural skills to make some money at it.
>
> —*Leticia, thirty*

Entrepreneurs start businesses that do just about everything. If you want to launch a firm that produces entertainment for goldfish and you are committed enough, there's probably a market out there for you. In this chapter, however, we'll explore the entrepreneurial careers that my survey participants found most attractive—including bed-and-breakfast innkeeper, blogger, boutique owner, event planner, health club owner, Internet-based business owner, inventor, pet sitter, and professional organizer. You'll learn what each job entails, as well as what you need to do to set up that type of business.

BED-AND-BREAKFAST INNKEEPER

> When I was a kid, my family took very long car trips up and down the East Coast. We didn't have a lot of money, so we always stayed in small hotels, some of which were like B&Bs. When we got home from vacation, staying over at the hotels was always the part I missed the most. I would go around the house putting numbers up on all the rooms so I could pretend we were still there.
>
> —Terry, thirty-five, bed-and-breakfast innkeeper

IN THE EARLY DAYS OF OUR RELATIONSHIP, my husband and I used to bond over our mutual love for B&Bs. Our favorite vacation involved taking the ferry to Martha's Vineyard and staying a few nights in a seventeenth-century, robin's-egg blue house on the Oak Bluffs shoreline. Inns that provide travelers with a morning meal have supposedly been in existence since the beginning of human history, though the descriptive term *bed-and-breakfast* originated in England a few centuries ago. In the United States, B&Bs popped up along the trails of early settlers making their way across the unexplored continent. When I began researching the profession, I was surprised at how much goes into running a B&B. If you've ever thought of ditching your office job and sharing a home with others in one of your favorite locations, I hope you'll find this section enlightening.

Although a lot of people romanticize the life of a B&B innkeeper, it really does take a special type of person to be one. Innkeepers are one part savvy entrepreneur and one part people lover. They have the benefit of meeting and socializing with people from all over the globe, and they also have to contend with those people when they call needing an extra blanket at three A.M. Innkeepers, like other entrepreneurs, enjoy the perks of earning a living their way, and they also get to create their dream home and show it off on a daily basis. The life of the innkeeper, though, involves sacrifice. First of all, it's not a one-person scenario. Even if you plan to hire staff to help with the upkeep, your loved ones will be involved to some extent, especially if they live with you. The early mornings, cooking, cleaning, shopping, bookkeeping, and marketing turn what many think will be a relaxing lifestyle into a seven-day-a-week, fifteen-hour-a-day job. And the fact that you can never leave can lead to burnout, which in turn leads to crankiness with guests, which can affect business. But now that you understand the pros and cons, let's move on to the particulars of starting a B&B.

You have plenty of education ahead of you before you can actually go out and purchase a piece of property. That's not to say that you have to go back to school, but it will behoove you to learn as much as you can about the business of running an inn. Some innkeepers recommend intensive seminars, including those given semiannually by Oates & Bredfeldt (www.oatesbredfeldt.com), and Innkeeping Specialists (www.innseminars.com). There are also good resources out there for home study, such as the books *So—You Want to Be an Innkeeper* and *How to Open and Operate a Bed & Breakfast,* and the video series from Innside Innkeeping (www.innsideinnkeeping .com). If you've targeted a location to set up shop, you should immediately join your state B&B association, which will provide you with the opportunity to network with seasoned innkeepers and learn the tricks of the trade. I've also heard that the Professional Association of Innkeepers International (www.paii.org) offers great resources for the aspiring B&B owner, including workshops, publications, real estate and innkeeper contact lists, and an active annual convention. "When I was preparing to open my inn, I stayed in lots of B&Bs, just to talk to the owners and see how they did things," says Terry, thirty-five, the owner of Artists Inn Residence. Of course, there's nothing more valuable than hands-on experience, so if you can get a gig working as an apprentice, or subbing for an owner on vacation, that's the best option of all.

Millions of homes have the potential to be excellent B&Bs, but whether buying one of them is the right decision depends entirely on its location, and on how much you're going to pay for it. Once you've targeted an area, take the time to do the market research. "Ask the important questions," says Elizabeth Arneson, in an article for the B&B guide of About.com. "Why do people visit this area? Are they seasonal travelers or year-round? How many other inns are nearby, and what will make yours stand out?"

You'll also need to determine early on if you can afford to buy in a particular area. "You'll probably have to come up with a bigger down payment for a bed-and-breakfast than you would for a home," says Elizabeth. And don't forget about the cash you'll need to put up for start-up costs pertaining to renovations, furniture and decorating expenses, food and supplies, utilities, and labor. It certainly helps to have a "day job" while in the process of opening the inn. While experienced owners with at least eight guest rooms available can earn a comfortable living in the high five or low six figures, it will take you a while to build up to that level of business.

The best way to find a B&B in your price range is to employ a real estate agent who specializes in historic homes, and if you can get a recommendation from another local owner, so much the better. Obviously, it's easiest to buy a property that is already functioning as a B&B, but if you can't find one that appeals to you, you could always buy a regular house that has lots of potential (and lots of bedrooms). "For Artists Inn Residence, we turned an empty building into a fully furnished mansion," says Terry. "And when you take on a project like that, you're dealing with endless contractors. Instead of getting frazzled by the unexpected, you have to learn to adapt, to do things in a different way." To Terry's point, you do want to know what you're getting into. Before you sign on the dotted line, check zoning laws and talk to other local innkeepers about the types of permits, licenses, and insurance you will need for that particular area.

Once you've made the grand purchase, you still have some work to do before you can open for business. Choosing a name for your inn will be one of the first things on your checklist. "Don't use your own name," says Sandy Soule, a contributor to BedandBreakfast.com. "Pick something that's easy to say and remember, and that's at the beginning of the alphabet." Then, you will need to set out to create an ambience for your guests, who, as typical B&B customers, will be looking for a special, out-of-the-ordinary experience. "Most bed-and-breakfasts decorate with a certain theme in mind," says the BedOwner.co.uk website. "Decorating themes often reflect the natural and cultural locale of the bed and breakfast. Themes are often expressed through color choices, linens, bedding, pictures, and accessories that appeal to the five senses." Some other preopening decisions involve:

- **Guest Rooms.** Your furnishings, especially the beds, should be in good condition. Rooms should be quiet and well lit. Provide private, *clean* baths if possible, or make proper arrangements for sharing.

- **Security.** Guests will need keys for the front door and for their individual rooms.

- **Policies.** You'll need to decide how you'll take reservations, and what you'll do if someone cancels. It's also not a bad idea to come up with a list of "house rules" in advance. "While you need to resign yourself that accidents will happen, making your policies clear up front will prevent guests from tearing apart your house," says Terry.

- **Breakfast.** Create menus for either simple continental breakfasts or gourmet breakfasts, and determine if they will rotate according to the season. Choose a style—sit-down or buffet—and make sure you have food on hand that will appeal to guests with special diets.

- **Housekeeping and Supplies.** Make checklists of the bedroom, bathroom, common room, and kitchen amenities you'll need on a regular basis, and make sure you're fully stocked in time for your opening. If you're not planning on cleaning the rooms yourself, you'll also need to hire help for this purpose.

- **Rates.** B&B guests are usually willing to pay more than they would for a hotel, but you want to make sure your inn is worth the price. Determine rates by considering what other inns in the area are charging, the type of room and bath, and any special services you may be offering.

- **Your Living Quarters.** Maintain a separate living area for your family that enables you to get away from the crowd and conserve some of your privacy.

The long-term success of your B&B, and your ability to sustain a career as an innkeeper, depends on how effectively you can attract guests to your establishment. The Bedowner.co.uk website suggests that you host a dinner or open house to get to know the owners of other tourist-friendly businesses and encourage them to recommend your inn to their customers. A search engine–friendly website with photos and rates is a must, for the majority of travelers will find your B&B via the Internet. You should also find out how to get listed in bed-and-breakfast guidebooks and online registries that cover your area, and have professional business cards and brochures printed. Finally, make sure you keep a guest register. Not only can you use it to send e-mail news, updates, and special offers, but it can also be a wonderful tool for keeping in touch with the scores of new friends you'll make in your new business!

BLOGGER

I chose to write about something related to my career, and I was lucky to be both an extrovert and an information junkie. Going from obscurity to being one of the top fifty bloggers online has been more ego gratification than anyone could possibly want. But I try to keep perspective. I look at it this way: in thirty years I'll have something cool to look back on.

—Steve, thirty-six, blogger

A FEW YEARS AGO, it seemed unthinkable that anyone could turn an egocentric hobby like blogging into a well-paying career, but that, along with several other unimaginable things involving the Internet, is exactly what has happened. For those of you who might still be unfamiliar with the concept, *blog* is an abbreviated version of *weblog,* a frequently updated website offering diary-like commentary and links to other articles or sites. Some blogs focus on one subject—such as politics or sports—while others cover a whole range of material. And they are so inexpensive and easy to create and run that any individual with good writing skills and strong opinions can attract big audiences, and, consequently, big profits. How can you be one of them? Let's take a look.

Before you attempt to earn a living as a blogger, most veterans say you should invest in your own blog, to prove that you can write with a unique, authentic style and that you can amass a following. "You need to get your name out there first," says Will, thirty, a blogger for Deadspin and former journalist who got his start in the blogosphere by launching an online sports journal with a few friends. "If you're diligent about it and do a good job every day, people will find you." It's easiest when you identify a subject and write about it intelligently. You will also need to spend several hours a week posting away, because the best blogs are updated often. Will has ESPN on all day so that he constantly has inspiration for his eighteen daily posts. Ideally, your blog should have an objective and target a specific market. For example, when I started my blog, Water Cooler Wisdom, the objective was to provide career advice, and the market was the twentysomething job seeker. Will's Deadspin, on the other hand, aims to provide up-to-the-minute sports commentary from the perspective of the average fan.

In order to get your personal blog up and running, you'll need to know a few basics. As many of you are likely familiar with these already, I'll keep them short. Most blogs have a few common features, including:

- a main content area with posts listed chronologically, newest on top
- an archive of older posts organized into categories
- a blogroll, or a list of the author's favorite blogs or websites
- a feed, or a way for readers to receive the latest posts in their Internet browser or e-mail, otherwise known as RSS (really simple syndication)
- a way for visitors to leave comments about the author's posts
- a way to inform the author when a reader cites a post on his own blog, called a trackback or pingback

Most blogging software has these components, and some of the best systems out there, including WordPress (www.wordpress.com), Blogger (www.blogger.com), and Movable Type (www.movabletype.org), require only a rudimentary knowledge of how websites work. Once you've set up your blog and have gotten into a posting groove, it's time to focus on building your audience and traffic. Here are some tips I've picked up along the way:

- Keep your posts short and easy to read and digest.
- Respond in real time to news or current events.

- Engage people in the discussion versus talking "at them."
- Link to other sites often, both in your blogroll and in your posts.
- Comment on other blogs whenever you have an opinion or information to share.
- Tag and title your posts with common keywords so it's easier for search engines to find you.
- Participate in blogging carnivals or be a guest blogger on a related site.

Steve, thirty-six, was a PR executive who developed a career around his wildly successful marketing blog Micro Persuasion. He attributes his success to constantly building his brand, being seen on and off the Internet, panning for information gold in his RSS reader, and stirring up a little controversy every now and then. Will agrees. "The best thing I can do is break a story, about an athlete on steroids, for example, and see it air on ESPN an hour later," he says.

In terms of generating an income from blogging, you'll understand in a minute why it's truly an entrepreneurial venture. According to *Business 2.0,* Web advertising is expected to grow by 50 percent (to $23.6 billion) by 2010, and with every passing day, more and more of those ad dollars are landing on blogs. Steve Pavlina, who has a widely read blog on personal development, says that it's possible to make a high-five-figure annual income blogging from home. He suggests developing an income-generating strategy for your site by taking a close look at how similar bloggers are making money and determining if a particular approach would work for you too. There is certainly an array of monetization options to choose from. ProBlogger (www .problogger.net), a fantastic resource for learning to make money from your blog, suggests these:

- **Advertising.** Google AdSense (www.google.com), Blogads (www.blogads.com), and hundreds of similar programs allow you to display relevant ads on your blog and earn money in the process.

Because the ads are related to what your visitors are looking for on your site, this is a way to both monetize and enhance your content pages.

- **Affiliates.** Programs like Amazon (www.amazon.com), LinkShare (www.linkshare.com), and ClickBank (www.clickbank.com) generate revenue for you every time one of your blog visitors clicks on an affiliate link.

- **Digital Assets.** Depending on your subject matter, you can sell e-books, white papers, research reports, courses, and teleseminars on your blog.

- **Merchandising.** If your blog has a cult following, you might sell branded products (T-shirts, et cetera) via e-commerce functionality on your site, or through programs like CafePress (www.cafepress.com).

- **Consulting and Speaking.** Blogging has the ability to establish people as experts on niche topics, and as a result, bloggers with no consulting or public speaking background can now charge for their time because of the profile that their blogs have built for them.

- **Blog Networking.** While it might be difficult to get a paid gig with one of the bigger blog networks (WebLogs, Corante, and so on), there are plenty of smaller networks that are always looking for fresh talent.

Speaking of getting paid to write on behalf of someone else, you may find yourself being solicited to blog for an established business or company. This happened to me when GetTheJob, a job portal, commissioned me to write their Water Cooler Wisdom blog. "It's great for your blogging career to plug into a site that already has traction, be it a regular website or an existing blog," says Steve. "However, when you're affiliated with a particular company, you might have to watch what you say, and bunt the ball a bit more carefully." Whether you're sponsored by a company or independent, both Will and Steve maintain that successful blogging has a certain cachet in the offline world. If your blog is popular, offline publishers may take notice of you, and next thing you know you could have a book contract or an offer to write for a newspaper or magazine.

At the time of this writing, becoming a professional blogger was one of the hottest career switches around, and if the experts are right, the blogging phenomenon is only getting more prolific. If you're the type of writer who thrives on change, is willing to speak your mind, and can keep pace with rapidly evolving Internet technologies, the blogosphere may have a home for you. Like other entrepreneurial jobs, blogging offers freedom and flexibility, and even if you're working for a network or company, you're usually afforded a great deal of autonomy and decision-making power when it comes to your content. "I love the control over my own destiny, and not having to answer to anyone," says Will. On the other hand, a high blogosphere profile usually results in more stress. "It's not really acceptable to make mistakes, and you can't be off," continues Will. "You have to 'bring it' every day." Adds Steve: "When you reach a certain level, there are always people who want to take you down, but there's nothing like the experience of having a blog with global reach. My bar is set very high, and I have to be resourceful in order to keep exceeding people's expectations!"

BOUTIQUE OWNER

My partner and I have to work hard at creating a brand and creating a name for ourselves, especially because we're new to the industry. On a daily basis, we are competing with stores that have been in business for thirty years! We have managed this challenge by being up front with our customers and turning what could be a negative into a positive. Our customers love that we are young and new, and they can see that we treat each customer as an individual, rather than as a number. It means we work twice as hard, but it has helped us quickly become a "must go" store in D.C.

　　—Carin, thirty-one, boutique owner

IF YOU LOVE SHOPPING and fashion, you are probably well acquainted with the boutique—a small retail shop offering specialized products and services, usually apparel or accessories. Boutiques, which are usually found in malls, shopping centers, or on busy city streets, differentiate themselves by selling unique merchandise while also providing a welcoming ambience and superior customer service. They make money by buying products at wholesale prices and reselling them at a profit. According to the National Retail Federation, at least a third of the 500,000 new enterprises launched each year are retail operations, and each year, this economic sector accounts for nearly 40 percent of the U.S. gross national product—more than $3 trillion!

Compared to other retail ventures, boutique ownership is a smart bet. Market demand for retail fashion is traditionally quite high, and because trends move at the speed of light, customers are always on the lookout for the next hot item from the latest hot designer. As a boutique owner, you'll plan and oversee your store's operations, from deciding on layout and putting together in-store displays, to purchasing inventory, hiring staff, bookkeeping, and interfacing with customers. "My day might include designer negotiation, magazine pitching, and a fascinating activity like cleaning the toilet!" says Julia, thirty, a co-owner of Hitched, a bridal boutique in Washington, D.C. "I get to wear many hats, experiencing both the glamour and the dregs of owning a small business."

Boutique owners are the supreme entrepreneurs: they are self-starters and born multitaskers, they're excellent salespeople, and they don't mind taking risks, or going into debt for a while, as they pursue their business goals. Boutique owners may know fashion, but they know business just as well. Although it's not necessary to have a master's degree in business administration (or even a bachelor's, really), many boutique owners will tell you that it's essential to learn core business skills—such as purchasing, pricing, inventory and labor management, accounting, sales, and marketing—either in an educational setting or by working in retail. "In the beginning, I had no experience in retail, but after college, I produced large-scale events and got experience juggling a lot of balls at once," says Carin, Julia's partner in Hitched. "Then I went to business school and discovered that it prepared me for owning a boutique in ways I never could have imagined."

There are a few steps involved in opening a boutique, the first of which is to select the type of boutique you want to open (women's clothing, formal wear, baby products, jewelry, et cetera). Since your boutique should fill a niche in the community, do some preliminary research to determine what's already out there and how your store can fill a need. "We attended bridal markets to meet designers and learn about the industry," says Carin. "We also interviewed boutiques across the country to help formulate how our boutique would function." Next, you'll need to choose a catchy name and a prime location. In the book *How to Start a Retail Store, Entrepreneur* magazine says that while a great location may not guarantee success, a bad location will almost always guarantee failure. Brianna, twenty-four, the owner of Brianna's Jewelry Store and More, agrees with this point. "Location is extremely important," she says. "I've moved three times in six years. Last summer I tried a fourth location without the knowledge that was needed for that location, and it failed."

A new boutique, says *Entrepreneur,* needs to be where the customers are. *Entrepreneur* suggests a location with a reasonable degree of security, access to public transportation for your customers and employees, adequate parking for commercial as well as personal vehicles, room for an office, and that all-important sales space. Ideally, you'll want to be next to noncompetitive retail businesses that have steady clients, because the overflow from these businesses will drive your walk-in traffic. Whether you lease space in a mall or shopping plaza, or rent the ground floor of a charming city brownstone, you'll want to learn about the demographics of the area to ensure that you're not opening an expensive couture boutique in a run-down area.

Before you finalize the arrangements for your new space, remember to obtain your business and resale licenses, a small business credit card, and insurance. Unless you have a lot of money saved or can borrow from a family member, you will probably need to apply for financing. In this case, you'll need to present potential investors with a business plan detailing objectives, strategies, operations, and finances. As you investigate loaners, look for straightforward options with the lowest possible interest rates.

Now it's time to select a high-quality inventory that will suit the theme and sensibilities of your new boutique. Research local and online wholesalers and manufacturers who carry the items you're interested in, and find out where and when you can attend trade shows and markets. The InfoMat (www.infomat.com) and Toronto Fashion Incubator (www.fashionincubator.com) websites are great resources for identifying supplier events. Take the time to sniff around online and at the markets, asking fashion experts and the buying public about the hottest-selling items and where the market is trending. While it's tempting to go wild on your first big shopping trip, be wary of overstocking and purchase only what you need to get your boutique off the ground. "You have to be a conscious buyer, because your success depends on your choices," says Brianna. "Spend money wisely and with a reason to spend it." Boutique owners also advise noting your suppliers' suggested real prices and what your competitors are charging for similar items so that you can price products appropriately. Your pricing should allow for the best possible markup while coming across as acceptable to your targeted clientele.

If you've applied for financing, you've probably already considered the physical design and layout of your boutique. In *How to Start a Retail Store, Entrepreneur* recommends using scale, colors, textures, materials, and amenities to convey your store's philosophy and set the stage for your customers. Whether you consult with an architect or an interior designer, or choose to do the work yourself, give your store plan a great deal of forethought. *Entrepreneur* suggests visiting boutiques similar to yours to spark ideas and get insights about why certain elements are working or not working. At the end of the day, your new boutique should be inviting, with special items placed in the windows to entice traffic, and with inside space allocated strategically so that customers have the easiest access to the most profitable items.

Once you near opening day, you'll need to focus on hiring the right employees and getting the store's operations (floor management, lighting, computers, security mechanisms, and so on) running smoothly. Remember to check off small but important details like business cards, store signage, hangers, price tags, and shopping bags. And don't forget about promotion! While strong word of mouth and stellar customer service will be the most effective ways to get new and repeat customers coming into the store, some low-budget marketing tactics you can employ include:

- Host a grand-opening party.
- Build a website that is easily indexed by search engines.
- Create an e-mail list to inform customers of new products and sales.
- Post flyers and signage in neighboring stores.
- Hold mini–fashion shows.
- Publish your own articles about fashion online.
- Advertise in your local paper.

Starting a boutique is a dream come true for many fashionistas. Not only do you get to be your own boss, but once business gets going and you develop a powerful brand, it's possible to make six figures, open additional stores, and even sell franchises. It won't be easy, though. You should expect losses in the first few years due to start-up expenses, and even if your income stabilizes, your working hours and your customers' demands may not. "You have to have a high tolerance for stress," says Julia. "A wedding is such an important day in a woman's life, which can cause unreasonable expectations as well as a lot of pressure on us."

Excited about the possibilities but think you might need some help? For more information on starting a boutique, I suggest reaching out to some of the resources I came across in my research, including the National Retail Federation (www.nrf.com), the Retail Advertising and Marketing Association (www.rama-nrf.org), and the U.S. Small Business Administration (www.sba.gov). You may find industry trade publications such as *Retailer News, Apparel News,* and the *Journal of Retailing* useful as well. "Opening a boutique is 100 percent consuming, so you should be at a place in your life, financially and emotionally, where you can handle it," says Carin. "It's a crazy ride!"

EVENT PLANNER

> When I was in high school, my friend's mom worked for Mattel. During the Christmas season, Mattel would have Barbie models go to stores to sign autographs and drum up business. At the time I was helping out, one of the stores had a drawing to receive a Barbie birthday party with Barbie as the guest of honor. I got paid to be Barbie and run the event. My party was so successful that I started planning and performing in my own events as Cinderella and Sleeping Beauty. That was when I knew I wanted to pursue a career in event planning.
>
> —Holly, twenty-two, event planner

UNTIL I HELD A JOB in public relations, I pictured an event planner as the person who, by day, charged through a conference purposefully, scribbling on a clipboard and barking orders on a two-way radio, and who, by night, sipped champagne and wore Chanel at the best parties with all the best people. The truth is, though, while event planning does have its perks and privileges, the meat of this career takes place behind the scenes, away from the spotlight and the glory. "About half of my time is spent in my office speaking to clients, researching vendors, reviewing contracts, preparing event timelines, and securing new business," says Lindsay, twenty-nine, the owner of Lindsay Landman Events. "Other times, I'm on the road, bargain shopping in Target for candleholders, or I'll be driving two hours to tour a new event site."

Monster defines an event planner as one who designs, organizes, and coordinates conferences, conventions, seminars, trade shows, or private parties. She is responsible for participants' accommodations, transportation, facilities, catering, signage, displays, audiovisual equipment, printing, and security, and must establish and monitor budgets to support these ventures. "The most appealing element of my job is the flow of event production," says Lindsay. "I book the event, work anywhere from weeks to years to complete the planning, and climax with the execution of the event. Then the next day, I'm onto something new, making a fresh start with new ideas and lessons learned."

Event planners typically have bachelor's degrees in business, communications, or hospitality management, but a college degree is not always required since most knowledge is gained on the job. Some people enter the field after working in lower-level positions in hotels or catering companies, and they may actually start with more responsibility than a recent college graduate with no experience who will inevitably pay her dues completing simple tasks under close supervision. But while their educational backgrounds may vary, event planners possess a few characteristics that are essential to success (and sanity) in the profession.

Great event planners must be detail-oriented, able to multitask, work autonomously, and function effectively in a pressure-cooker environment. "We're organized and neurotic in a good way," adds Kori, thirty-two, the president of Kori Elizabeth Events. "You have to be a quick thinker, managing the client through the process smoothly and with candor, and anticipating the client's needs. For example, before a clambake at the navy yard, the forecast called for rain, so I had 1,200 rain ponchos delivered overnight. There is always a mini-disaster, or at least a challenge, and there's no crying in event planning. Everything might look wonderful on a spreadsheet, but it is how you react to trouble when it arises that makes the difference."

If, despite the stressful elements, you think event planning might be the career for you, I'd recommend you first check out the Convention Industry Council website (www.conventionindustry.org) and the Meeting Professionals International (MPI) website (www.mpiweb.org). MPI in particular has a great suite of personalized services, including a skills assessment, which identifies your proficiency level in over 160 skills, a gap report, which analyzes where your skills are compared to the industry standard, and a listing of recommended resources based on your unique results. The MPI job bank, along with websites like Meetingjobs.com (www.meetingjobs.com) and the MeetingConnection (www.meetingconnection.com), are good places to seek specific employment opportunities in the industry, for most event planners suggest you get a few years of experience working for someone else before venturing out on your own. "The best way to get started is to work for a hotel or catering company as a banquet server, because catering is the backbone of how an event flows," says Kori. "I got a strong catering background working as a corporate planner and then at a small catering company, and from there I was able to launch my own business."

Additionally, while independent planners like Lindsay and Kori are the fastest growing segment of the meeting planner population, nearly 60 percent of people in the profession work for corporate or nonprofit organizations. If you have some time, volunteering at a local association may be the easiest way in the door. "Every nonprofit plans countless events each year and looks for young volunteers to help pull everything together," says Lindsay. "This is valuable, hands-on experience in event planning that cannot be attained in any college course or certification program, and when it comes to getting that first job, any event experience at any level is priceless."

The lifelong journey of an event planner varies from person to person, but you'll want to be prepared with some basics. At the beginning, you'll likely face some obstacles. "Finding a job in event planning can be difficult if you're not living in a metropolitan area, and some positions involve a lot of traveling," says Holly, twenty-two, a university event planner in Philadelphia. Fortunately, within a larger organization, there is usually ample opportunity for growth as you move from the entry level to the managerial level and, finally, to the director or vice president level. Though the pace at which your responsibilities increase depends mostly on how well you prove yourself on the job, continuing education does play a role. The Convention Industry Council offers the Certified Meeting Professional (CMP) credential, which is based on professional experience and an academic examination. You can also seek professional development opportunities through MPI or organizations like the International Special Events Society (www.ises.com) and the National Association of Catering Executives (www.nace.net). And what can you expect regarding salary? According to Salary.com, half of all event planners earn between $45K and $64K, and your income can be much higher if you advance to the top level of an organization or form your own planning firm.

As an industry, event planning is ripe with opportunity. MPI says that its members are collectively responsible for nearly 700,000 meetings per year, with expenses totaling $10 billion. The hours may be long, and you may lose your weekends more often than you'd like, but those with the right combination of skills and entrepreneurial spirit thrive on rewards that extend beyond simple job satisfaction. "This job allows me to build lasting relationships with a huge variety of people from many backgrounds and religions," says Lindsay. "I learn a great deal about the world from my clients, which translates to being a much more interesting, knowledgeable, and cultured person." Adds Holly: "I love watching everything fall into place, but the best part is seeing people enjoying themselves and knowing that I created that happiness."

HEALTH CLUB OWNER

> My biggest reward is the clients. I love when they improve. It's not just the cosmetic stuff—although that's fun too—it's when a client comes in and says something like, "This is the first time I can remember when I woke up and my back didn't hurt." It was really satisfying, after six months of working with a ninety-four-year-old woman, to see her out of her Barcalounger and down from a walker to two canes and then one cane. She was going out to dinner with her daughters and enjoying Boston again. I felt so grateful to have been able to help her get her life back.
>
> —Lisa, thirty-nine, health club owner

THE INTERNATIONAL HEALTH, Racquet & Sportsclub Association (IHRSA) expects that the number of U.S. club memberships will exceed 50 million by 2010. In this era of obesity and heart disease, this is good for America, and if you're an entrepreneur who loves fitness, good for you. Starting a health club sounds like it would be both a fun job and a gratifying career, but it does require the same disciplined business-minded approach as other sole proprietorships.

Health club owners who are also smart businesspeople have a few things in common. They are self-motivated, have a head for planning, get along well with different types of people, are capable of making decisions quickly, and have a great deal of physical and emotional stamina. "There's a lot involved in running a gym that people don't think about, and it doesn't get easier for a while," says Scott, thirty-three, a health club owner in Texas. "You give a lot of your personal life, and you worry about when the money's going to come in." Sounds like par for the entrepreneurial course!

Your career as a health club owner will most likely succeed if you pace yourself. Over time, perhaps while you're still employed in another job, you should take the time to study business. Formal education, such as a master's of business administration (M.B.A.) is ideal, but you can also learn what you need to know by taking seminars or adult education classes, reading top business books, or even partnering with someone with extensive business experience. Also, given that you cannot expect your health club to make a profit for three to five years, you will have to start with a great deal of capital. According to the Fitness Consulting Group, you must save or borrow enough money to see you through a full year of losses in your health club business, at the very minimum. If you're taking out a bank loan, make sure the interest rates won't bankrupt you. "I made very little money the first four years as I built the business and kept reinvesting in the studio and in my training," says Lisa, thirty-nine, owner and president of Studio Elle Pilates. "It wasn't until last year that I finally made more than my top trainer!"

Developing a strong business plan at the outset is a step that, when skipped, comes back to bite the owner later on. One of your first major decisions involves whether to start your club from scratch, buy an existing club, or purchase a franchise license. An established business brings a built-in location, equipment, and membership roster. A franchise license, on the other hand, offers national name recognition, predetermined costs (and expensive license fees), and a predetermined management model. The Internet provides a wealth of franchising information and opportunities—groups like Gaebler Ventures (www.gaebler.com) often offer thousands of franchise options in a single online directory.

Both the established club and the franchise options are easier and less intense than opening an independent, brand-new facility, but you do give up a lot of freedom and decision-making power. You may also have to adopt the existing culture. "The big-name clubs are only focused on membership numbers," says Scott. "As an independent, we focus on personal service and helping our clients reach their goals." In any case, once you've made your selection, it's time to put your plan in writing. Assuming you don't have the guidance and direction of a franchise, consider the following:

- **Mission Statement:** what your health club will provide and to whom
- **Situation Analysis:** the current status of the market in your area (competitors, et cetera)
- **Operations:** how you'll run your club (proposed location, equipment, customer service, staffing, et cetera)
- **Marketing:** how you'll let people know about your club (advertising, PR, online marketing, et cetera)
- **Sales:** how you'll address the needs of existing members and bring in new members
- **Finances:** your budgeted costs and how your health club will turn a profit over the next thirty-five years

All of the elements listed above can be discussed in much more detail, and for more information, I suggest checking out helpful fitness industry resources such as the magazines *Fitness Management* (www.fitnessmanagement.com) and *Club Industry's Fitness Business Pro* (www.fitnessbusiness-pro.com). For the purposes of this section, however, I'll call out a few things that I think are particularly important based on my research. First and foremost, again assuming you're not going the franchise route, you'll need to think carefully about which fitness center model you'll want to employ (women only, racquet club, yoga studio, et cetera) and what profit centers your club will have in addition to memberships (personal training, spa, a pro shop, et cetera), because a strong health club won't be all things to all people. Second, I heard from just about everywhere that the physical location of your club can make or break your business. In choosing a space, ask yourself the following questions:

- Is there enough demand in the area for your type of club?
- Is the space easily accessible by car?
- Is the area lean on competition?
- Is there enough parking?
- Does the building structure meet your business needs?

Purchasing or leasing a commercial space will involve some details you should be aware of, including having the appropriate licenses and permits, getting an inspection done, and coordinating with the professionals who will help you realize your vision for the club's interior and exterior (architects, contractors, interior designers, et cetera). Determining the precise layout of a new club without the assistance of a franchise requires a dizzying amount of critical decisions and purchases. It's a sad truth that all the work that goes on behind the scenes of a club is not nearly as important as what your customers will see and experience when they walk through the door, and you must be strategic and systematic in the location and appearance of your reception area, locker rooms, class studios, and workout rooms. There are literally thousands of equipment and furniture options available, so get recommendations from non-competing health club owners you respect. Marketing is another area you'll want to pay close attention to. Trial memberships, referral rewards, and e-mail newsletters are just some of the tactics health club owners use to keep existing customers and attract new ones.

Even once your club is up and running, you'll still be busy. "As far as the business stuff goes, I'm the big picture person," says Lisa. "I'm always trying to figure out how to get the studio more prominence and better marketing. Is our advertising working well? What will the fall or spring campaign be? Is it time to write a newsletter? What are our competitors charging? Do we need to hire anyone?" But you'll inevitably experience the type of satisfaction that comes from seeing people every day and watching them transform their bodies and lives, and if you're good at what you do, the money will eventually be there too. "Owners can make anywhere from $40K to over $100K," says Lisa. "It depends on how large you decide to grow your business, how many instructors you have working for you, and if you open multiple locations. I always wanted to work in the fitness industry, but I used to think it wasn't possible. How wonderful to realize I could make money doing it!"

INTERNET-BASED BUSINESS OWNER

My company, Rivalfish, is responsible for helping me find my path. Had I not taken the risk a few years back, I would've likely jumped into the nearest grad school program. When Rivalfish didn't make me a million-aire overnight, as I foolishly thought it would, I struggled for a few years of being a nobody, armed only with a company that had no track record. I faced a number of challenges, primarily of friendship and finance. In time, the company began to succeed, and thanks to the long, difficult process, I'm finally content with the somebody I've dis-covered.

—Jonah, twenty-four, Internet-based business owner

YOU CAN'T SURF THE WEB these days without coming across a million propositions to start your own business. The idea is certainly attractive. Internet entrepreneurship, after all, offers the ability to control your own work environment without the significant financial investment of an offline business, and the opportunity to participate in any and all aspects of running a company. "I spend every day working closely with my customers, designers, programmers, and other staff," says Alyah, thirty, the owner of ActiveNation. "I make sure our bills are paid, that we are meeting our financial goals, and that we are doing the right things to get our name out and build relationships." Jonah, twenty-four, the CEO of Rivalfish, is pretty busy too. "I do a bit of graphic design each day, I get on the phones and pitch local media outlets, I talk with our legal counsel, I connect with bloggers to build readership for our online magazine, and I sit down with friends and brainstorm creative promotions." Whew!

In terms of answering one of those Google ads, however, if something sounds too good to be true, it probably is. Becoming an

Internet-based business owner is a strategic career move like any other, and you'll be better off if you approach your move to the e-business marketplace with careful thought and preparation. Here's how to start.

Ana Rincon, an About.com online business guide and the owner of On Target Internet, says that your first steps are to determine your new company's business model and how you'll make money. While the primary focus of your business might be to sell a particular product (or line of products) or service (or group of services), you should also consider additional ways to generate revenue, including selling advertising space or recommending affiliate products on your site.

You'll also want to select an appropriate name for your business that is easy to remember, spell, and type into a Web browser. At this point, you should set up your business legally and formulate a business plan that outlines your company's purpose, objectives, competitive advantage or value proposition, target customers, offerings, sales strategies, and finances. Your business plan can be either formal or informal, depending on whether you'll be using it to secure a loan, and you can get help with it by visiting several useful resources:

- About.com guide to online business (onlinebusiness.about.com)
- *Entrepreneur* magazine (www.entrepreneur.com)
- PayPal's Online Merchant Network (www.onlinemerchantnetwork.com)
- U.S. Small Business Administration E-Business Institute (www.sba.gov)

When you own an Internet-based company, your website is a major part of business. If you're selling products or services, Rincon suggests that your online store be simple to navigate and search, and reflect the brand image you're trying to project (professional, upscale, et cetera). Like an offline store, your e-commerce website should offer easy checkout, accept credit cards, and make it easy to find and contact live customer service. Depending on how complex your offerings are, you can either build the site yourself or purchase an e-commerce solution. If you don't have substantial Web design and programming expertise, your best bet is to go with a professional host like eBay's ProStores or Yahoo! Merchant Solutions. These all-in-one solutions provide a mix of site-building tools, product catalog tools, shopping-cart technology, payment processing, shipping and inventory management, accounting tools, tracking and reporting capabilities, and domain registration. Rincon advises choosing a host that is always open, can handle a lot of traffic, and responds to your questions quickly. Whether you have help building the site or not, make sure it's tested repeatedly before you open for business. You'll want to be certain that transactions run smoothly and that the site can handle heavy customer traffic.

Speaking of eBay, I can't write a section on Internet-based business owners without mentioning that nearly one million people earn a part- or full-time living selling products here. If you're new to the e-business world, opening an eBay store can be a great way to get your feet wet, and you may find that you're making so much money you don't need to do anything else! Janelle Elms, the author of *eBay Your Business,* says in an *Entrepreneur* magazine article that people who are successful using this medium make an effort to incorporate best practices via the eBay University (www.ebay.com/university) and employ a combination of eBay auctions, an eBay store, and a personal e-commerce website to maximize cross-marketing opportunities between all three channels.

If you're not selling your own products or services, you will need to round up some good suppliers. Types of suppliers include manufacturers, distributors or wholesalers, independent craftsmen, and foreign import sources. While price is important in choosing suppliers, reliability and stability are equally critical factors, because their timeliness and accuracy will be essential to managing your inventory effectively, and you need them to be responsive if there's a problem with a product. Remember—once you sell to the customer, it's your reputation that's on the line!

It may be wise to choose suppliers who will handle order shipping for you (aka "drop shipping"). This way you don't have to worry about using your home as a storage facility. Search on Google or ThomasNet (www.thomasnet.com) to find drop shippers who sell appropriate products, and then set up accounts. Once your customer pays you online, you will place an order with the drop shipper, who will in turn send the product to the customer using your company name and address.

The saying "If you build it, they will come" does not necessarily apply to e-business. If you want a steady stream of paying customers visiting your site, you have to proactively find your target audience online and spread the word. Here are a few tips for marketing your Internet business efficiently and inexpensively:

- **Make your site search-engine friendly.** Make your domain names, page titles, and copy relevant to your business and industry, and link to similar sites with good reputations and high traffic.

- **Promote your topical expertise.** For example, if you sell baby products, you might publish articles about infant care on your site and others. Develop an e-newsletter or start a blog for new moms in which you regularly offer useful content.

- **Develop cross-selling partnerships.** Research other e-commerce sites in your industry that offer compatible products, and talk to the owners about collaboration opportunities. For example, the seller of baby products might hook up with an online retailer of baby clothing to provide both sets of products on both sites.

- **Purchase search engine ad space.** Use Google and Yahoo! paid advertising options to bid on your most relevant keywords and secure top search engine results.

- **Drop in on online communities.** Find social networks and online communities where your target audience gathers and converses. Listen, get a feel for the community, and then offer your expert opinion on issues without blatantly hawking product.

Now that you know the steps to becoming an Internet-based business owner, what should you be prepared for? The first thing is the importance of education. Although there are obviously no formal requirements, you'll need to learn business basics first, and it helps to be versed in the technology that will power your online presence. "You have to know every aspect of how a business operates, from filing and bookkeeping to sales and administration," says Alyah. Adds Jonah: "It's important to take basic Web design and graphic design classes, because you don't want to have to rely on other people to perform simple tasks for your business."

The second thing is early poverty, a concept with which nearly all entrepreneurs are familiar. "The money is terrible at first. We raised seed capital from family and friends but we quickly learned that the dollar we used to order late-night pizza doesn't go far in the real world," says Jonah. "Even once established, the compensation for Internet business owners varies considerably."

Like other entrepreneurs, e-business mavericks also face stress, uncertainty, and periods of self-doubt, but their aggressiveness, persistence, and interpersonal skills usually carry them through. And most think the hard times are worth it. "I am my own boss, and I'm the one making the decisions regarding how the company is run," says Alyah. "I can do my job anywhere in the world there's Internet access, and if a competitor comes down the road, I can take steps to reinvent immediately. For the first time in years, I look forward to working."

INVENTOR
• • • • • • • • • •

> I became an inventor at the age of eleven. Like many successful prod-
> ucts, my creation was simple. I had a paper route in my neighborhood,
> and I was always wasting time and annoying customers by repeatedly
> showing up and harassing them for cash. So I came up with a payment
> envelope that I would just slip under the door. Customers would put a
> check in at their convenience, and I would pick up the sealed envelope
> the next day. Twenty years later, all of *Newsday*'s paperboys in Long
> Island use this payment method.
>
> —Brian, thirty-two, inventor

WHEN I'M STANDING IN A BAR or at a cocktail party with friends,
someone in the group always pipes up with a great idea for a new
product. If you're one of those people, you'll be especially interested in
this section on making a living as an inventor, one of the most entrepreneurial jobs of all time. In my quest to discover how one actually
becomes a professional inventor, I came across the unfortunate statis-
tic that fewer than 10 percent of independent inventors who try to
bring their ideas to market ever succeed. Here we'll explore the ins and
outs of creating and selling an invention so that you can decide if it's
truly worth the gamble, or if, like your product idea, your career as an
inventor simply sounds good in theory.

Unlike other entrepreneurial careers, inventing doesn't require
formal education, and virtually anyone can try his luck in the field.
But Jack Lander, an inventor with twelve patents, author of *All I Need
Is Money: How to Finance Your Invention,* and the creator of the Inventor
Mentor website (www.inventor-mentor.com), says that your success
depends on your intellectual honesty in analyzing your inventor personality. First and foremost, you must be innovative. People throw this

word around a lot, but essentially it means that you can identify a particular need brought on by societal change or weakness and determine a product or service that addresses that need. Like other entrepreneurs, you also have to be a talented salesperson and a risk taker who's willing, as Lander says, to face down creditors or bankruptcy for a chance to come back for another round. "You can't be a procrastinator or a talker, you have to be a doer," says Brian, thirty-two, an inventor of household kids products in New York. "Follow-through is incredibly important, as is the ability to think long term and communicate persuasively about your ideas."

Think you have the chops to give this career a shot? Let's look at the process for turning rough sketches into real products that generate real income. As a novice inventor, your first instinct might be to run out and file a patent for your idea, but given that the average cost to do so is around $7,500, you'll want to do your homework first. The first step is to make sure someone hasn't thought of your idea already. Go online and look for products similar to your idea in indexes such as ThomasNet (www.thomasnet.com) and the Harris InfoSource (www.harrisinfo.com). You should also research the companies that make these products to see if their items would directly compete with your invention or if they are better than your invention in some way. Then search the U.S. Patent and Trademark Office's online database (www.uspto.gov) to find related patents that have already been filed.

If the preliminary data indicates that your product idea is unique, you can more carefully consider its positioning. What is the hole in the market that your invention can fill? Is your customer target among a small group of people (niche market) or a large group of people (mass market)? How will your invention improve your target's life, and what are the specific, distinctive features she will benefit from? Brian, for example, saw how his kids were always losing their expensive mylar balloons at theme parks and shows, and in response, patented and licensed a weight wristband for keeping migrant balloons in check. "I talked to other parents, and kids who liked to buy balloons as souvenirs," says Brian. "I went to the *Sesame Street* show and passed out a few, and then gauged people's reactions. It really helped me get a sense of the market and the opportunity." Knowing your customers, and what will motivate them to buy your invention, will help a great deal when you attempt to sell your product down the road.

If you want to be extra sure you're making a good investment in hiring an attorney to file a patent for you, first get a professional patent search firm (such as Patent Search International, www.patentsearchinternational.com) and a market evaluation service (such as the WIN Innovation Center, www.wini2.com) to confirm the viability of your invention. Then you can rest easy knowing that you're shelling out big bucks to protect a product idea that's worth protecting.

Once you have your patent, you'll want to decide how you're going to sell your product. Nearly all invention experts warn against using an invention submission company that advertises on TV or online. Instead, they suggest two courses of action: licensing (getting an established manufacturer to buy your invention and pay you a royalty on those sales) and venturing (starting a business to manufacture and sell the product yourself). We'll start with licensing. To do this, you should go back to the list of manufacturers you found on ThomasNet and contact a VP of marketing or research and development at each company. In your call or e-mail, ask where you can send a short proposal, and make sure you get the name of an individual as opposed to the address for a nebulous "new products committee." Then write a one-page letter that describes your product in general terms. You don't want to reveal specifics until you are invited to pitch the manufacturer in person. During this last stage, you will be well served to have a prototype of your product, which Brian suggests you produce inexpensively through a local university engineering program.

In the event that you have trouble connecting with manufacturers one-on-one, you might consider some alternative tactics. Networking at high-profile inventor trade shows such as the Yankee Invention Exposition (www.yankeeinventionexpo.org), launching a publicity campaign, or entering your invention in a new-product hunt sponsored by a company like Radio Shack, Staples, or the Dial Corporation may attract the attention of a new-product scout. If all else fails, you could engage a licensing agent who will find you a manufacturer in exchange for 20 to 50 percent of your net income from the product. This is a hefty amount to pay considering that most inventors only earn around a 5 percent royalty on every licensed product sold. You can, however, expect your agent to negotiate an up front lump sum (usually in the high four or low five figures) that is an advance on your royalties. So assuming you have several inventions in the pipeline, it is possible to survive on licensing income.

Jack Lander tells us that the advantage of a successful licensing deal is that it frees up an inventor to pursue new products while still profiting from the last great idea. It also requires much less capital. Your other option, venturing, will require more time, money, and effort in the beginning, but will also pay greater financial dividends over the long term. Even if you can borrow money to start your new business or have enough saved to devote to the cause, you'll still want to start by preparing a business plan similar to what you would create for potential investors. The plan will include how you will handle manufacturing (for instance, the method and materials used, the sources employed), how you will store and move inventory, how you will price your product, and how you will market it. Specific sales tactics—such as meeting with retailers and developing collateral materials—should be incorporated, as should a budget and timeline.

Planning, however, is only the beginning, and in order to be a profitable entrepreneurial inventor, you'll need to get out there and hustle. Tamara Monosoff, a columnist for Entrepreneur.com and the CEO of Mom Inventors, recommends a phased approach that starts by selling directly to end users in order to create referenceable customers and get valuable feedback. Once you've ironed out your product and packaging wrinkles, you can try selling to independent specialty stores and online stores, and then to larger regional stores and catalogs. Depending on the nature of your product, achieving sales with these retailers may lead you to approach the big guys—mass-market sales channels such as Wal-Mart and Target.

Whether you decide to license your products or sell them on your own, the life of an inventor can be emotionally and financially draining. Seasoned inventors advise joining a local inventor support group, which you can find through your local chamber of commerce or through industry organizations such as the Professional Inventors Alliance (www.piausa.org), the National Congress of Inventor Organizations (www.inventionconvention.com/ncio), and the United Inventors Association (www.uiausa.org). Subscribing to industry resources such as *Inventors Digest* magazine or the newsfeed at InventorEd.org will help you keep tabs on the industry, but a support group affords the incomparable opportunity to network with potential mentors, brainstorm with your peers, and learn what's working and what isn't. No one understands what it's like to be an inventor better than another inventor, so go out and meet a few today.

PET SITTER
● ● ● ● ● ● ● ● ● ● ● ●

In college, I had three majors, and once I thought I wanted to be a lawyer. I've done every kind of job imaginable: fixing computers, tutoring, babysitting, and nannying, but by far the best was working with pets. It is so rewarding when you go to a house and there is a dog or cat waiting for you at the door to give you affection. A big part of this business is selling myself, because customers need to like and trust me with their most valuable possessions: their pets and homes. Once I saw I could be successful and mapped out a long-term plan, I decided that I had to devote myself to the business 200 percent. I haven't looked back since.

—Joey, twenty-six, pet sitter

FOR THOSE OF US WHO LOVE ANIMALS, it doesn't come as a surprise that over 70 percent of U.S. homes contain at least one pet. Americans spend over $14 billion on 65 million dogs and 77 million cats, and each and every one of these critters is considered a cherished member of the family. This means that when today's busy owners go to work or on vacation, their pets require a high standard of care and treatment. Enter the professional pet sitter. If you're an entrepreneurial type who wishes you could spend every day frolicking in the dog park, starting a pet-sitting business could be your ideal career. Besides being your own boss and enjoying a flexible schedule, you'll be able to grow a business by offering rewarding services that help others. A pet-sitting business has two major advantages over many other entrepreneurial ventures. You don't have to move to a particular area to do it because pets are everywhere—from the busiest city to the one-stoplight town—and you'll need very little money up front to launch the business.

It's understood that pet sitters provide for the welfare of domestic animals, but what are their specific responsibilities? The majority of sitters offer some combination of the following services: home visits, dog walking and exercise, pet taxis to the vet, groomery, or dog park, house sitting (security checks, watering plants, taking in mail, et cetera), and boarding. Most care for pets in the owners' residences so that they don't have to spend time traveling and the animals don't experience the stress of being in a strange location, but some others own good-size homes and prefer to supervise pets there. If you choose the latter option, however, you will need to purchase supplies to make pets feel at home, and ensure that there won't be conflicts between your charges and your own animals. Pet sitters' daily tasks also vary depending on whether they care for clients on their own or employ a staff to help them. "When a pet-sitting business expands, you might hire people to work for you, and then your job involves supervising them," says Joey, twenty-six, who owns Ruff Ruff Pet Care with his wife, Bettina. "Sometimes employees quit unexpectedly, so you have to be able to easily disperse assignments to other sitters as well as cover some yourself."

Like other entrepreneurial pursuits, starting a pet-sitting business requires some substantial forethought. First, you must determine your suite of services. Do you want to be a full-service sitter, or would you prefer to stick with walking dogs? Do you have the knowledge to care for exotic animals, such as rodents and reptiles, in addition to mainstream dogs and cats? On which days, and at which times, will you make yourself available to visit an owner's home? Next, scope out what your local competition is offering (and how much they're charging for various services), and figure out how you can differentiate your new business. For example, if there is already a doggy day care center in your neighborhood, perhaps you can fill a niche for owners who want their dogs to get top-notch care without leaving home. On the other hand, if your area is cluttered with dog walkers, consider catering to kitties instead. Identify a creative name for your pet-sitting business that also accurately describes what you do, and put together a price list for your services that gels with commonly accepted rates in your area. You may also wish to develop a brief business plan that addresses the following:

- Your long-term business goals
- Days and hours you will work
- Employees you will need (if any)
- Your client process
  - Complementary introductory visit
  - Background information to collect and questions to ask owners
  - Contracts
  - Reporting at the end of each day of care
  - Payment
- Your expenses and budget
- Revenue forecasting and tracking

You're almost ready. But before you hit the accelerator, you'll want to do two more things: prepare for the responsibility of caring for certain pets, and decide how you will recruit clients. Don't overlook the obvious step of learning about the pets you'll be sitting for, including what they eat and drink, how they behave, how they play and show affection, how they sleep and exercise, and the signs they'll exhibit if they're ill. This is especially important if you'll be dealing with rare animals. A great way to gain experience is to work for an existing pet-sitting business. "When I was researching how to start a pet-sitting business, I came across the website of an organization that did exactly what I wanted to do, so I applied," says Joey. "If you're not quite ready to start your own business, a good option is to contact pet-sitting companies in your area and find out if they're hiring."

It's also a smart idea to join a professional association such as Pet

Sitters Associates (PSA, www.petsitllc.com) or the National Association of Professional Pet Sitters (NAPPS, www.petsitters.org). These organizations offer valuable networking and education, as well as the opportunity to learn best practices from experienced sitters. NAPPS has a home study certification program that instantly increases your credibility as a pet care professional—even if you don't have years of experience under your belt.

You should also be bonded and insured against liability before you walk into a new client's home. Some pet-sitting associations, PSA included, offer this type of insurance as part of their annual membership dues. "I recommend checking with your local Red Cross to see if there's an animal first-aid class you can take," says Nola, thirty-three, a pet sitter in Georgia. "Hopefully you'll never have to use what you learn, but you and your clients will feel better knowing you can handle an emergency." Finally, you'll be able to get up and running more quickly if you start out with a few strong references. You can get these easily by offering a few people you know free services in exchange for their good words. Just make sure you get their permission for future clients to call or e-mail them!

Speaking of future clients, how can you find them? The answer is in effectively marketing your new business. First, using a logo with your business's name, create colorful, animal-friendly business cards and flyers to put up in local pet, grocery, and retail stores. Peggie Arvidson, the founder of Pet Care Business Success University, recommends trying to get face time and make alliances with community groups that can help you get the word out, such as the chamber of commerce, pet-rescue organizations, veterinarians, and housekeeping services. Since many people find pet sitters online, make sure you are listed in all of the pet directories, especially those sponsored by professional organizations like NAPPS. A professional-looking website for your pet-sitting business is a must: include services and rates, your professional affiliations and certifications, animal photographs, frequently asked questions, contact information, and an e-mail inquiry form. Begin collecting the e-mail addresses of clients and people you meet, and send out a monthly e-mail newsletter with fun stories and helpful pet care tips.

Although you may do a superb job marketing your business, the biggest factor in how successful you'll be as a pet sitter is your personality. In addition to getting along well with pets, you must come across as warm, trustworthy, and reliable with their owners. It's a tall order making people feel comfortable enough to allow a stranger into their homes, but as a pet sitter, that's what you have to do. In some ways, this is a selfless profession: caring for animals' needs before your own, forgoing your own holidays so that owners can go on vacation worry-free, and always checking in to see that your customers (human and animal) are getting what they need. But let's not forget the entrepreneurial side of this equation. "In addition to being an animal lover, you have to be a smart businessperson," says Joey. "You can't be solely one or the other or you will only succeed for a little while." Fortunately, if you're good at it, pet sitting can be a reasonably lucrative career too. According to NAPPS, independent pet sitters earn anywhere from several hundred to several thousand dollars a month. "After a few years in the business, I make enough money to spend every day playing with my favorite creatures on the planet," says Nola. "When I'm walking outside in the fresh air with a doggy client, I can't believe how lucky I am!"

PROFESSIONAL ORGANIZER

> One day I was just hanging out helping a friend of mine, an interior designer, organize her old photos. Then, out of the blue, one of her clients calls and says she needs a professional organizer. So I went online, found other organizers, and gathered as much information from them as I could. I went to my appointment and just followed my instincts. From there, I was hooked and started telling everyone I was a professional organizer. Word of mouth spread, and I found myself in an exciting new career!
>
> —Gina, thirty-nine, professional organizer

I AM ONE OF THE MOST compulsively organized people on earth. I always have been, and had I known about professional organizing when I was choosing a career, my life might be very different today. Professional organizers, who are for the most part entrepreneurs and work for themselves, provide personal assistance, planning, and products to help people organize their homes and offices. Specifically, they're often involved with setting objectives for a space, cleaning out clutter and identifying whether items should be saved or thrown away, moving and packing, and creating storage or filing systems.

Professional organizers also help to change behaviors that cause disorganization, like procrastination, an inability to focus, and the accumulation of unnecessary "stuff." They achieve this by teaching simple organizing techniques that aim to reduce waste, make everyday processes easier, and simplify daily responsibilities. "My clients and I spend time assessing where the problems lie and how the clutter develops, and putting together a game plan for how to tackle the situation and prevent it from happening again," says Gina, thirty-nine, a professional organizer and the owner of It's an Organized Life. It sounds like a lot more than dumping the contents of a room into a trash bin, that's for sure!

How does one become a professional organizer? It's actually fairly easy. While the National Association of Professional Organizers (NAPO, www.napo.net) does offer a certification program involving a mix of paid work hours and coursework, most organizers agree that formal education isn't necessary. According to the very useful website OnlineOrganizing.com, a career as an organizer requires business savvy, interpersonal and problem-solving skills, and the ability to teach new ideas. "You have to be able to read people and listen to what they're really saying," says Beth, thirty-three, a professional organizer in Chicago. "It's important to be patient and even-tempered even when a situation seems overwhelming, and to recognize that people have different lifestyles and preferences. What works for you might not work for the client, and inevitably things won't turn out as perfectly as they do on TV."

Before you rush out and get a credit card for your new organizing business, you should read up on the industry so that you can be sure it's something you really want to get into. NAPO recommends several books, including Maria Gracia's *Ultimate Guide for Professional Organizers* and Julie Morgenstern's *Organizing from the Inside Out* and *Time Management from the Inside Out*. It's also a good idea to peruse websites such as OnlineOrganizing.com (www.onlineorganizing.com) and Get Organized Now! (www.getorganizednow.com). Both are chock-full of tips and resources on how to start, manage, and grow an organizing business, and both have monthly e-newsletters and referral networks that will keep you plugged in over the long term. And if you can afford to, join NAPO immediately. The only nationwide association for professional organizers has twenty-five local chapters, each of which offer courses on how to become an organizer and lots of networking opportunities. I've heard that NAPO's annual conference and organizing expo is a great forum for gaining insights, generating ideas, learning about the latest products and techniques, and meeting experienced organizers.

NAPO tells us that clients expect organizers to be competent, honest, and responsible, and able to agree on expectations up front and maintain confidentiality. Competency, however, usually requires practice, so you should offer to organize your friends and family before you solicit paying clients. In exchange for your services, ask people to give you feedback about the experience and serve as references. You can also gain experience by applying with NAPO to work with a member as an intern, apprentice, or assistant. "I got my start at another organizing company in Chicago, which I found by doing a search on the Illinois NAPO website," says Beth. "However, if you are going to work for someone else, be careful of noncompete agreements that may prohibit you from starting your own business in the same area."

Once you feel comfortable enough with your organizing skills, you should consult the U.S. Small Business Administration (www .sba.gov) for information regarding setting up your business. In addition to choosing a name and a focus (for example, houses, offices, closets, or kids' rooms), you will need a home office, business cards, a small-business license, and liability insurance to protect you when you're working in other people's homes. In her book *FabJob Guide to Become a Professional Organizer*, Grace Jasmine provides valuable templates to use with your clients, including a task-planning worksheet, a time-activity log, a personal organizational assessment, a room analysis form, a rate sheet, and sample invoices, contracts, and feedback forms.

You will also have to decide what you are going to charge for your services. OnlineOrganizing.com says that your fees should be determined by your level of experience, the difficulty level of your work, and what clients in your area are willing to pay to get organized. Each organizer charges differently—some are paid by the hour, some by the day, and some by the project. While hourly rates can vary from $15 to $150, the average in the United States is typically between $45 and $65.

As a professional organizer, your biggest challenge by far will be attracting clients. This is still a new field, and there is a general lack of awareness of the benefits organizers can provide. "People don't need organizing services like they need a dry cleaner or a cleaning lady," remarks Beth. The most obvious thing to do is to tell everyone you know about your business and ask them to refer you to their disorganized friends and family members. Join as many referral networks as you can find, including the ones mentioned in this section, and offer prospective clients a free consultation to get them in the door. NAPO suggests public speaking as a great way to get your name and face out in the community. Ask to speak about organization tips at your local service or nonprofit organization meetings, make contacts at chamber of commerce functions, or teach adult or continuing education classes. In terms of advertising, a yellow pages listing should be a given, as should a website listing basics such as your services, rates, and contact information. Your website will be most clients' introduction to you, so make sure it reflects your orderly persona and includes lots of text references to organization so it's easy for search engines to find. In order to enhance your business's online presence, you might create a monthly e-mail newsletter of organizational tips and techniques, and look for sites that will publish your expert articles (with a link to your website) for free.

Professional organizing is widely perceived to be one of the fastest-growing fields in home-based business, and every year organizers help tens of thousands of clients bring order, calm, productivity, and control to home and office life. Like other entrepreneurial jobs, having your own organizing business is not for the faint of heart. "Dealing with adult ADHD, and staying open-minded and nonjudgmental, can be hard sometimes," says Beth. "And professional organizing is not a steady job where you work seven or eight hours every day."

But according to Maria Gracia, the author of *Ultimate Guide for Professional Organizers* and the website Get Organized Now! (www.getorganizednow.com), if you're a go-getter, the professional organizing field can be a very lucrative one. You can make thousands of dollars a month on organizing projects alone, and there's the opportunity to expand your services by holding seminars, writing books, and/or hiring employees. One thing's certain: combing through other people's possessions can be interesting. "Sometimes I feel like I'm doing therapy," says Gina. "We're purging 'stuff,' and a lot of stories come up related to the 'stuff.' Clients have told me things they haven't even shared with their spouses or children!"

The Investigator

There are many days when I will spend all of my time looking through files only to find one or two tidbits of useful information. In order to succeed as a historian, you have to really want to find out something, whether you end up proving something happened in the way you have always heard or whether you debunk some myths and wind up finding out that the stories that have been passed down through the ages happened in a fashion wholly other than what everyone had thought. Days can be long and tiresome, but when you finally have all of your research materials collected and you see how things fall into place, it's worth all the effort.

—Gregg, thirty-eight, historian

REMEMBER BEING IN SCHOOL with investigators? They were the ones always asking the teacher questions, and the ones you wanted on your team for group projects because they were so darn smart and motivated. They could be frustrating to work with too, though, because they'd be so focused on finding something interesting that they'd sometime lose sight of the big picture. You'd have to remind them that the point of dissecting the frog was to do exactly what the teacher asked so that you could get a good grade, not just to tool around in there!

Investigators place a high value on learning—with a few exceptions, they're the best educated of all of the passion profiles. The pursuit of knowledge is second nature to them, and they do it not because they have to in order to advance in their careers, but because it fulfills them. "At the gallery, we have a seriously huge library," says Yvette, twenty-five, an art curator. "I'm always reading the books and discussing them with the owners. And when something comes up I'm not familiar with, I get to do research on it, learning the who, what, where, why, when, and how of a particular piece."

> It would be really cool to be an art curator because I'd be responsible for creating and managing collections that help the world understand certain artists and ideas.
>
> —Adam, thirty-four

Indeed, investigators excel at research—usually, but not always, scientific in nature— and in using the information gained through their senses to solve abstract problems. "Psychological research involves gathering as much data as you can, and then putting it all together to see what insights you can glean," says Susan, twenty-three, a psychology research assistant. "We learn all we can about an individual's history, and then have to comb through it, zeroing in on the particular question the study is trying to answer." Although investigative types tend to be patient and like to focus on the work at hand rather than a specific outcome, nothing thrills them more than a big find. "Even under circumstances that would cause the average person to give up, the forensic scientist is always analyzing and brainstorming about how to solve the mystery," says Rob, twenty-seven, a forensic scientist. "And then there's that adrenaline rush that's typically experienced when you find the smoking gun."

Intellectual and introspective, investigators are happiest when they're using their significant brain power to pursue what they deem as a worthy endeavor. "Criminology is the perfect job for the socially conscious inquiring mind and for those who are always asking questions of society and wondering what we could collectively or individually do better," says Michelle, thirty-six, a criminologist. "The pursuit of a safer society involves representing people of endless ethnicities, cultures, occupations, educational backgrounds, religions, lifestyles, and value systems. Such diversity brings countless perspectives, and I am so lucky to be in the position to learn from so much of it."

Investigators also prefer their work to make a difference in the education of others. "I want to find out the real story and hopefully uncover facts that people have long since forgotten. I love to share my discoveries with people, and hope that through my writings, websites, and lectures others will become curious about the past, and we can make sure that history is never lost," says Gregg, thirty-eight, a historian. Adds Erin, a thirty-one-year-old field archaeologist: "On every project, I have the potential to discover things that teach us about people, the environment, and people's manipulation of the environment. My findings are scientifically documented, and artifacts are stored in curation facilities. I feel my work contributes to the archaeological record."

> As a historian, I'd get to be the top geek. I'd actually get paid to start sentences with "Well, no, actually, it didn't happen that way at all." Who could ask for more in a job?
>
> —*Cris, thirty-seven*

Investigators like to do things their own way. They aren't fans of overly structured environments that necessitate a set response to challenges. "One thing I love about the antiques business is that you can tailor your job to fit your personality," says Heather, thirty-four, an antiques dealer. "You can have a shop, exhibit and sell at antiques shows, buy and sell through auction, buy and sell online, deal from your home—the possibilities are endless." Says Sarah, twenty-seven, a field archaeologist: "I don't work behind a desk all the time, and every day my job is different. Every day is another question, every project holds unknowns: Is there something significant there? What will we uncover as we look at the property?" While most of their careers involve some type of collaboration with others, interpersonal difficulties can occasionally get investigators down. When I asked my investigative interviewees what aspect of their jobs they found most taxing, I heard answers like "inefficient co-workers," "speaking in front of people," and "the social obligations." Says Jaye, thirty-five, a historian: "Whether they are extreme micro-managers or insufficiently attentive to their professional duties, deal-ing with bosses has proven to be my biggest challenge. The only way I have found to cope effectively with a dysfunctional boss is by trying not to take the person too seriously."

Investigative types are highly vigilant when it comes to keeping up with the formal or informal education necessary to be on top of their fields. "I'm actively working toward moving back to academia, because if you know you want to be at a certain place, you have to keep educating yourself," says Kreg, thirty-four, a field archaeologist. How-ever, they can be impatient when they have to put important work on hold to focus on another task. "I really enjoy conserving precious arti-facts and doing full-blown excavations that save a site that's about to be destroyed, but the reality is that my day often involves mundane and miserable surveying through briar-, tick-, and mosquito-infested forests, doing tests that result in nothing at all," says Kreg. Laments Michelle, a criminolo-gist: "Unfortunately, when I'm immersed in other tasks, I don't have the opportunity to use my data analysis expertise, and I get rusty. I then have to work hard to refresh these skills."

> Forensic science is nerdy-cool because it's a job that uses science and tech-nology in ways that are always chang-ing and evolving, with the goal of solving crime and re-creating recent history.
>
> —*Amanda, twenty-eight*

The investigators profiled in this chapter work every day to ensure that we continue to celebrate the achievements of the past while paving the way for a productive future. Let's now take a look at nine investigator jobs—antiques dealer, art curator, classic car restorer, criminologist, field archaeologist, forensic scientist, futurist, historian, and psychology lab assistant—that mix a little bit of romance with a lot of hard work and perseverance.

ANTIQUES DEALER

Antiques dealing is a treasure hunt! Searching out great pieces while my competition is out there doing the same makes my job feel like an adventure every day. It's a wonderful feeling when you walk into a shop or an antiques show and see "that" piece—the one that is a great example of whatever you're dealing in. When you think about it, you're handling a piece of history. The piece has been through a lot of hands and now you're the one who'll place it in just the right hands.

—Heather, thirty-four, antiques dealer

WHEN I'M VISITING sleepy little towns in New England, occasionally I'll stop into the antiques stores and just chat with the owners. It seems that the stories that antiques owners have to tell about their lives are almost as interesting as the tales behind the items they find and sell. And although their journeys to arrive at this career vary greatly, they have certain things in common—namely, a house crammed with antique furniture, a fascination with history, and a healthy appetite for treasure hunting at flea markets. Is there a tried-and-true formula for breaking into the antiques trade? Not exactly. But the dealers I spoke with were happy to share tips that will be useful to you as you consider antiquing as a career.

According to the StyleCareer.com website and the e-book *Break-*

ing Into and Succeeding as an Antiques Dealer, an antique is any object—including furniture, quilts, clothing, knickknacks, clocks, jewelry, accessories, paintings, photographs—that withstands the test of time and increases in value due to its rarity, beauty, functionality, or uniqueness. An antiques dealer is someone who finds these objects—either for free or for purchase at auctions, estate sales, flea markets, garage sales, and thrift stores—evaluates their condition, has them restored if needed, reviews their documentation, assigns them a monetary value, and sells them to the public, collectors, and museums.

Heather, thirty-four, is an antiques dealer in New York City who recently opened her own shop, Heather Karlie Fine Art. "Every day I'm out searching for merchandise," she says. "Today, for example, I went to two antiques shows, an auction preview, and I can't remember how many antiques shops. I purchased a beautiful pair of hand-carved gilt eagles. Tomorrow, I'll be up at three A.M. and at the local flea market."

Antiques dealing is one of the few professions that requires no formal education whatsoever. While an undergraduate or graduate degree in art, art history, or business can provide some of the background you'll need, most experts will tell you that it's much more important to acquire a comprehensive body of knowledge about the type or period of antiques you want to specialize in (for example, pottery versus textiles, Arts and Crafts versus Edwardian), either through self-study or by actually working in the field. "Some people may feel comfortable in a paid environment at first, just while they're getting their feet wet," says Heather. "Maybe a gallery, antiques shop, auction house, museum, or another place where you'll be in contact with the arts. Some other people may just want to dive right in. This business is great for both types."

The British Antique Dealers' Association's article "Making a Career in Antiques" suggests a do-it-yourself course of reading and studying; visiting museums, country houses, salesrooms and dealers' shops; asking questions and handling objects whenever possible; and attending evening classes and museum and gallery lectures. Online resources you might check out include:

- About.com: Antiques (antiques.about.com)
- AntiquesDealer (www.antiquesdealer.com)
- *Antiques Magazine* (www.antiquesmagazine.com)
- *Art & Antiques* magazine (www.artandantiques.net)
- Art Dealers Association of America (www.artdealers.org)
- The British Antique Dealers' Association (www.bada.org)
- GoAntiques (www.goantiques.com)
- The National Antique and Art Dealers Association of America (www.naadaa.org)

Because the start-up costs for independent antiques shops are so high, most get their start in the profession by working as interns at major auction houses such as Christie's (www.christies.com) or Sotheby's (www.sothebys.com) or as assistants to established dealers. The Princeton Review says that in these types of positions, you'll learn inventory systems, bookkeeping methodology, and payment schedules, and assist with client contact and valuation decisions. The hours are long and the pay is low (consider a full-time starting salary of less than $20K!), but the responsibility in terms of inventory management and presentations is significant. And once you're able to secure one job in the field, the contacts you'll meet there will make finding your next position much easier.

The StyleCareer.com e-book also reminds us that there are ways to try your hand at buying and selling on your own without having to raise a huge amount of capital for your own store. You can sell whatever you have in your attic, buy pieces from family and friends, set up booths at flea markets and community fairs, rent a space in a local antiques mall, or use an online auction service. Selling on websites like eBay only costs a few dollars a month, and might provide the income to eventually move your store to a brick-and-mortar location.

After several years of experience, many antiques dealers who work for other employers do open independent shops, a move that typically involves assembling a collection of pieces and offering to buy them from the current employer. Although average salaries for tenured antiques dealers don't rise much beyond $50K across the board, you'll make more money if you do well on your own. However, with increased earning potential comes greater pressure. Independent antiques dealers must invest heavily in their inventory, which means that they have to assess carefully the value of items before purchase, and then sell those items aggressively after purchase. "Working for yourself is tough," says Heather. "Business is linked to the economy, and when times are slow, sales are slow. Being able to hold on to great merchandise during a slow time is critical. It goes back to believing in yourself and being patient."

Good antiques dealers are the supreme investigators—they're always looking for the right find at the right price. Success requires a great deal of knowledge and hard work, and also an elusive quality that some refer to as artistic flair. "Taste is subjective, but quality speaks for itself," says Heather. "You have to understand what separates the common from the special. Also, going with your gut and knowing when to buy and when to sell is key." Antiques dealing is a career in which you answer to no one, and make your own luck by relying on your instincts out in the field. "In this job, the sky's the limit," says Heather. "With hard work and good luck, you can expect to eventually be very happy. And in the meantime, you're surrounded by beautiful objects!"

ART CURATOR
● ● ● ● ● ● ● ● ● ● ● ● ● ●

I love this job. Given my age and experience, the owners have put an immense amount of trust in me and I do my best to keep that. I love that every day is different. New people come and go. Old clients of the gallery have become friends to me. I form new relationships all the time. I am constantly surrounded by beautiful artwork of every medium. I work in an environment where continuing your education is a priority. The owners are always willing to teach me something new and impart their hard-earned knowledge to me. The people here act as a family, caring for each other and helping each other.

—Yvette, twenty-five, art curator

FOR PEOPLE WHO LOVE ART, curator tops the list of dream jobs. And even for those like myself, who have no talent for art and only appreciate looking at it occasionally, there's something fascinating about the person who gets to work in a museum and decide how precious items are stored and displayed. This career was thrust into the public consciousness with popular books such as *The Da Vinci Code*, and as a result art curating is now considered hotter than ever. Let's have a look at what the job entails.

The Princeton Review tells us that curators collect, exhibit, interpret, maintain, and protect objects of historical and aesthetic importance primarily in museums, galleries, and private collections. They are responsible for the safety and proper presentation of the works, and their daily responsibilities include creating exhibitions, acquiring works for the collection, meeting with and educating trustees, labeling exhibits, accurately and carefully keeping track of inventory, and overseeing research on collection pieces to make certain the integrity of the piece is maintained (such as dating tests for fossils or X-ray analyses of paintings to determine origin). Curators also educate the public about objects through tours, lectures, and workshops, and work in concert with collection managers to write grants and raise funds on behalf of the institution.

Thirty-nine-year-old James is a decorative arts curator in Baltimore, Maryland. "My day consists mostly of meetings with staff, collectors, and donors. I'm also engaged in studying objects, cataloging, researching, and answering letters, telephone calls, and e-mails relating to the collection and general departmental administration," he says. "Then, after the normal five o'clock quitting time, the curator's responsibilities begin anew with 'social' meetings—dinners, cocktail parties, lectures, et cetera—with supporters."

Becoming an art curator is a tough proposition, because the interest in the field usually exceeds the number of available jobs. If you want to work in a museum, your point of entry will be as a museum technician, a position that involves assisting curators with research and public inquiries, as well as the preparation and maintenance of museum art. In order to be considered for most museum technician jobs, you'll need an undergraduate degree, preferably in a related subject such as art, art history, or museum studies.

Because even entry-level jobs are hard to come by, you might consider starting your career at a local museum or gallery. Smaller organizations are more likely to need the help, and they will be more willing than the Smithsonian or MoMA to hire you without a master's degree and allow you to take on a wide range of responsibilities as you work your way up. If you have your heart set on a position at a more prestigious museum or gallery, then you should be prepared to do your time as an assistant or even as an intern or part-time volunteer. "My first job was a barely paid internship at a gallery in New York City," says Yvette, twenty-five, an art gallery director. "I met a man at an exhibition opening my senior year of college and talked his ear off about the research I had been doing. He turned out to be the vice president of the gallery and proceeded to offer me an internship for the summer . . . at a whopping $10 a day!"

In case you're not quite as lucky as Yvette, below are some online resources you may find useful as you search for curator opportunities. You should note that even if you're applying for volunteer or internship positions, interviewers will want to see that you know something about the art world, so do your homework first. Review your notes from your college art history classes, read over informational websites such as Internet ArtResources (www.artresources.com) and About.com: Art History (arthistory.about.com), and get in touch with professional organizations such as the American Association of Museums (www.aam-us.org) and the Association of Art Museum Directors (www.aamd.org). "The more you know about art history, the better," says Yvette. "Clearly you can't know everything about every period—but you should know a great deal about every artist who was working at the time. For example, when I walk into a room, nine times out of ten I can at least give the painting a specific period."

Curator Job Openings
- ArtJob (www.artjob.com)
- ArtSchools (www.artschools.com)
- Museum Employment Resource Center (www.museum-employment.com)
- Museum Jobs (www.museumjobs.com)
- Museum Market (www.museummarket.com)
- Museum Resource Board (www.museumwork.com)

The art curators I spoke with also suggested that you look outside the box for curator opportunities. Everyone who wants to become a curator heads to the art museums first, but they might not think of alternative avenues such as restaurants, bars, or coffee shops that host art exhibits; libraries and schools; and companies that provide services to museums such as Museum Services (www.museumservices.org) or Museum Services Corporation (www.museumservicescorporation.com).

Also, while you're hunting for your first position, don't discount experience that might at first seem irrelevant. "I was interviewing for an assistant curatorial position that involved a series of historic houses," says James. "In the last few minutes of my interview, I revealed that I had worked my way through high school running a house-cleaning business. It was something I was embarrassed about, and something I chose to leave out of my résumé. But the revelation no doubt appealed to the chief curator, who was concerned with having someone familiar with presentation and detail to maintain his standards. I got the job."

Whether you start your career in a small or large institution, in order to advance in the field you will probably need to obtain a master's or doctoral degree. It's easy to see why graduate education is necessary when you consider that full-fledged art curators need a working knowledge of art, history, chemistry, digital imaging, restoration, museum studies, public relations, and business administration. According to the U.S. Bureau of Labor Statistics' *Occupational Outlook Handbook,* in large museums or galleries curators may advance through several levels of responsibility, eventually becoming the museum director. Curators in smaller museums often move to larger ones. Like academia, career prestige is obtained through research and journal publications.

Across the board, curating is not a particularly well-compensated profession. The most recent numbers from the *OOH* show median annual earnings as a little under $45K, with assistants making mid-$20Ks and large museum directors sometimes exceeding $78K. "There is recognition, but there is no money," says James. "There is just the satisfaction of knowing that you are contributing to the recording of history."

The Princeton Review reports that while the years 1950 through 1984 were strong for museum growth and funding, beginning in 1985 and continuing into the present, museums have been under severe financial pressure due to lack of government funding and general economic trends. In these lean-funding years, curators who are successful at advancing to the top of the field are highly organized and detail-oriented. They have impeccable written communication skills, are good multitaskers, and are great at implementing workable systems and at coordinating a staff. And when required to charm trustees or people who are just browsing, they come up big. "I have to deal with really wonderful people and really painful people," says Yvette. "But because I'm extroverted, I'm able to be patient and nice to everyone!"

CLASSIC CAR RESTORER

I have the best job in the world. I get to build cars that most "car guys" only dream about building. One of the neatest aspects of my job is that with every car comes a story or a piece of history from the owner that really gives the build that much more meaning—maybe it was the first car he ever bought or maybe it was a gift from a relative or a way to remember a family member who has since passed away. There is almost always a great personal story to go along with the car. It is like I get to restore a fond memory or a small piece of someone's life and that feels good. It becomes much more than just another car that I get paid to work on.

—Dave, thirty-five, classic car restorer

PEOPLE WHO LOVE CARS really love cars. For some, like my cousin Ed, building or fixing up a classic automobile is the ultimate hobby.

But others dream of making a career out of restoring cars like Buick Skylarks, Jaguar XKE convertibles, Ford Model Ts, Trans Ams, and Cadillacs, and it's not out of the realm of possibility to do so. Vintage cars are big business in the United States, and investigator types who have a talent for re-creating the vision of the original manufacturer can earn quite a good living. The path to becoming a car restorer is, in many ways, similar to what you might experience in seeking a career as an automotive technician. Let's take a look.

Most car restorers work in private restoration shops that they may or may not own themselves. Depending on the particular shop's focus, they may perform restorations and customizations on all makes and models of classic foreign and domestic cars, trucks, and race cars. They must do careful research to ensure that restorations are absolutely true to the originals, which often includes ordering or making special parts and accessories. Automobile restorers inspect vehicles, evaluate their mechanical condition, repaint, reupholster, and reassemble vehicles, and coordinate delivery. If he is a sole proprietor, the restorer is also usually responsible for scheduling activities at the shop, coordinating purchases and sales, and managing ongoing relationships with owners and vendors. Car restorers are concerned with marketing their work as well, and so they often attend and compete in collector car events and shows such as the Barrett-Jackson and Leake auctions, Pebble Beach Concours d'Elegance, and Mercedes-Benz StarTech.

Michael, thirty-four, is a manager at Corbett's Auto in North Carolina. "I spend a lot of time on the phone with customers and suppliers," he says. "In dealing with the customer, I have to take into account what the budget is, how he wants the final product to look, and what he thinks is most important to achieve that end result. When it comes to suppliers, we get most of our parts from sources whose quality and service we've come to appreciate over the years.

Other times we have to search contacts out, either online or through the network we've already established."

Continues Michael: "In managing a restoration shop, the biggest challenge is breaking out of the cookie-cutter mold of the 'Paint and Body Shop' category that most people want to put us in. Restoration is so much more involved—it means bringing a thirty-plus-year-old car up to a level that in many cases exceeds the way it left the factory."

Opinions are mixed as to whether or not it's useful to obtain a formal education in automobile service. According to the U.S. Bureau of Labor Statistics' *Occupational Outlook Handbook,* voluntary certification by the National Institute for Automotive Service Excellence (ASE) has become a standard credential for automotive service technicians. Certification is available in one or more of eight different areas of automotive service, such as electrical systems, engine repair, brake systems, suspension, and steering. Many car restorers get their start in the industry by attending schools through which they are able to get ASE-certified as automobile technicians. Some schools, such as Ohio Technical College (www.ohiotechnicalcollege.com), offer degrees in classic car restoration. These programs are usually between one and two years in duration and are designed to teach both automotive and auto body technology, including everything from engine, drivetrain, and suspension restoration to tuning, upholstery, trim work, metalworking, painting, and refinishing. They also come in handy in helping the student obtain the hands-on internship or apprenticeship that will launch her career in car restoration.

Dave, thirty-five, a restoration technician for Antique and Classic Restorations in Pennsylvania, got his first position after he took a leap of faith and responded to a help-wanted ad in the local paper. "I figured they would want a tech school graduate or certified mechanic, but I sent my résumé in just for kicks," he says. "When I got the call to interview, I just wanted to jump at the chance to look around a real restoration shop. To my surprise, though, I got the job with no formal education in automotive."

Whether you've gained automotive service experience through schooling, on-the-job training, or just tinkering around with cars on your own like Dave, several online resources are available to assist with your job search in car restoration.

Automotive Job Opportunities

- AUTOjobs (www.autojobs.com)
- Automotive Employment Resource Center (www.needtechs.com)
- Automotive Jobs (www.automotivejobs.com)
- Best Auto Jobs (www.bestautojobs.com)
- CarCareers (www.carcareers.com)
- The Car Jobs Network (www.carjobs.net)
- National Automotive Technicians Education Foundation (www.natef.org)

Car Restoration Resources

- About.com: Classic Cars (vintagecars.about.com)
- Auto Restorer On-Line (www.autorestorer.com)
- CarJunky (www.carjunky.com)
- ClassicCar (www.classiccar.com)
- Collector Car Restoration Videos (www.carestoration.com)

It may take a little while to find gainful employment, especially in more rural areas with a limited number of operating restoration facilities. But that doesn't mean your budding career has to come to a standstill. "If you can't get into a shop for on-the-job training, do what the rest of us have done . . . take stuff apart," says Dave. "Build your own cars, document them, and take pictures—and you have your portfolio." Adds Michael: "Read, read, read, and then read some more. Ask questions, and buy tools. You can never have too many!"

The U.S. Bureau of Labor Statistics' *Occupational Outlook Hand-*

book provides a typical career path for automobile service technicians, and the trajectory is similar for most car restorers. Those who are brand-new to automotive service usually start as trainee technicians and gradually acquire and practice their skills by working with experienced technicians and mechanics. While some graduates of post-secondary automotive-training programs are often able to earn promotion to the journey level after only a few months on the job, it typically takes two to five years to become a journey-level service technician, who is expected to quickly perform the more difficult types of service, repairs, and restorations. Experienced technicians who have leadership ability sometimes advance to supervisor or service manager, or open independent shops.

Job prospects and earning potential appear to be strong as well. As reported in the MSN Encarta article "Auto Technician Careers: Your Fast Track to Success," the Automotive Aftermarket Industry Association states that for every ten automobile technicians who retire or change careers each year, only two to three new technicians enter the workforce, and according to the National Automotive Technicians Education Foundation, automobile technicians can earn up to $70K or more annually. Additionally, as a car restorer, the majority of your customers are likely to pay substantial sums to ensure that their valuable classic cars are meticulously cared for by highly skilled technicians, and so this area of the field can be more profitable than standard automobile service. However, you shouldn't get your compensation hopes up too high. "As far as monetary figures go, don't expect to get rich doing auto restoration," says Michael. "I know there are some big names out there that seem to have made this into a very lucrative profession, but if you look closely, they earn money off of other things, such as making parts, doing TV shows, et cetera. The compensation for me and the majority of guys like me is the idea of a job that lets me go to work smiling because what I do doesn't feel like work."

There's no doubt that a huge component of a restoration career is loving cars—their power, their speed, and their beauty. But there's more to it than that. The successful car restorer is a true investigator. He enjoys seeing how things operate, working with his hands, and problem solving. He's artistic and intuitive, certainly, but also has a comprehensive understanding of electronics, mathematics, and engineering, and the ability to keep up with constant improvements in technology. "You have to be multitalented to be in this business," says Dave. "Not only do you have to be mechanically inclined, but you also have to pay attention to the details, because when the car is done, people will pick up on that one paint flaw on the fender. And sometimes that one flaw is the difference between a first-class restoration and a hack job." Michael echoes that point. "You have to know what the customer wants and how to give him exactly what he expects," he says. "You have to have the desire to do every task better than 'industry standard.' You can't view it as a job or work, it has to come from the inside."

CRIMINOLOGIST

This summer, I brought a colleague on her first prison visits. In the past, I've taken research staff to prisons for the first time and have helped them acclimate to working out of correctional environments. But I'd almost forgotten the range of emotions that even trained researchers may go through the first time they step inside a prison and are led through it. When I got excited about the offer to eat prison food with the staff, served up by the inmates, I thought she was going to kill me!

—Michelle, thirty-six, criminologist

CRIMINOLOGY, OR THE SCIENTIFIC STUDY of crime as an individual and social phenomenon, has been around since the late 1800s, but gained momentum in the last half of the twentieth century when the FBI and urban police departments began commissioning studies of crimes and criminals. Although the definition of criminology sounded fairly straightforward to me, few professions I explored in this book were prone to as much confusion. Criminology is not forensic pathology or forensic psychology, although it is related to both of those fields. If you've seen the movies *The Silence of the Lambs* or *The Usual Suspects,* you've seen criminologists in action. Let's take a look at what makes them tick.

Criminologists study how certain factors influence people to deviate from normal social behaviors, and try to establish patterns at the root of crime. Their daily responsibilities often involve going to crime scenes, attending autopsies, questioning potential suspects, generating psychological profiles of suspects, and compiling reports about their findings. Michelle, thirty-six, is a criminologist for a nonpartisan economic and social policy research organization in Washington, D.C. "My institution conducts research and collaborates with practitioners, public officials, and community groups to inform the national dialogue on crime, justice, and community safety," she says. "One of my recent projects involved managing a study of the effects of college education on offenders, both during and after incarceration. This entailed conducting focus groups with inmates, interviewing prison staff and education providers, and working with data from several state departments of corrections."

It's possible to enter the criminology field with only a bachelor's degree, but employers will want to see coursework in psychology, sociology, and statistics. Increasingly, those who become criminologists obtain bachelor's, master's, or doctoral degrees in criminal justice, in which they learn, among other things, theories of crime, brain patterns of criminals, current prevention techniques, and the components of the criminal justice system (police, probation, the courts, et cetera). Criminal justice programs range from those at accredited four-year colleges such as John Jay College of Criminal Justice (www .johnjay.edu) or the University of Illinois at Chicago (www.uic.edu), to those offered part-time and online by institutions such as the University of Phoenix (www.phoenix.edu).

Trained criminologists are employed in a variety of work settings. The Criminal Justice USA website says that some conduct research while teaching legal studies, criminology, sociology, or law at a university; others work for state and federal justice agencies as policy advisers; and some work in private practices consulting on crime statistics, juvenile justices, adult corrections, and law reform. The majority of criminologists I identified, however, were employed by law enforcement, and they recommended the sources below for seeking your first job in the field. As you're applying, be aware that for most government law-enforcement agencies, background and security checks are standard, and, depending on your state, you may be required to pass a written examination that will license you as a criminologist.

- 911 HotJobs (www.911hotjobs.com)
- The American Society of Criminology (www.asc41.com)
- CopCareer (www.copcareer.com)
- The Corrections Connection (www.corrections.com)
- Federal Bureau of Investigation (www.fbijobs.gov)
- FedWorld (www.fedworld.gov)
- Government Jobs (www.govtjobs.com)
- Officer.com (www.officer.com)
- USACOPS (www.usacops.com)
- USAJOBS (www.usajobs.gov)

On the research side of the house, Michelle recommends researching nonprofit and private research organizations that do the kind of work you're personally interested in, and making contact even if there are no specific openings at the time. If you're lacking criminal justice experience, a volunteer stint can improve your chances. "By the time I graduated from college, my résumé included work in an alternative to incarceration for female offenders as well as a homeless shelter," says Michelle. "It's this experience that qualified me for my first job at the Research Institute on Addictions even though I was significantly younger than the other applicants."

The Princeton Review provides a potential career trajectory for people entering a criminology career. According to the site, junior criminologists are in charge of data collection, report proofing, and computer work. These years are marked by low responsibility, average hours, and average levels of pay (around $44K, says the U.S. Bureau of Labor Statistics), and much of the time is spent learning the specific methods, protocols, and procedures involved in law enforcement. Five-year veterans work as part of a team, assembling the data collected by more junior members and providing analysis. Fieldwork is more common, and many criminologists now are involved in discussions of policy and procedure. Ten-year professionals have, for the most part, become chief or head of criminology at their agencies. Many are project developers and manage staffs of junior criminologists, overseeing their research and directing projects through final report status.

The Victoria University Career Development and Employment department's *Career View* names several skills necessary to become a competent criminologist. These include analytical thinking, or the ability to pull together conclusions from the essential points; critical judgment, or the ability to evaluate situations and information and pick out what is logical and relevant; and the ability to understand research methodologies, statistical analyses, and computer-based information systems. And it takes a certain type of person to enjoy this line of work. "Criminology is not for the faint of heart," says Michelle. "You have to be flexible and able to adapt to all types of environments and people. You may encounter uncomfortable situations, like the bowels of a prison or a private area with a violent or mentally ill offender. It's important to remain neutral and avoid reacting to what you might see, like prostitutes with severe track marks on their arms and legs, and hear, like vulgarity and un–politically correct comments."

Indeed, a criminology career has its tribulations. The work can be emotionally draining and even damaging at times. Those who yearn to make a difference to society sometimes find their work mired in bureaucracy, and mid-career switches into different areas of the field can be hard to pull off. But most longtime criminologists meet challenges with enthusiasm. "When asked what I do for a living, I often receive a response such as, 'Oh, how depressing!' That couldn't be further from the truth," says Michelle. "Yes, you see a lot of frustration because criminal behavior continues and society continues to be affected by crime and the fear of crime. But working with service providers, law enforcement agents, policy makers, program developers, and others who are working to make a difference for victims, offenders, communities, and the larger society is so invigorating. I get to see and experience hope and advancements on a regular basis—how could that be depressing?"

FIELD ARCHAEOLOGIST
•••••••••••••••••••••••••

I've had the opportunity to witness an American Indian burial cere-
mony, which took place after graves were accidentally dug up by a
backhoe. After the archaeological excavation, the individuals were
reburied near their original place of internment. To witness this cere-
mony, filled with tradition, new and old, with music and singing and
prayer, I felt really attached to my work and had a new respect for the
past that I did not have before.

—Pamela, twenty-six, field archaeologist

A FEW YEARS AGO, my dad quit his corporate human resources job
to get a master's degree in archaeology. He'd spend his weekends sleep-
ing under the stars while on a dig with the Crow Canyon Archaeological Center, and his morning commutes on the New York City subway
poring over the latest issue of *Historical Archaeology*. Many twenty- and
thirtysomethings share my dad's dream of participating in the discovery of lost civilizations, which is why archaeologist tops the list of
dream careers. But lest we think archaeology is just about Indiana
Jones and the Discovery Channel, I've recruited several young field
archaeologists, or "shovel bums," to tell us what it's really like.

Archaeology, officially, is the study of past human cultures
through the analysis of the material evidence they left behind. According to the About.com: Archaeology website, the field archaeologist, or
field technician, performs archaeological survey and excavation under
the supervision of a principal investigator. This involves spending a
great deal of time physically working at a site, taking notes, drawing
maps, excavating archaeological features, and taking botanical and
radiocarbon samples. Back in the lab, field archaeologists clean and
catalog artifacts, analyze data, and write reports of their findings.

Sarah, twenty-seven, is a field archaeologist and cultural resource specialist with Langan Engineering and Environmental Services. "My division generally evaluates properties for permits associated with development or redevelopment, identifying whether or not historic or prehistoric remains might be found there," Sarah says. "Often this involves field investigations with shovel testing, preliminary excavation, and full-scale excavation. Shovel testing is a method of subsurface testing in which we dig pits about a half-meter in diameter and try to get a picture of the soil below the grass. As we dig, we screen the dirt and save any materials we find."

Twenty-six-year-old Pamela specializes in CAD/GIS, or computer-aided design. "Using ESRI and Autodesk software, I make maps of project areas for archaeologists to use in the field," she says. "When the project is complete, I add to the map the locations of all the shovel-test pits and units and everything else that is important to the interpretation of the area. Artifact density maps, soil survey maps, profile and plan drawings are also made for each project area. Occasionally, I will hand draw artifacts in the field or in the office."

The Society for American Archaeology's (SAA) brochure *The Path to Becoming an Archaeologist* says that most archaeologists working in the United States today have degrees in either anthropology or history, and that archaeologists specializing in ancient Greece or Rome have degrees in ancient history or classics. A B.A. or B.S. is usually sufficient to obtain a position as a field archaeologist, although most employers will want to see that you've already put in some time learning the basics in a summer archaeological field school like Crow Canyon (www.crowcanyon.org) or Poplar Forest (www.poplarforest.org). "Field school is a must. It is usually a requirement for employment, and it also teaches you what they don't teach you in college. It's a hands-on experience, and it helps you figure out what the work is actually like," says Pamela. "I got my first paying job at a large, local excavation of a cemetery. Because I was in my last year of college and had completed field school, I was hired."

Most shovel bums work either for the state or federal government (in organizations such as the Bureau of Land Management, the U.S. Army Corps of Engineers, and various state historic preservation offices) or for private firms that conduct cultural resource management (CRM) investigations and help the government and industry adhere to laws that protect archaeological sites (such as the Berger Group and Langan).

In *The Path to Becoming an Archaeologist*, the SAA offers several tips for breaking into the field as a newbie. In addition to field school, the SAA suggests obtaining a volunteer field position or internship through a state archaeological society, a state historic preservation office, or one of the following organizations:

- Advisory Council on Historic Preservation (www.achp.gov)
- American Anthropological Association (www.aaanet.org)
- The Archaeological Conservancy (www.americanarchaeology.com)
- Archaeological Institute of America/*Archaeological Fieldwork Opportunities Bulletin* (www.archaeological.org)
- Center for American Archaeology (www.caa-archeology.org)
- Earthwatch Institute (www.earthwatch.org)
- PreserveNet (www.preservenet.cornell.edu)

"My first paying job came directly after graduation, through the ShovelBums listserv [www.shovelbums.org]," says Kreg, thirty-four, a field archaeologist in Louisiana. "I gathered up my college experience and volunteer work, sent my résumé to the company hiring, and within a few weeks I was headed to Missouri. When it comes to getting a job in this field, education is the key, no matter how or where you get it. Learn how to survey, learn GPS, excavate in a cave shelter or underwater, get good at mapping, et cetera. All this combined makes for an awesome CV!" Adds Erin, thirty-one, a field archaeologist in Indiana, "There are several great job websites that anyone interested in the cultural resource management field should check out in order to see the different options, like Archaeology Fieldwork [www.archaeologyfieldwork.com] and the National Trust for Historic Preservation [www.nationaltrust.org], to name a few."

But the individual who beats out the competition for a coveted position on a field crew won't just have the right experience, he or she will possess the right skills and the right personality too. "Analytical skills are critical. Everything in archaeology is broken down into sets. How many fish vertebrae of a particular species were excavated from site X? What's the total number of pot shards with a particular pattern from site V? That's really the nitty-gritty of it," says Kreg. "Also, patience is the most important personality trait anyone can have in this field. It often takes months or years to research, excavate, record, and then produce reports about a site."

You also have to be prepared to deal with the hardships, including seasonal employment that's unpredictable and sometimes hard to come by, and precarious working conditions. "People often do not realize the dangers associated with true archaeology," says Erin. "There's trench cave-ins, toxic chemicals polluting your sites, and an endless list of possible injuries that come with the job."

And then there's the low pay. Annual salaries for field archaeologists range from approximately $23K at the entry level to $55K after several years of experience. However, in order to advance to a supervisory role on a field crew, you will usually have to obtain a master's or doctoral degree in archaeology or anthropology. After completing graduate studies, you will also have the option of moving into a university or museum appointment that will typically pay a bit better.

Some of the archaeologists I spoke with had gotten, or were in the process of getting, advanced degrees, while others were content with their current work as field technicians. It's the possibility of an amazing discovery that keeps them in the game despite the challenges. "When I told one of my professors what I wanted to do for a living, he said I would never make any money," says Sarah. "When I said it didn't matter, that I just couldn't imagine doing anything else for the rest of my life, he said, 'Well, then, welcome to the field.' "

FORENSIC SCIENTIST

Television shows such as *CSI* have really brought the forensic sciences into the spotlight in recent years. However, in reality, those who are wishing to get involved with forensics will soon realize that a crime is hardly ever solved in an hour. Some crimes can easily go unsolved for years; that smoking gun won't always be staring us in the eye.

—Rob, twenty-seven, forensic scientist

FORENSIC SCIENCE WAS AMONG the top five coolest careers in my survey, and I'm willing to bet that everyone who voted has the same mental picture of the profession as I do. The scientist gets a call at midnight about a murder. She arrives on the scene, and carefully examines the body and the environment in which the body was found. She gathers any and all evidence pertaining to the crime, including DNA, blood, and skin samples, and then returns to the lab to analyze the material and derive brilliant answers that will help investigators solve the case. We have this impression as a result of years of watching *CSI* and *Law & Order,* but the reality of the forensic scientist's job tends to be a bit different. For one thing, the American Society of

Crime Laboratory Directors' website tells us that forensic scientists who actually process crime scenes *and* work in the laboratory are increasingly rare. Crime scene technicians, who are dispatched to crime scenes and are responsible for securing and photographing the scene, and collecting and preserving the evidence, are usually police officers. True forensic scientists, on the other hand, spend more of their time in the lab, conducting physical evidence examinations on ballistics, bones, blood work, teeth, drugs, and toxins, or even computers. Other daily activities might include writing reports, meeting with attorneys and detectives, fielding phone calls, assisting with quality-assurance monitoring, and testifying in court trials as an expert witness.

The excellent Career Prospects in Virginia* (www.careerprospects .org) also reminds us that forensic scientists don't just solve homicides. Rather, they help determine the facts in all sorts of criminal and civil cases. For example, a scientist in wildlife forensics might collect evidence related to the death of an animal to determine if that animal was illegally poached. Twenty-seven-year-old Rob specializes in computer forensics. "On any given day, my job can entail provisioning digital media in preparation for an upcoming engagement, performing a forensic acquisition in the laboratory or on-site at a client's, validating the integrity of evidence acquired, performing forensic analysis on one or more pieces of evidence, or consulting a client on proper approaches to data preservation," he says.

Ideally, prospective forensic scientists will have obtained a B.S. degree in one of the natural sciences, such as chemistry or biology or, in the case of computer forensics, computer science. Coursework in forensics, criminal justice, psychology, and statistics will prove useful as well. According to the Career Prospects website, though, forensic

* Even though this website focuses on Virginia, much of its information can be helpful to people in other locations.

scientists who become laboratory directors and/or routinely give expert testimony in court usually need the credibility provided by an advanced degree, or accreditation by a professional association such as the American Academy of Forensic Science's Board of Scientific and Technical Advisors (www.aafs.org). Even with the right educational background, though, competition for entry-level forensic scientist jobs is fierce given the attention the profession continues to receive in the entertainment world.

The Midwest Forensics Resource Center (MFRC, www.mfrc .ameslab.gov) suggests doing an internship or applying for a trainee position at a crime laboratory, an experience that will expose you to the real world of forensic science. In order to find these opportunities, you'll have to contact crime labs directly or get a recommendation from a trusted professional. Twenty-eight-year-old Allison is a forensic scientist for a crime laboratory in New York City whose primary responsibility is to examine biological stain evidence from sexual assault and homicide cases. "A forensics instructor at my university recommended me for my first position," she says. "Someone from the lab contacted me after receiving the recommendation and asked for a résumé, and I later had an interview." You'll have a better shot if you're geographically flexible and willing to relocate, but if you must stay local and you can't score a crime lab internship in your area, the MFRC recommends starting with a more general laboratory technician job involving biology or chemistry. The experience you'll gain with respect to lab techniques and procedures, instrumentation, and safety will prove invaluable.

At the beginning of your career, your focus should be on learning. "Read science journals and newspaper articles on your topics of interest," suggests Allison. "There are always new developments in forensics, and you can learn a lot from other investigators' failures and successes." It's also critical to seek advice from those who have a few years on you. "Early on, I was fortunate to have mentors who were former law enforcement personnel," says Rob. "My curiosity caused me to ask many questions, and soon enough, I was thinking outside the box and realized I had a knack for it. By listening to the stories that my mentors shared with me, I learned how to deal with certain situations that come about during the course of seizing or analyzing computers."

With a year or two of experience and knowledge under your belt, you'll find that career opportunities are a bit easier to come by. Forensic scientists are employed by dozens of publicly operated crime laboratories, in addition to federal, state, and local government agencies, law enforcement organizations, universities, private consulting firms and laboratories, and law firms. For specific openings and information that could lead to the forensic science job of your dreams, check out the online resources listed here:

Professional Associations
- American Academy of Forensic Sciences (www.aafs.org)
- American Board of Criminalistics (www.criminalistics.com)
- American College of Forensic Examiners (www.acfei.com)
- American Society of Crime Laboratory Directors (www.ascld.org)
- International Association of Computer Investigative Specialists (www.iacis.com)

Employers
- Federal Bureau of Investigation (www.fbijobs.gov)
- LabCorp (www.labcorp.com)
- Orchid Cellmark (www.orchid.com)
- state crime laboratories (www.dna.gov)
- state law enforcement agencies (www.usacops.com)
- U.S. Drug Enforcement Administration (www.dea.gov)

Information Sites
- Computer Forensics World (www.computerforensicsworld.com)
- Forensic DNA Consulting (www.forensicdna.com)

- *Forensic Magazine* (www.forensicmag.com)
- Reddy's Forensic Page (www.forensicpage.com)
- Science Careers (www.sciencecareers.org)

You should be aware that most crime laboratories and government agencies require job applicants to undergo an evaluation prior to employment that often includes a polygraph, a drug screen, and a background investigation. In addition to being drug-free and having no criminal record, a successful candidate will have a high aptitude for science and math, excellent attention to detail, innate inductive-reasoning capabilities, and strong writing, public-speaking, and critical-thinking skills. "Forensics requires a high level of focus," adds Allison. "There's only one set of evidence for each case, so there are no do-overs!"

To do well and to enjoy your work to the fullest, you'll want to have realistic expectations of the field before plunging in. Several sources pointed out that the profession is really nothing like how it's portrayed in the media. The American Society of Crime Laboratory Directors says that those interested in forensics should have a natural love of science and respect for public safety, because most cases are routine and mundane. Forensic science can be frustrating as case backlogs grow and feelings of being overworked arise. The trajectory in many crime laboratories is rather flat, and your promotion opportunities will be limited without a master's degree in science. Also, in public sector organizations, salaries tend to be low—starting around $30K at the entry level and capping out around $70K for the most experienced forensic scientists.

Still, there's a great deal to be said for having a career that allows you to use your investigative skills to fight crime and contribute to the safety and well-being of your community. And despite the competition, forensic scientists continue to be in demand as the number of crime laboratories expands and law enforcement agencies place an increased emphasis on new forms of DNA and computer-based evidence. "The nature of the evidence and the tools used to analyze it are constantly evolving," says Rob. "But the forensics community is a very close-knit network of individuals, all of whom are willing to help one another overcome an obstacle. And it's the sharing of knowledge among those in the field that truly makes this a remarkable career."

FUTURIST

> A futurist must be inquisitive and open to diverse viewpoints. If you think the world is black-and-white, you will not do very well understanding it, because it isn't. The future is not found in one ideology or one book. You need to be ready to listen, because getting more viewpoints will always improve your grasp of future possibilities. You should be optimistic on some level, so that you can help people prepare for and shape better futures, while not being blind to real problems.
>
> —Josh, thirty-nine, futurist

WHEN I WAS WRITING THIS BOOK, countless people asked me which job I thought was the coolest. And while I certainly tried hard not to play favorites, I couldn't help being especially intrigued by this one. As a kid, I wrote a lot of science fiction, and I remember the day my dad took me to visit the headquarters of the World Future Society (WFS) in Bethesda, Maryland, so that I could do research for a story on future climate change. Looking at that story now, I can see that many of the predictions regarding global warming, which I obtained from the WFS in 1988, actually turned out to be true.

The formal study of the future in the United States began after World War II when Herman Kahn of the RAND Corporation started using scenarios to explore the consequences of nuclear war. The question of what a professional futurist does is a good one, for if we use the dictionary definition of "one who studies and predicts the future on the basis of current trends," then millions of writers, scientists, and laypeople with an interest in the topic could call themselves futurists. Using data from the past and present, futurists use a wide range of methods to understand how the present will evolve into possible alternative futures and how humans will adapt to the resulting technological, demographic, political, environmental, and sociological changes.

Joseph Coates is a well-known consulting futurist based in Washington, D.C. In his article "On Being a Futurist," Coates states his purpose as helping people and organizations think about their possible futures and shape their present actions and policies to move toward their most desirable future. His work involves the systematic monitoring and tracking of trends and developments in all sectors, and then perceiving relationships among developments in order to create accurate futures scenarios. His hypotheses are constantly tested through workshops and focus groups, for according to Coates, one of the things that separates the serious futurist from frauds, clairvoyants, and astrologers is that legitimate futurist work is all public and open to scrutiny.

As a futurist for Washington-based firm Social Technologies, thirty-nine-year-old Josh spends his days trying to discover what is changing in the world and what that means for the future. "I devote part of each day to learning: looking at that day's flow of scan hits to see what they might hint about the future," Josh says. "Every company, organization, and government is interested in the future, so I've worked everywhere from U.S. intelligence agencies' headquarters to an eighteenth-century fortress island off the coast of Helsinki. Popular interest is high as well, so I've often found myself on TV and the radio. My visions of the future have been used in movies, and I've been featured in media like *Entertainment Weekly* and CNN."

The futures field is small—only around two thousand professionals worldwide call themselves full-time futurists—but it's growing rapidly. While it's still the case that few people possess formal academic degrees in futures, many with backgrounds in the hard and soft sciences are entering careers as consulting futurists, educational futurists, and organizational futurists. A handful of firms, like Josh's Social Technologies, focus on futures thinking specifically, and futurists are also employed in Fortune 500 companies, government agencies, and nonprofit institutions.

There are currently no standard educational requirements to become a futurist, although the majority of jobs do require an undergraduate degree. In what, you ask? "I'd recommend a solid education in both liberal arts and business disciplines," says Robb, thirty-five, a futurist in New York City. "And studying human behavior through a classic social science education lets you cross the two and gives you the ability to see trends in behavior and data more easily." If you went to college and this section has sparked your interest, your best bet is to learn as much as you can about the profession by penetrating its close-knit community. Start by visiting the websites of the Association of Professional Futurists (www.profuturists.org), the Millennium Project (www.unmillennium project.org), the World Future Society (WFS, www.wfs.org), the World Futures Studies Federation (www.wfsf.org), and the independent site Futurist.com (www.futurist.com). Use the available information to learn about futures concepts and methods, review the

existing body of literature, and participate in educational conferences and events.

In seeking your first job, you may uncover specific opportunities
by checking out the WFS's directory of consulting futurists and either
applying for openings listed on their websites or doing informational
interviews with firms located in your area. Both futurists I spoke with
indicated that taking an internship was a good way to break in—if you
can afford it. "I've always been into watching PBS and reading science
fiction, and I got my first job in the field by applying for a summer
internship with a futurist consulting firm in D.C.," says Josh. "The
interview was a little unusual: the company owner asked me to invent
a game to replace golf—and he meant right then. I got the internship,
and worked my way up from there." If, through your exploration, you
decide you might be up for pursuing a graduate degree in futures, use
your newfound contacts to secure a recommendation to one of the
twelve plus respected programs.

What qualities do successful futurists have in common? The
Association of Professional Futurists cites big-picture thinking,
strong pattern recognition, innate curiosity, openness to new experiences, a global outlook, and the ability to question and challenge
assumptions. "You have to know how to research, and you have to be a
good critical thinker, seeking out underlying and hidden truths," says
Josh. "And you need to convey your ideas effectively, so you have to
have good writing and speaking skills." Adds Robb: "You have to be
obsessed with keeping up with trends, and always willing to consider
the 'what if?'" Compensation and career trajectories for professional
futurists vary widely depending on the organization. Consulting
futurists for companies and governments, however, can do quite well,
often hitting the six-figure mark within a few years.

There's no end to the potential of a futures career in the
twenty-first century. But as the pace of global change continues

to speed up, the profession faces increasing challenges. "Keeping up with how quickly media is fragmenting to micro levels is difficult," admits Robb. But most seem to agree that the futurist's horizon is bright. "I am glad to have a job for which I have to think, and especially grateful to have to learn all the time," says Josh. "We have to keep an eye on everything, from how people spend their time to new technologies to the evolution of China. And I feel that it is a privilege to know a little bit about the future—with only the slight downside that we sometimes have to wait a while for things we know are coming."

HISTORIAN

My favorite part of my job is exploring old buildings during the documentation process. Some of the most interesting abandoned buildings that I have explored include a 1920s-era movie palace, a former police headquarters and jail, a train station, and a naval training campus. Despite the mold, standing water, penetrating darkness, fleas, bees, quasi-satanic altars, dead birds, and potential for unknown danger, the excitement and sense of mystery is what draws me to the work.

—Jaye, thirty-five, historian

MOST OF US ASSOCIATE HISTORIANS with those academic-looking people on the History Channel, who sound as if they have filled up every available space in their brains with detailed knowledge of ancient Rome's agricultural economy or the Tudors's favorite recreational activities. We imagine a life of sniffing around dusty libraries, always on a quest to uncover a new fact or perspective that could change the way people view the world of the past. If you're like me, and read extra chapters of your high school history books just because you thought they were interesting, you probably think that becoming a career historian would be fascinating. But what does being a "career historian" mean exactly? As you'll see in this section, many things!

Work in Primary, Secondary, and Higher Education. On some level, most historians enjoy teaching, and because formal education is the method through which most people learn about history, classroom opportunities abound. In grades K–5, teachers usually teach historical subjects (American explorers, the Civil Rights movement, et cetera) as part of a broader curriculum that includes other subjects as well. Secondary school teachers are often able to specialize in history, and may in fact only teach one or two courses, such as U.S. history or European history. In the university setting, the breadth of a history professor's teaching responsibilities depend on the size of the school. History professors, like other academics, also engage in independent research projects that bring money to the school and prestige to the individual. In order to become a history teacher for grades K–12, you will need a bachelor's degree, and, if you're planning on applying for jobs in public schools, you'll have to pursue certification as well. Graduate work in history is essential for positions in higher education.

Work in Museums. According to the American Historical Association's book *Careers for Students of History,* museum historians research, write, and design exhibits that hold the attention of the visitor and express an understandable and compelling interpretation of a historic subject. In re-creating historical subjects or incidents, they are always on the lookout for sources that provide factual descriptions, as well as items that help the visitor to visualize the period. Museum historians also lecture to groups. "I love teaching kids about history, because a lot of them don't see the point in learning about things from the past. I enjoy correlating past events to things in the present, showing that where we are going, as a people, does indeed depend on where we've been," says Melissa, twenty-six, a museum historian in Texas. Based on the size and status of the museum, you may be able to get an entry-level or volunteer position with just a B.A. degree in history, but advancement in the museum hierarchy usually requires that you complete some amount of graduate-level education along the way.

Work in Archives. Archivists arrange and provide access to source collections, analyzing and classifying historically relevant information in a way that benefits the collection and addresses researchers' needs. *Careers for Students of History* describes archives as falling into two categories—those that preserve the permanently valuable records of their own institution, and those that collect the historically valuable documents of others outside of their institution—and suggests that professional archivists may work in either or both. Some archivists in small repositories have no formal graduate education and learn on the job or through professional association workshops, but the majority of archives now require employees to hold a graduate degree in archival studies, history, or library science.

Work in Historic Preservation. The preservationist, says *Careers for Students of History,* appreciates the built environment and is committed to saving these valuable resources for future generations. Most preservationists work within a framework of regulations intended to protect the historical integrity of the structures, districts, and landscapes that help to define our cultural identity. While preservationists can be found in architectural firms, economic development agencies, and construction companies, many more are employed by federal, state, and local government agencies. You'll need at least a bachelor's degree to enter the historic preservation field. "I was working on my master's degree and heard through one of my professors that a local historic preservation architecture firm was in desperate need of people to help finish off a major district survey," says Jaye, thirty-five, an architectural historian in California. "I wanted to break into historic preservation, so I took the job even though it only paid about seven dollars an hour—that was less than half of what I had been making a year earlier as a museum archivist. After the project was completed, the firm gave me a raise and hired me on a permanent basis."

Work as a Federal, State, or Local Historian.   According to *Careers for Students of History,* federal historians work in a variety of capacities that range from providing research services for politicians and developing public policy to interpreting the stories behind our national parks. State historians offer information of interest about the state and hold archives for genealogical and historical research, while local historians collect artifacts for display, provide access to manuscript archives, provide reference services to the community, fundraise, and assist schools with educational programs. "I'll spend hours in libraries, newspaper offices, courthouses, or visiting individuals to gather all of the information I can for a research project," says Gregg, thirty-eight, a local historian in Oklahoma. "Photos, film, and recordings can take several hours to go through in order to find nuggets of information." Federal historian positions typically require a graduate degree, while state and local historian qualifications vary greatly.

Depending on which of these areas interests you the most, you'll want to consult different avenues when it comes to pursuing a career as a historian. Useful online resources, complete with job openings and networking and training opportunities, include:

- Academy of Certified Archivists (www.certifiedarchivists.org)
- American Association for State and Local History (www.aaslh.org)
- American Association of Museums (www.aam-us.org)
- American Historical Association (www.historians.org)
- American Institute for Conservation of Historic and Artistic Works (aic.stanford.edu)
- American Library Association (www.ala.org)
- National Association of Government Archives and Records Administrators (www.nagara.org)
- National Center for Preservation Technology and Training (www.ncptt.nps.gov)
- National Park Service (www.nps.gov)
- National Trust for Historic Preservation (www.nationaltrust.org)
- Organization of American Historians (www.oah.org)
- Senate Historical Office (www.senate.gov)
- Smithsonian Institution (www.si.edu)
- Society for History in the Federal Government (www.shfg.org)
- USAJOBS (www.usajobs.gov)

Job hunting in this field will undoubtedly be easier if you're able to get as much hands-on experience as you can, as early as you can. "As a history major with a forestry wildlife minor in college, I was an ideal candidate for a local museum dedicated to forestry and the forest product industry," says Melissa. "Working there gave me a jump into the museum world after graduation, because I knew people who could give me leads and recommendations, and that's how I learned about my current job."

The U.S. Bureau of Labor Statistics' most recent survey indicated that the median annual earnings of historians are just under $45K. This isn't a lot considering the long, often solitary hours, and the diverse range of skills the successful historian must employ. Using substantial investigative prowess, historians of all types must understand how to use the historical method (a systematic approach to solving problems of the past) and know how to interpret historical questions in a larger context. They are adept at finding and critically evaluating primary sources, or raw materials that constitute the historical record, and secondary sources, or existing literature pertaining to a historical issue or event, and integrating all relevant information to formulate a coherent total picture. Historians must be able to communicate their findings in a manner that makes sense not just to other historians and academics, but to the public as well. "Patience and inquisitiveness are critical skills for historians," says Gregg. "And the ability to think analytically is important as well, because many times history can be like a puzzle and you have to put the pieces together."

Nevertheless, it's a career that incites passion in the hearts of people who really love history. "Doing historical research is like detective work," enthuses Jaye. "It's extremely rewarding to discover a rare image at a historical society, or to learn a fascinating fact about a former occupant or owner. I sometimes feel a sense of emotional closeness with the people I research. This type of work forces one to see the big picture in terms of the human condition and its relationship to the progression of time."

PSYCHOLOGY LAB ASSISTANT

> I have had a strong interest in child psychology for a long time, so every job I have had up to this current position has been in some way related to children and/or psychology. I have previously worked at a summer camp, preschool, learning center, psychiatric institution, and a nonprofit organization. With all of these jobs, I was able to take away something that I felt directly related to my long-term goal of studying child psychology in graduate school.
>
> —Margaret, twenty-four, psychology lab assistant

CONSIDERING OUR COLLECTIVE obsession with why people act the way they do, it's interesting to think that psychology, or the science concerned with the behavior of human and nonhuman animals, is only about 125 years old. What began with James, Pavlov, and Freud is today a broad discipline, focusing on the intersection of two critical relationships—one between brain function and behavior and the other between environment and behavior. Although psychology sometimes gets bashed for being a "soft science," its practitioners follow scientific methods and use careful observation, experimentation, and analysis to uncover essential truths.

The American Psychological Association (APA) tells us that psychological research runs the gamut—from studies of basic brain functioning to the behavior of complex social organizations, with participants that include rats, human infants, the emotionally disturbed, and the elderly. It can take place in laboratories where study conditions are carefully controlled, or in the field where behavior is studied as it occurs naturally. Regardless of the specific situation, however, one individual is usually at the center of the process: the entry-level research assistant (RA).

If you went to a college with a psychology department, you might already be familiar with the RA. He's the first person you met when for extra credit in your freshman Psych 101 class you participated in that study on the effects of diet soda on concentration. Lots of RAs are in fact undergraduate students who are currently majoring in psychology, but if you've already graduated, have no fear. There is still an RA position out there for you.

And once you find it, you'll never be bored. A day in the life of an RA is certainly busy enough. Working in universities, medical schools, community or government agencies, and independent institutes, RAs are typically engaged in major coordination efforts on behalf of a specific research study. Their responsibilities include designing aspects of studies; collecting and managing data; scheduling, running, and monitoring study participants; conducting interviews; and gathering and reviewing relevant scientific literature. They may also supervise more junior RAs, prepare conference presentations on research findings, contribute to the maintenance of the lab, and participate in regular status meetings.

Twenty-three-year-old Susan is currently an RA with the Thresholds organization in Chicago, in which she helps to run a study that links people with persistent mental illness to employment opportunities. An experienced RA, Susan previously worked on an HIV intervention study and a teen smoking study. "The RA is effectively the ambassador for a study, because we're the ones responsible for recruiting people, telling them what the research is all about, and then screening them for eligibility," she says. "In the study I'm working on now, I also administer neurocognitive assessments to assess the mental functioning of our applicants."

There are hundreds of thousands of studies going on around the country at any given time, and most researchers need help in some form or another. If you're in touch with any social science professors at your college, this is a terrific place to start. Tell them what you're interested in doing, ask them if they've come across any research opportunities in their e-mails or in listservs they subscribe to, and see if they can write you a letter of recommendation. Twenty-four-year-old Margaret, an RA with the Stony Brook Temperament Study at Stony Brook University, found her first position the summer after graduation. "I heard about this job through the psychology department and career development center at my college," she says. "The primary researcher of the study had sent out a nationwide advertisement regarding the research project and available positions."

You can also scout out opportunities online. Your first stop should be the human resources websites of local universities—they nearly always have RA positions listed. Other places to check out include medical schools, which often have bigger grants and therefore more money to fund RAs anyway, and private research firms such as the RAND Corporation (www.rand.org) and Future Search Trials (www.fstrials.com), which run drug studies for pharmaceutical companies. You should also become familiar with the job-posting sections of the National Institutes of Health (www.jobs.nih.gov) and the American Psychological Association (psyccareers.apa.org), and nonprofit career sites such as Idealist (www.idealist.org) could help you identify jobs with community and social service research studies funded by the government.

Successful RA candidates usually have a B.A. in a social science discipline and are highly conscientious, responsible, detail-oriented, and self-motivated. They are intellectually curious and either have or can pick up computer skills quickly. If you're going in without any relevant education or experience, you may have to look for a volunteer position to start, or a very basic RA job entering data or calling subjects. "My advice is to take the time to think about what research topics interest you early on," says Susan. "Most studies are underfunded, so if you're new to psychology but you show genuine enthusiasm, they'll probably be happy to have you volunteer for even a few hours a week."

Once situated, most RAs really enjoy their work. "The best part is meeting someone at his lowest point in life and then following him through the process of getting the help he needs," says Susan. However, there are challenges. "Research is complex," says Margaret. "When you work on a large-scale research study things can get chaotic and messy, and as a result it is easy for breakdowns in communication among your fellow co-workers to occur. I have learned that good communication and the ability to cooperate with others takes work and is crucial to making sure all parts of the study are running smoothly and efficiently."

RA jobs are short term, low paying (between $12 and $20 an hour, or approximately $30K annually), and, unfortunately, only last for the duration of a particular study. However, if you've proven yourself, you can probably find additional opportunities with the same organization or through the contacts you've made there. It's possible to have a lifetime career as an RA, and if you develop a specialized skill like clinical interviewing or statistical analysis, you can easily make up to $50K doing it. But most RAs use the position as a pit stop on the way to a graduate career in psychology. After receiving letters of recommendation for Ph.D. or master's programs as a result of their RA stints, many budding psychologists go on to do their own research as university professors and clinicians. "Because this job has provided me with the opportunity to collaborate with others and complete independent research projects, it has really prepared me well for graduate school," says Margaret.

According to economists at the U.S. Department of Labor (as cited by the APA), opportunities for people with graduate degrees in psychology are expected to grow between 10 to 20 percent by 2010. Every day, research psychologists apply scientific principles to solve problems of behavior, such as drug addiction, relationship violence, and environmental abuse, which are affecting our society. "Our work makes a measurable impact on people's lives," says Susan. "We help them go from being so depressed they can't get out of bed to having a well-paying job that's allowing them to support their children on their own for the first time."

The Networker

> Being part of the marketing team has allowed me to formulate some very rewarding friendships and find mentors, and I am grateful for all these people give to me as a friend and co-worker. I recently established myself as the "social planner" for the group of eight associates who are all new to the company within the past five months. We have monthly meetings where we hear from a senior executive, and it's also an opportunity for us to share ideas and vent.
>
> —Jessica, twenty-five, marketing executive

WHILE LOTS OF THE PERSONALITY TYPES in this book appreciate the value of working on a team, surrounded by other people, the networker derives unique satisfaction from it. He couldn't be happy sitting in an isolated cubicle, interacting with a computer screen all day long. Inherently social, the networker needs to have his phone ringing off the hook in order to feel like he's making a substantial contribution. "Agents are the ones everyone wants to talk to," says David, thirty, a talent agent. "I'm always on the go, having dinner or drinks with studio execs and managers and clients, or attending entertainment-driven events. This is a job of late nights."

And he likes it that way. The networker has boundless energy, and she thrives on balancing a full plate and managing an ever-changing roster of responsibilities that emphasize personal contact.

"I'm constantly interacting with people, from customers to sales representatives, and the relationships that develop are a lot of fun," says John, thirty-seven, a wine merchant. "I'm enriching customers' lives by enriching their dining experiences." Adds thirty-two-year-old lobbyist Tanya: "I'm in contact with people on a daily basis, including clients, colleagues, and members of Congress and their staffs. To be successful as a lobbyist you have to be fairly outgoing and love working with others."

As a book editor in New York, twenty-five-year-old Danielle would be quite bored if locked in her office with a pile of manuscripts to read. "I work in an office of more than four hundred people," she says. "Every day, I speak with co-workers in the art, publicity, marketing, production, design, and sales departments, as well as authors and agents from all walks of life, all across the country."

> Speechwriters are responsible for taking what a person is thinking and feeling and presenting him in a favorable light. Oftentimes, speeches are quoted in the press and remembered for ages, and I'd love to have that kind of influence.
>
> —*Lynaye, twenty-six*

The networker prefers interpersonal fulfillment and influencing change over financial reward. "One of the best things about my job is that the work I do has an impact on the business. It's really rewarding to sponsor an event and then receive positive consumer feedback afterward," says Prita, thirty-seven, a marketing executive. Phil, a thirty-year-old television producer, says: "You don't get into producing for the money, but having the responsibility of being in charge of a newscast that people rely on for critical information is a huge honor."

Networkers excel in leadership roles and only feel comfortable when they're respected by those with whom they work. "In my job, being able to manage others is critical," says Prita. "Fortunately, I have a team of six great people who help to get everything done!" Twenty-eight-year-old Barry, a speechwriter, loves the part of his job in which he has the opportunity to meet with distinguished political leaders and dignitaries. "I've been a fly on the wall for some incredible meetings and have been told secret information by candidates," he says. "Earning my clients' trust and then guarding it are very important to me."

> **My dream is to be a wine merchant. Learning about the world's wines, where and how they are produced, and then sharing my recommendations with others sounds so exciting.**
>
> **—Lucas, thirty-one**

Although generally well liked due to impeccable social and persuasive skills, networkers can come off as oversensitive or too emotionally invested in the job, always warding off fears that they don't fit in or that others don't appreciate them. "My confidence takes a hit on a daily basis, and I'm always worried about offending people," says Phil. Tanya agrees. "Lobbyists face rejection all the time, usually in the form of unreturned phone calls and e-mails, and you eventually have to develop a thick skin," she says. Indeed, several of the networkers interviewed for this chapter felt that the people-centric nature of their jobs presented some of the largest obstacles, as well as some of the most significant rewards. "Tour groups and visiting constituents can be difficult to deal with, and callers are sometimes downright abusive," says Jack, thirty-two, a congressional staffer.

Networkers are known for their graciousness and generosity with those who share their values, and are happy to consult the team before making an important decision. "I always seek the feedback of other editors and other departments before I acquire a book, because they have insights I might not necessarily have thought of," says Jennifer, twenty-six, a book editor. However, supportive as the networker might be, she won't want you on her team unless you're willing to commit yourself fully and give 100 percent to the task at hand. "One frustrating aspect is having to work with an egotistical client who doesn't meet deadlines or take my input kindly," remarks Jennifer. Adds Meredith, thirty-four, a television producer: "Less-than-competent

My dream careers are book editor and marketing executive, because they satisfy my desire or proclivity toward meeting people, satisfying their needs, and filling certain voids like providing information, making goods and services readily available, and passing on valuable ideas. These jobs would encourage me to develop my capabilities and gain a worldview about life and its intrigues.

—Akinloye, twenty-eight

co-workers definitely present a challenge."

For the networker, life is a never-ending stream of voice-mails, meetings, and cocktail party conversations. Highly extroverted, he makes friends wherever he goes, and, as a result, usually manages to find some fun in the most stressful of days. In this chapter, we'll explore several jobs suited to networkers, including book editor, congressional staffer, image consultant, lobbyist, marketing executive, pro sports team manager, speechwriter, talent agent, television producer, and wine merchant.

BOOK EDITOR

I've always loved books, and when I was growing up, my parents read to me every night. My mom in particular has always been an avid reader, and a lover of language. I had a tendency when I was young to take on elaborate, detail-oriented projects, from extra-credit art projects to exhaustive personal scrapbooks. Projects like these, which required a lot of planning, concentration, and kid-size passion, helped prepare me for the drawn-out, detail-oriented process of seeing a book through from the proposal/idea stage to the finished product— a process that often takes a year or more.

—Danielle, twenty-five, book editor

AH, THE LIFE OF A BOOK EDITOR! A young woman sits behind a cluttered desk, squinting behind reading glasses, a pencil behind her ear. It's an image coveted by those who love to read and have imagined themselves surrounded by books all day long. But after talking to a few book editors for this section, I realized that there is a lot more to this profession than meets the eye, for modern book publishing is a complicated business, and the editor, a networker in overdrive, is at the center of it all.

To start, while we typically think of the book editor as the person who selects and perfects brilliant works of literature, those in this profession actually perform a variety of roles in many different types of organizations. Some editors, such as Danielle and Jennifer, the two I interviewed, work for trade publishers, which produce commercial books for the general consumer. Some trade publishers are held by a parent company, while others are independent and therefore have more freedom to print a more eclectic, but usually smaller, list of titles. Academic or scholarly publishers publish books marketed to professionals in industries such as technology, medicine, law, business, and the sciences, while educational publishers print textbooks and accompanying learning materials. Today, editors may also work for book-packaging companies, which create books that are then sold to a publishing house, or self-publishing companies, which require the author to pay fees for editing, production, and marketing.

Book editors in most of these organizations generally fall into two categories—acquisitions editors and copy editors. Acquisitions editors are responsible for purchasing books from literary agents and authors on behalf of a publishing house. "My daily activities include corresponding with authors and literary agents, speaking with potential authors, meeting with different in-house departments to discuss everything from book jackets to book sales, sending advance copies of books out for blurbs, and preparing manuscripts to go into production," says Danielle, twenty-five, an acquisitions editor for Hudson

Street Press, a hardcover imprint of Penguin Group. Acquisitions editors are also usually responsible for developmental and line editing of manuscripts. Copy editors then edit author manuscripts for grammar, spelling, and punctuation. It's important to note that depending on the publisher, an editor might serve both the acquisition and copy editing functions.

How does one break into what is considered by many to be one of the most competitive industries in the world? First and foremost, you must have a college degree to be hired into the entry-level position of editorial assistant, although an English or journalism major is not required. After that, it's all about relationships. Your best bet is to see if you can score an internship in a large New York publishing house, a small local or university press, or a literary agency. While there's a good chance the internship will be unpaid, there's no better way to master how the publishing process works and what's hot in the marketplace, and to make personal connections that will help you move forward in your career. "When I was still in college, I did an internship with a literary agent who had tons of contacts and single-handedly got me my first full-time editing job," says Jennifer, twenty-six, an assistant editor for a large New York–based publishing house. Danielle adds: "My current job resulted, in large part, from an internship I had with Penguin the summer after my sophomore year in college. During the two years following, I stayed in touch with the editor I interned for, and when it came time for me to apply for jobs, she graciously passed my résumé along with a note of recommendation. Not only can interning help you secure contacts, but it looks great on your résumé and gives you an opportunity to prove your mettle editorially."

You might also consider enrolling in a four-to-eight-week intensive publishing course—if you can afford it (they cost $4K–$6K). Because these programs are taught by working editors or other publishing professionals, they often serve as a valuable ticket inside the tightly knit publishing community. The most prestigious courses include those given by Columbia Univeristy (www.journalism.columbia.edu) and the University of Denver (www.du.edu/pi), which will prove far more useful than, let's say, a graduate degree in English.

Another insider tip my sources shared pertained to informational interviews. Like most networkers, book editors like talking about their work and are usually happy to chat with aspiring professionals about what's involved. Not only will you learn a ton, but an intelligent conversation will also render you top of mind for any open positions the editor may be aware of. Where can you find editors to approach for informational interviews? "Look in your college alumni directory," says Jennifer. "Or even better, go to the bookstore and check out the acknowledgments section in books you like. Editors' names will usually be listed."

Although the best way into publishing is through a personal contact, it can't hurt to keep your options open and to stay up-to-date on what's happening in the industry. Here are some resources to consider while you're gearing up:

- Association of American Publishers (www.publishers.org)
- Bookjobs (www.bookjobs.com)
- BookWire (www.bookwire.com)
- *Copy Editor* newsletter (www.copyeditor.com)
- iHirePublishing (www.ihirepublishing.com)
- *Publishers Lunch* newsletter (www.caderbooks.com)
- Publishers Marketplace (www.publishersmarketplace.com)
- *Publishers Weekly* magazine (www.publishersweekly.com)

Before you apply for specific editorial assistant jobs, you should think about the kind of books you want to edit, and the type of organizations you'd prefer to work for. For example, you might determine that you'd rather start at a small press, where you could get much broader experience acquiring your own books, designing catalogs, and doing marketing plans, as opposed to a large New York house, where a majority of your day would likely be spent on administrative tasks. The more research you do and decisions you make up front, the less stressful it will be to assimilate into your role as an editorial assistant.

And you'll need all the help you can get. By all accounts, the life of an editorial assistant is tough. You'll be at the beck and call of more experienced editors who aren't always tolerant of newbies, and even in a small press, administrative and clerical tasks will be a reality. Your weekends will be spent reading manuscripts, and you'll face enormous competition for promotions and raises. The career information website Vault tells us that the best editorial assistants are detail-oriented, hardworking, and assertive, and they have sharp reading and comprehension skills and are able to write clearly. It is these individuals who manage to avoid burnout and get promoted to the next level, assistant editor, after a year or so.

As you progress in your publishing career, more and more of your networker skills will come in handy. "In order to advance up the editorial ladder, you need to acquire books, and in order to acquire books, you need both to make yourself known to literary agents and be able to convince the powers that be to support the projects you're enthusiastic about," says Danielle. From an assistant editor, you will become an associate editor, then on to editor and senior editor, and finally an executive editor or an editor in chief. Full-fledged editors "spend a lot of time schmoozing" and are required to "spot new talent and manage people and their egos."

Though publishing in general is not the most generously compensated field, the $80K you'll likely make as an executive editor is a far cry from the high $20K to low $30K you'll bring in at the beginning. And many editors become literary agents or publishing administrators, often increasing their annual incomes to surpass six figures. One thing is for sure—despite the hardships, most book editors truly believe they have a dream career. "As someone who has always idolized writers, getting to work in such a literary, intellectual environment is amazing," says Danielle. "I feel so fortunate to have the opportunity to help authors—from celebrities to experts to ordinary people—tell their stories and put their expertise into words. Being a book editor is an ideal job for those literary, bookish types who are excited and energized by the idea of working in an environment that's Bergdorf's meets Barnes & Noble."

CONGRESSIONAL STAFFER

My first year on the job, which was after 9/11, I was meeting with officials from our state police regarding their budget request, and we were discussing how quickly they could get a new communication system running. We talked for about twenty minutes on how hard it would be, and I finally asked for what the bottom dollar figure would be to get the system up in the next year instead of the next three. When they answered that it would take $1 million, I said that was no problem and waved it off, and was actually annoyed that I just wasted twenty minutes talking about a mere $1 million. Right after I said that, I had to stop myself and realize that at the age of twenty-three I had just waved off $1 million like it was the pocket change in the cushion of my couch.

—Clint, twenty-eight, congressional staffer

FOR MOST PEOPLE IN THEIR TWENTIES and thirties, having a voice in government means going to the polls every two or four years and voting. Congressional staffers, though, have a much more influential role, doing business every day in the offices of America's 100 senators and 435 representatives, or on one of 300 committees and subcommittees (Senate Foreign Relations Committee, House Committee on Foreign Affairs, et cetera). Many who aspire to a career in politics start as staff assistants, and whether you're immersed in the action on Capitol Hill or working in a remote local office, a congressional position offers the opportunity to learn the inner workings of government, make indispensable contacts, and demonstrate an interest in public service that will serve you well even if you decide that politics isn't for you in the long term.

According to the Opportunities in Public Affairs' "Capitol Hill Job Guide," the best way to get a paid professional position in a legislative office is to first gain experience by working as an intern in a member's office or on a campaign. Interns perform a wide range of duties including answering phones, running errands, and putting together mailings. The staff assistant is a paid entry-level professional who performs many of the same duties as an intern, but with a higher level of responsibility, assisting senior-level staffers with legislative or press-related tasks, researching legislation, writing speeches, meeting with lobbyists, arranging tours, and liaising with office visitors.

From the amount of administrative work this job involves, you wouldn't think a college degree would be necessary (though it is). However, as the *Vault Guide to Capitol Hill Careers* points out, the proximity to power is key. By working directly for a member of Congress, the staff assistant positions herself for far more interesting jobs in the future. For instance, Clint, twenty-eight, began his career as an intern, and then as a staff assistant, for an Illinois representative. At a relatively young age, he's now a legislative analyst who attends committee hearings and assists elected officials in deciding how to vote on bills. "I'm responsible for listening to various arguments on a piece of legislation, and combining all of them into one, nonbiased, explanation of what the bill does," he says.

As you might expect, staff assistant positions are pretty tough to come by, and many are unadvertised. The congressional staffers I interviewed indicated that the best way to get any job with a member's office, including an internship, is to network like there's no tomorrow. The Johns Hopkins University School of Advanced International Studies suggests trying to connect directly with people employed in the offices of your own representatives, or with alumni of your college who are working in politics. The high turnover rate and the large size of some congressional offices can provide enterprising job seekers with lots of chances to get in the door, especially just after an election, because newly elected representatives need to staff their offices quickly. Below are some resources you may find helpful in getting the lay of the congressional land and proactively contacting individuals about job openings:

- Congress.org (www.congress.org)
- Congressional Quarterly (www.cq.com)
- Congressional Staff Directory (csd.cqpress.com)
- Congressional Yellow Book (www.leadershipdirectories.com/products/cyb.htm)
- FedJobs (www.fedjobs.com)
- *The Hill* (www.hillnews.com)
- Opportunities in Public Affairs (www.opajobs.com)
- *Roll Call* (www.rollcall.com)
- U.S. House of Representatives placement office (www.house.gov)
- U.S. Senate placement office (www.senate.gov)

As you're applying, keep in mind that it's likely you won't be contacted by the office or committee even if your materials have been accompanied by a referral. Congress is a busy, harried place, so the Johns Hopkins University School of Advanced International Studies says that if you don't hear anything after two weeks, you should touch base with your contact or the appropriate staffer to make sure you're still in contention and to reiterate your enthusiasm for the position. "I pursued an active job search on both the House and Senate sides during an unpaid, four-month internship in the House," says Jack, thirty-two, a legislative assistant on Capitol Hill. "After considerable persistence, I was eventually offered a staff assistant job in the same office I was interning in."

When that job offer finally comes along, you'll probably be on top of the world, but don't spend too much time celebrating, as you'll be expected to prove yourself immediately. The *Vault Guide to Capitol Hill Careers* says that the typical staff assistant stays in the position six to sixteen months before getting promoted to legislative correspondent, and how quickly you advance depends at least in part on talent. You'll be required to have an in-depth understanding of your member's committee work, and strong written, oral, and interpersonal communication skills are critical. Flexibility, a naturally energetic personality, and the willingness to work hard despite long hours and low pay will come in handy as well. "You need to know how to make the most of your opportunities, and you need to be patient with the process," advises Jack. "You will not change the world, and if you come in thinking that, you will get burned out. But with the right attitude, you can have a positive impact and feel good about what you do for a living."

Once congressional staffers progress beyond the entry level, their career paths begin to diverge. Some continue to be promoted within a single member office or committee, moving from legislative correspondent to legislative assistant to legislative director, and then possibly press secretary or chief of staff. This type of upward mobility is slow, however, because in order for you to be promoted, someone above you typically has to move up or leave. You may find that you can ascend the ladder faster if you jump to another office when an appropriate position opens up. However, there is something to be said for remaining loyal to a particular member of Congress, for if he respects you and values your service, he'll take you with him as he advances in his own career and assumes greater responsibility. "I've managed to climb up significantly over the last five years due to better-than-average work product, and because I have gained the complete trust of the officials I work for," says Clint.

Since compensation for congressional staffers is poor compared to the private sector (staff assistants typically make $25K, legislative correspondents around $32K, legislative assistants around $42K, and legislative directors around $65K), many transition to the private sector, taking positions with lobbying firms, think tanks, or Fortune 500 companies. Regardless of what you decide to do with your congressional expertise, though, my sources assure me that the time is well spent. "Working on the Hill is an experience that will stay with me for the rest of my life," says Jack. "It's not an easy job, but you are surrounded by history, and in your own small way, you are a part of history. Even after working long into the night, you can still walk outside and see the lights of the Capitol dome."

IMAGE CONSULTANT

This job is all about relationships—with your clients and with the people who work in the stores. I've met some of the most amazing people, and it's incredible how well you get to know your clients when they spend most of their time with you in their underwear in a dressing room! Every day is different and there are always new and unexpected challenges. One day you may be outfitting a woman for the opera opening and the next you may be looking for vintage gold necklaces or creating a list of gift ideas for a ten-year-old.

—Amy, thirty-seven, image consultant

ARE YOU THE PERSON your friends drag shopping when they have a promising job interview or a hot date? Does your significant other tell you that you should replace one of the experts on *Extreme Makeover* or *Queer Eye*? Maybe you should consider being an image consultant, one of the coolest jobs a savvy networker can have. According to the Association of Image Consultants International (AICI, www.aici.org), an image consultant provides services for individuals and corporations through coaching, presentations, seminars, and workshops. Intuitively understanding how to bring out the best in people, she offers assistance in image enhancement (appearance, body and color analysis, wardrobe development and management), effective communication, business and social etiquette, and personal branding. She shows people with discretionary income how to make positive impressions in order to get ahead in their careers and social lives, and boosts their self-confidence in the process.

The *Fab Job Guide to Become an Image Consultant* outlines some of the typical daily activities of an image consultant, which include:

Personal Makeover Counseling
- identifying the client's "season" based on skin tone, eye color, and so on
- determining the right makeup
- advising a client on the most flattering hairstyle and color
- providing grooming tips
- choosing the right clothing colors
- selecting and putting together outfits that conceal body flaws
- teaching a client the mechanics of how to shop
- deciding what clothing items to keep, fix, and get rid of
- selecting the right accessories

Social Consulting
- advising a client on verbal communications, including voice, vocabulary, and pronunciation, and nonverbal communications, such as body language, posture, and eye contact

- improving conversation skills (icebreakers, topics, et cetera)
- improving dining and telephone etiquette

Corporate Image Consulting
- understanding a company's brands and corporate culture
- doing a needs analysis for a company
- developing a corporate dress code
- presenting training programs on dressing for success
- teaching effective customer communication
- coaching company representatives for media interviews

If this sounds like your dream job, you're in luck, for image consulting has a pretty low barrier to entry. You don't need a college degree—in fact, no formal education at all is required. However, you're going to need some training if you want to do well. Organizations such as the Training Institute School for Image Consultants (www .newyorkimageconsultant.com) in New York City offer coursework in color analysis, wardrobe and style analysis, and personal shopping, and AICI has a well-respected certification program that will earn you credibility with prospective clients. AICI's first-level certification can be obtained by passing a written exam measuring core knowledge of personal image consulting, and subsequent levels of certified image professional (AICI, CIP) and certified image master (AICI, CIM) can be achieved as you grow your business and move forward in your career. You should be aware, though, that image consulting isn't something you can just jump into. Most image consultants start their careers by working part-time in the profession, or volunteering to "make over" friends and family, while they are employed in another job. Most are also a little bit older. "Life experience and age are assets in this profession," says Amy, thirty-seven, an image consultant in Northern California. "Usually the people who can afford you are in their thirties and up, and I think it would be hard for them to trust someone who's barely out of college."

Like all successful networkers, the best image consultants love working with people. "Being a good listener is critical," says Leslie, thirty-six, an image consultant in New York City. "I always begin by meeting with a client, just to chat about what she wants to get out of our relationship. A client doesn't always have a clear picture of the end result, she just knows she wants a change. It's up to me to help her figure out how her personality, lifestyle, personal taste, and budget will come together to create an appealing new look." Adds Amy: "A good image consultant is creative and organized, and has lots of shopping stamina and skill. Even though someone may like to shop, it doesn't mean she can explain why a certain print does or doesn't work on a client, where her necklaces should hit and why, or what colors they should be wearing. Having that innate knack really helps, but you also have to be educated."

Both Leslie and Amy also mentioned the importance of understanding how to run a business. Since the majority of image consultants are self-employed, they do need to spend a substantial amount of time managing and marketing their companies. "I'm not crazy about the administrative aspects," admits Leslie. "Billing clients, writing contracts, figuring out taxes, hiring someone to take before-and-after pictures that I can put on my website, hiring someone else to do publicity—these are things I could do without, but they're a necessary evil." Accounting and bookkeeping skills are key," says Amy. "I actually hired a CPA to set up my books and give me basic training so that I could do my own books." You should also expect that it will take at least a few years to build up a strong clientele, as well as a network of partners—such as hairstylists, cosmetic dentists, personal trainers, and boutique owners—who can offer good service and product discounts to you and your clients. Joining AICI and taking advantage of their resources and events can move this process along, as can hooking up with a more experienced image consultant who can show you the ropes and help get the word out to individuals and companies who will take advantage of your services.

Having an image consultant used to be a privilege reserved for Hollywood actresses, politicians, and CEOs, but now that everyone's doing it, the field is growing fast and isn't showing any signs of slowing down. According to AICI, membership has grown 133 percent in the past five years. And if you play your cards right, you can make quite a good living. "Image consultants charge based on their experience and what the market will bear," says Amy. "I think you can earn more if you work in an urban area. I am currently at $150 an hour, and I know consultants in the San Francisco Bay Area who charge anywhere from $50 an hour to $500 an hour. My gross income has increased about $10K a year since I started, and I'm now in my eighth year of business!"

LOBBYIST

In lobbying, you are in constant contact with people on a daily basis, whether those people are clients, co-workers/colleagues, or members of Congress and their staffs. Additionally, on occasion you may have the opportunity to work for a client who truly helps people and is not just a business trying to get a tax break or something similar; on these occasions, you can feel like you are helping to make the world a better place by getting research funding to help find a cure for a disease or securing money to help build a shelter for the homeless.

—Tanya, thirty-two, lobbyist

AS LONG AS THERE HAVE BEEN politicians, there have been lobbyists. The term *lobbyist* derives from the fact that pioneers of the profession worked the lobbies and anterooms of political buildings. Because it is a profession that is strictly protected by the Constitution, lobbying will no doubt be around for years to come despite the negative attention it sometimes receives from Washington circles. In fact, according to *The Washington Post*, the number of registered lobbyists in Washington has doubled since 2000, and the fee lobbying firms charge new clients has increased by 100 percent. Are you a networking type who wants to work in Washington without the pressure of being or toiling under an elected official? Let's take a closer look at what the job entails.

Lobbying, also called government relations, involves individuals and organizations actively engaged in promoting the legislative interests of their employers or clients—which may be governments, private sector companies, nonprofit associations, or unions. As the Princeton Review explains, lobbying can be direct or indirect. Direct lobbying means actually meeting with congressmen and their staffs, providing them with credible data pertinent to a bill, and sometimes helping to draft legislation. For instance, a lobbyist with AARP might lunch with a legislative aide to discuss and hopefully influence her opinion on proposed changes to Social Security. Direct lobbyists research current issues, create reports and presentations, and attend congressional and regulatory hearings. Indirect lobbying, or grassroots organizing, enlists the community to influence politicians by writing, calling, or demonstrating on an organization's behalf. These lobbyists also report to politicians about the concerns and reactions they have gotten from the community.

Although there are courses in professional lobbying—the Public Affairs and Advocacy Institute at American University being one of them—most lobbyists get by just fine with a college degree or even a master's degree in another field such as law, journalism, or communications. The majority of those seeking lobbying careers break in by volunteering on a political campaign or interning for legislative staff on Capitol Hill or in government agencies. The American League of Lobbyists (www.alldc.org) claims that such experience provides an understanding of the process and issues unlike anything in a classroom, and also a valuable network of congressional contacts. Thirty-two-year-old Tanya, a Washington-based lobbyist, agrees. "You really do need the benefit of having worked on Capitol Hill or in the federal government to really appreciate and thrive in a lobbying job," she says. "I got my first job in the field after spending nearly five years in various jobs on the Hill. At that point, I was getting tired of the long hours and low pay and decided that I was ready to take what I had learned and the relationships I'd built and move to the private sector. I think this is a fairly typical course for entry into the lobbying field."

Even securing campaign volunteer positions or legislative internships, however, can be difficult in the competitive realm of politics. Obviously, your best bet is to know—or get to know—someone working for a legislator who can introduce you to the right people. Sending introductory e-mails to well-connected individuals in your alumni or online social networks, as well as those in your local government infrastructure, might prove useful in this regard.

Another option is to apply for an internship directly with lobbying organizations, which may include government PR firms such as Edelman, lobbying firms such as Morgan Casner, public interest groups such as the Children's Defense Fund, trade organizations such as the National Federation of Independent Business, and political groups such as the Democratic National Committee. Some of these organizations have formal internship programs, while others may be amenable to allowing you to create your own. Here are some additional resources you may find helpful in your search:

Books and Directories

- *The Complete Guide to Public Employment* (Ronald and Caryl Rae Krannich)
- *Lobbying and Government Relations* (Charles Mack)
- *The Lobbying Handbook* (John Zorack)
- *Washington Representatives* (Columbia Books)

Periodicals

- *Congressional Quarterly*
- *Government Executive*
- *National Journal*
- *The Washington Post*

Websites

- American League of Lobbyists (www.alldc.org)
- Lobbyist Education Center (www.lobbyist.org)
- LobbySearch (www.lobbysearch.com)
- Washington Center for Internships (www.twc.edu)

As a younger person starting in the lobbying profession, you will be in the minority, for many lobbyists arrive fresh from careers as politicians. This makes sense, because senior-level lobbyists are often hired more for who they know than what they know. The substantial number of people who habitually move in and out of government, often known as the "revolving door," also means that there is no hard-and-fast trajectory when it comes to lobbying careers. For example, you might start as a congressional aide, then take a position as an analyst at a lobbying firm, and later become a director in a government agency.

The Princeton Review tells us that lobbyists who can prove their ability to advance their agendas regardless of the party in office are the ones most likely to climb the ladder successfully. And climbing the ladder in the lobbying world can be lucrative. Though private sector companies and firms are known to pay more than nonprofit organizations, it's not unusual for well-connected or veteran lobbyists to exceed the low six figures. "People who are 'rainmakers,' and bring in lots of business for the firm or company they're working for, are extremely well compensated," confirms Tanya. If you're a newbie with no experience to speak of, however, be prepared to start low, with an unpaid internship followed by a paltry entry-level salary in the $20Ks.

Like other networking jobs, relationships are really the name of the game when it comes to lobbying. On a daily basis, lobbyists call upon their friends in high places to garner support and sway votes. The best lobbyists have loads of personal charm and natural persuasive ability, coupled with excellent written and oral communication skills and a mastery of the legislative process and current issues. Assuming you've got those traits in the bag, though, lobbying can still be a challenging job. Hours are long, especially when Congress is in session and eighty-hour weeks are typical, and the reputation of the profession is periodically tainted by the questionable practices of a few unscrupulous individuals. Also, a warning for the women: "Lobbying is still an old boys' club," says Tanya. "Most of Washington's most well-known and top lobbyists are still men, requiring women to work harder to achieve the same level of success." Still, lobbyists lead what many consider a glamorous life, rubbing elbows with influential people at expensive dinners and cocktail parties while promoting causes they believe in. "A job in lobbying affords you the opportunity to meet many famous and interesting people—politicians, actors, rock stars, and everyday people who have great stories to tell," says Tanya. "And that's one part of my job that I never get tired of!"

MARKETING EXECUTIVE
• •

> My group once sponsored a segment on *The Martha Stewart Show*. Shortly thereafter, we received some great feedback through our 1-800 number. One e-mail came from a consumer who saw our product on the show and, as a result, decided to try our pasta sauce. She enjoyed our product so much that she vowed to be a continued consumer after years of making her own sauce.
>
> —Prita, thirty-seven, marketing executive

IF THERE'S ONE THING I KNOW—besides writing books—it's marketing. I've spent the first nine years of my professional life in this career, and I'm still having trouble breaking away even as my schedule gets crazier by the day. What's so special about marketing? Well, in addition to being one of the most dynamic, creative, people-oriented professions out there, there are also a variety of jobs you can do, and equally as many ways you can break in.

From a big-picture perspective, a marketing executive understands the branding and details of a company's product or service, the potential and historical market for that product or service, and how to effectively communicate the value that the product or service delivers to the customer. According to the About.com article "Exploring Careers and Jobs in Marketing" by Laura Lake, marketing serves as the intermediary function between product development and sales and encompasses, among other things, market research, brand management, advertising, promotions, and public relations.

Market research involves developing a comprehensive understanding of the customer and is conducted using surveys, focus groups, and more formal controlled studies. Brand management involves assuming ownership for a particular brand, such as Weber grills or Dove soap. It is the brand manager's job to devise new products and decide how to package, price, and promote them through multiple channels. Advertising, which can be either an in-house or agency function, includes developing and placing creative online or offline ads that are in sync with the brand's overall marketing strategy. Promotions teams use direct mail, displays, and special events to offer purchase incentives such as coupons, gifts with purchase, rebates, and sweepstakes. Twenty-five-year-old Jessica, for instance, is a promotions specialist with an international consumer magazine who is responsible for developing programs that induce clients to advertise. "I spend most of my time doing research and creating proposals and presentations," says Jessica. "I also do a lot of brainstorms, always trying to figure out the right strategy to provide value to the client based on their audience and the message they're trying to deliver." And last but not least, public relations entails managing and planning communication with the media and other brand constituents like investors, employees, and the general public.

Nearly all entry-level marketing positions require at least a college degree, and a major in business or communications is desirable. If you're interested in starting your career in advertising, promotions, or public relations, your job prospects will be most promising in an agency situation. The big communications agencies, many of which have offices in nearly every major U.S. city, experience high turnover at the junior level, which means they are always looking for smart college grads to fill empty positions. By reading industry publications such as *Brandweek, Adweek, Marketing News,* and *PRWeek,* you can identify agencies that are working on projects you're interested in. After that, I recommend setting up informational interviews with junior-level employees at each so that you can get a sense of the work environment and daily responsibilities at that particular agency. While you're preparing to apply for available slots, you'll want to make sure that your résumé reflects your experience in skill areas important to the marketing function, including writing, researching, data analysis, public speaking, and project management.

"If you don't have a formal degree in marketing, you have to be creative about getting the education you need," says Prita, thirty-seven, director of integrated marketing communications for Barilla America, a consumer goods company. "To be successful, you really need to know how marketers think and what they want, and you have to be able to speak their language. You can show employers that you're serious about breaking in by building your knowledge of basic marketing principles, and by doing a marketing internship or volunteer work with an organization like the American Marketing Association [www.marketingpower.com], or your favorite charity." Additional resources you might consult to learn more about the industry and uncover specific employment opportunities are:

- American Association of Advertising Agencies (www.aaaa.org)
- Direct Marketing Association (www.the-dma.org)
- Direct Marketing Careers (www.directmarketingcareers.com)
- Interactive Advertising Bureau (www.iab.net)
- KnowThis (www.knowthis.com)
- MarketingHire (www.marketinghire.com)
- MarketingJobs (www.marketingjobs.com)
- MarketingProfs (www.marketingprofs.com)
- Promotion Marketing Association (www.pmalink.org)
- Public Relations Society of America (www.prsa.org)

If your goal is to become a brand or marketing manager at a Fortune 500 company, or a marketing director for a government or nonprofit organization, you're probably going to need more education. Most of these positions require a master's of business administration (M.B.A.) with a focus in marketing. In fact, even if you manage to work your way up the ladder in an agency environment, the headhunters recruiting you will need to check off the fact that you have the advanced degree before sending you on interviews. Without an M.B.A., you can ascend to a senior agency position, but with it, you'll have the credentials to gain access to the Fortune 500 fast track. Most M.B.A.s start as assistant brand managers for a year and a half to two years and then take on brands of increasing size for the next few years. Successful brand managers often move on to manage a category such as deodorants or cereals, and eventually to C-level general management. The higher you move in an organization, the larger the teams you will oversee. It's not unusual for the VP of marketing or the chief marketing officer to manage hundreds of people.

In her marketing management role, Prita supervises six people internally and several large vendor teams. "My projects utilize people that work in other disciplines within the company as well as partners. In order to get things done, I have to be able to communicate objectives clearly in this cross-functional environment, and motivate the teams against timelines and goals. Once in a while, I have to push back on vendors who are emphasizing their own agendas or not pulling their weight. You have to be nice, but also firm."

The marketing field, both on the agency and the corporate side, is generally a lucrative one. According to several sources, including the National Association of Colleges and Employers and the Princeton Review, starting salaries in marketing are approximately $35K, and advancement prospects are such that you are likely to hit six figures within ten years. You'll have to work hard for that money, though.

Most marketing executives work fifty-plus hours a week and travel on business quite a bit. Because their projects are highly visible and their plans are often frustrated by political and financial circumstances they can't control, marketing executives must also cope with high levels of stress.

In addition to being able to thrive under pressure, marketing professionals must be creative thinkers, confident and assertive communicators, compassionate managers, and effective decision makers. "You have to balance being a team player with working well independently—tracking down resources and taking the initiative to jumpstart projects," says Jessica. "Multitasking is important too, because you have to simultaneously monitor the progress of all the assignments in your current stable of work." Adds Prita: "Marketing managers have to be able to sell their projects to management in order to get funding, because otherwise they're just ideas. We have to synthesize a wide range of information in order to arrive at the necessary strategic insights, and we also have to understand how programs impact the company's bottom line." But the diverse skill set required is precisely why marketing executives are rewarded handsomely when they do well. "My work situation is great," says Jessica. "I get to work in a midtown Manhattan high-rise, in a creative industry for a highly regarded company with a historic reputation. Our work space is new, clean, and bright and we have the tools we need at our fingertips. My company has superb benefits and I am very well taken care of. I absolutely love it."

PRO SPORTS TEAM MANAGER

Growing up in Boston, I always felt a great passion for our area teams. Going to the Super Bowl in 1986 when the New England Patriots played the Chicago Bears was one of the most memorable experiences of my childhood, and I've been personally involved with sports for as long as I can remember. I always knew I wanted to work for a professional team in some capacity, but I'd heard that those jobs were impossible to get. So I was surprised that contacting team VPs directly about an entry-level job in administration actually worked. It took a lot of planned networking, of course, but once I got to know the right people, I was in.

—Kelly, twenty-seven, pro sports team manager

AS KIDS, many of us dream of careers as professional athletes, but as we grow older, we realize the limitations of our athletic prowess and try to think of ways to incorporate our love of sports into jobs we can realistically obtain. Some ambitious networkers like Kelly apply for positions in team administration right out of college and find themselves immediately thrust into the chaotic but adrenaline-filled world of the professional sports organization. What does it mean to work on the management side of the house? Let's look at a few positions.

For the uninitiated, the most visible administrative position on a professional sports team is the general manager. You're probably familiar with the phenomenal rise of Theo Epstein, who at the age of twenty-eight became the youngest general manager in the history of Major League Baseball. However, Epstein's trajectory was atypical. General manager job openings are few and far between and require years of experience in the industry. However, most general managers do have assistants or business managers who work underneath them. Assistant general managers and business managers are typically responsible for the nuts and bolts of ensuring that the team functions smoothly, from obtaining supplies cost-effectively and negotiating contracts with vendors to managing the team's accounting and hiring personnel.

According to Shelly Field, author of *Career Opportunities in the Sports Industry,* another popular entry point into team management is marketing. If you are a recent college grad, you probably won't have any marketing experience, which means you would likely come in as a marketing assistant. Marketing assistants are essentially clerical positions, but you will have the opportunity to learn and participate in the daily duties of a team marketing director, which include coordinating advertising, PR, and promotional campaigns, developing and sustaining corporate sponsorships, and licensing the team's name and logo to outside organizations. The marketing director is primarily responsible for bringing more people into the stadium, and this means exploring ways to open new markets.

Several sources told me that if you want to make money in sports administration, go into ticket sales. Ticket managers generate income for professional teams by selling season tickets, securing group sales, and booking stadium suites. If you don't have much experience, scout out bigger teams with ticket sales departments, for which you could interview for an entry-level clerk position that requires little or no experience working in the box office.

Whether you're interested in a position in business administration, marketing, or sales, you should be prepared for a challenging job search. In the incredibly competitive sports industry, getting your foot in the door requires more than having sports experience and blindly sending a résumé and cover letter to team HR departments. "Connections are absolutely the way to get these jobs," says Kelly, twenty-seven, a pro sports team manager in New England. "If you don't know anyone who can help you, you'll have to go out of your way to meet people." Spoken like a true networker.

Start by contacting alumni from your college who are working in sports. Ask them if they would have time for a half-hour phone call to provide you with general information and advice about the industry. Do not, however, ask a contact for a job right off the bat, for this can be a turnoff. If she is aware of an available position for someone with your experience, either in her organization or another, she'll let you know as the relationship develops.

Research and attend tournaments, coalition events, or general manager meetings where top team administrators are speaking, and hang around to introduce yourself. At sporting events, most people are interested in getting close to the players, but you should be keeping your eye out for the men and women in suits with the large VIP badges. These are the individuals you want to talk to. Just make sure you know what you want from the person (such as an informational interview) before you approach him, and wait politely for a break in his conversation.

As in most fields, joining related associations can be a helpful step up. Minor League Baseball, for example, has an organization called Professional Baseball Employment Opportunities (www.pbeo .com), which offers members access to a huge database of open positions and an annual job fair in conjunction with its winter meeting. I've heard good things about the National Sports Marketing Network (www.sportsmarketingnetwork.com), which is the national organizing body for networking opportunities, education, and industry discussion in the sports business industry and has a great job-matching service. Note, though, that you must have some form of sports business experience in order to be accepted as a member. If you're a woman, you might think about joining Women in Sports Careers (WISC, www .wiscfoundation.org), a nationwide network serving the business and career networking needs of women with an interest in sports. WISC has local chapters in more than twenty U.S. cities that regularly host events, where you can meet seasoned sports professionals in your geographic area.

The sports industry is a tight-knit community, and you'd be surprised how making the right impression on the right person can open up all sorts of doors. The more things you try, the more likely you are to strike gold. For instance, one guy I talked to was visiting the top sports job site, TeamWork Online (www.teamworkonline.com), every day, and taking an online course with Sports Management Worldwide (www.sportsmanagementworldwide.com), an accredited training program for those aiming to break into sports careers. He was confident that he would be employed by a professional team within the year, even if, like many sports industry newbies, he had to accept an internship first.

Once you're fortunate enough to get invited for an interview with a professional team, how can you prepare for the experience? Well, for one thing, all of the standard interviewing rules apply. Approaching sports positions differently from other jobs is a mistake, for the sports business is just that—a business. Also, if you're interviewing for a team and you've attended every game since you could walk, you may want to downplay your enthusiasm a bit. "Acting like a crazed fan is a red flag," says Kelly. "Passion is great, but in order to be an effective member of the team, you have to be objective about it."

Despite the advantages of snagging free tickets and chumming around with superstars, only a particular type of person can be happy working in the sports industry. A sports administration position, whether in business, marketing, or sales, does not necessarily lend itself to a balanced lifestyle. You have to like what you do enough to work obscenely long hours leading up to and during your season. Because most of the income goes to the players, even a prestigious team's front office is pretty small, so no matter who you are or what you're supposed to be doing, inevitably you'll be getting your hands dirty and wearing two or three hats at once. Since you never know what's going to happen with a team in a particular year, sports professionals have to be flexible and cope well with ambiguity. They must also forgo healthy advancement prospects, for while there may be several entry-level positions in a front office, there are usually only a few senior ones, and you could spend years, or even your entire career, at the bottom of the ladder as you struggle to achieve that coveted six-figure income.

Here, I should also mention that the lucky few who do obtain the top administrative positions on a well-recognized professional team are often encouraged to get an advanced degree, such as a master's of business administration (M.B.A.), a master's in sports management (M.S.M.), or a masters in sports administration (M.S.A.). Some master's degree programs, like the one at Ohio University, integrate the M.B.A. and the M.S.A. in a two-year curriculum that combines traditional business leadership teachings with specific instruction in sports management, journalism, marketing, facility and event management, sponsorships, licensing, and financial administration. Your organization may or may not subsidize the cost of your education.

The twenties and thirties are the ideal years for networker types to try a career in professional sports administration because you have the adaptability, hunger, and stamina to give it your all. And although working in this high-octane industry has its challenges, most veterans agree that it's a labor of love. After all, on a day-to-day basis, you're riding a wave of contagious excitement that fills nearly every American home. Behind the scenes, you're playing an important game of your own, and you're just as influential to the team's success as the players being cheered on the field, court, or ice.

SPEECHWRITER
● ● ● ● ● ● ● ● ● ● ● ● ● ●

> I spend my mornings combing through the major newspapers and watching TV to ensure that I'm current and topical in my material. I will blog for a while to get my brain going, and then I'll begin organizing and drafting speeches. I have a little trick that really helps me change my voice or tone for each client—I read comic books. You see, each comic book hero has his own secret identity, strengths, and weaknesses. They all have an archenemy too, and this creates the building blocks for great oratory. I assign a comic book hero to each client, so that I can be distinct and unique as I write for each one. I know I've done my job when the client receives a standing ovation.
>
> —Barry, twenty-eight, speechwriter

SPEECHWRITING IS SOMETIMES KNOWN as "the silent profession" because most people associate it with behind-the-scenes, low-profile work. But in fact, the successful speechwriter is a supreme networker. First, she must keenly understand the person she's writing for, including how the remarks relate to the speaker's core identity, and the purpose the speaker would like to see the remarks achieve. And because in-person communication is still such an important method of persuasion, the speechwriter also has to instinctively know how to connect with and positively influence the audience to adopt a belief or take a particular action. She must accurately assess the personal and environmental factors surrounding the speech so that the speaker can communicate with conviction, and so the audience will genuinely believe the words are the speaker's own. "Everything I draft for my candidates has to speak to the people and has to resonate," says Barry, twenty-eight, a political speechwriter. "It has to be honest and powerful—and it has to mean something."

In this era of authenticity, you might think that speechwriting is going the way of the fax machine. But people all over the world, from politicians and business leaders to entertainers and activists, still speak in public all the time. If they can't write well, they often need help expressing themselves in the most appropriate, truthful way. Says Rob Cottingham, a professional speechwriter, in his article for *Social Signal:* "Maybe busy speakers would write every word themselves in an ideal world, but I'm noticing more people trying to carve out time by focusing on their core strengths and outsourcing everything else." And speechwriting, whether in the private or the public sector, can be lucrative. According to an article by Lynn Wasnak in the *Writer's Market,* the average thirty-minute speech earns between $2 and $6K, with the average compensation per speech being about $4,064. If you're as busy as the speechwriters belonging to the Washington Speechwriters Roundtable, 78 percent of whom write more than twenty speeches a year, you can do quite well for yourself once established. What are the typical responsibilities of speechwriters, and what's the best way to become one? Read on.

"Speechwriting is its own medium," says Rob Cottingham. "It has far more to do with writing music than it does with writing an essay, and if you've ever had to sit through a speech that was written as an essay, with long sentences and complex grammatical structures that you have to navigate through like a dense syntactical jungle, you'll know that there is a craft to speechwriting." Some mechanics of that craft include:

- interviewing the speaker and listening carefully; partnering with her to develop the core content and then later coaching her as to how the speech should be delivered
- researching speech topics via the Internet and primary sources
- listening to other speeches similar to those you write, and staying current on rhetorical trends influencing how people are speaking in formal and informal settings

- understanding how and when to leverage particular speech formats (PowerPoint lecture, commencement address, toast, et cetera)
- outlining the flow of a speech so that ideas are organized effectively, with an overview at the beginning followed by the body and a forceful conclusion
- preventing boredom by sticking to the topic at hand, and keeping things simple
- drafting prose designed to be spoken and heard rather than printed and read
- including conversational language to keep the audience engaged
- knowing how and when to use key speech elements such as anecdotes, quotes, imagery, hard data, jokes, and pressure points
- integrating the speech content with existing communications platforms or messaging

There's a lot that goes into a good speech, certainly, but if you've got that winning combination of writing and people skills, you may find that it comes easily to you. More challenging will be getting established in the business. Nearly all speechwriters will tell you that the best way to get started is to start writing and making speeches, whether it's by volunteering for a political campaign or nonprofit organization, or offering to write remarks for an executive at the company where you currently work. "I broke in by giving away my services for free early on," says Barry. "When there's an election on, candidates are always looking for able volunteers, and I honed my craft through lots of practice. Persistence was key. I had to chase one client for a year, asking him over and over to give me a shot before he finally said yes. You can also get involved in the PR and communications industries—that's where the speechwriters often work and hang out."

Another workable strategy is to define a niche for yourself—or a topical area you know well and would like to focus on—but follow the news and brainstorm creative topics outside your area too. Tell every-one you know that you're looking for speechwriting work, and offer substantial discounts to new clients in order to get things moving. Attend networking events such as Ragan Communications' annual speechwriters conference (www.ragan.com), and take advantage of every opportunity to learn from the experts—either in person or through books and articles written by vets such as former presidential speechwriters Peggy Noonan and Michael Waldman.

Marketing your services effectively will be important throughout the course of your speechwriting career, not just at the beginning. Because speechwriters don't receive public credit for their remarks, you need to demonstrate your talent and gain critical exposure by writing for publication as well. Look for chances to byline opinion articles or book reviews in trade publications, newspapers, or online outlets that your prospective clients read. Teach workshops in writing or communications, and sign up for speaking slots at appropriate conferences. Rob Cottingham also emphasizes the importance of building a strong online presence. "I've been hired three times purely on the strength of my website and blog," he says. "Using a blog to write about topics in your niche will help establish your authority, not to mention make your site a magnet for people searching about those topics. Definitely make sure that your site includes your latest contact information and a professional profile establishing your speechwrit-ing bona fides." Cottingham and other seasoned folks recommend the following resources as you launch your career as a professional speech-writer:

- Bartlett's Quotations (www.bartleby.com)
- The Elements of Style (www.bartleby.com)
- *The Executive Speaker* resources for speechwriters (www.executive-speaker.com)

- IdeaBank (www.idea-bank.com)
- rhetorical terms glossary (www.uky.edu/Classics/rhetoric.html)
- The SpeechWriters (www.nvo.com/speechwriters)
- Speechwriter's Manual (www.speechwritercity.com)
- Washington Speechwriters Roundtable (www.washingtonspeechwriters.com)

A speechwriting career can lead to prestigious opportunities working in high places, and it can certainly be exhilarating to see your words brought to life by charismatic and powerful individuals. However, this path does have its disadvantages. The lack of acknowledgment, for instance, is a bitter pill for many networker personalities to swallow. Clients, especially those used to getting their way, can be difficult to work with and hard to please. "Speechwriters have to be willing to be ghostwriters in many respects," says Barry. "When you work with experienced clients, they'll often hack and maul your writing to make it their own. You have to be okay with that, and realize that collaborating makes for better oratory." Finally, speechwriting can be compared to the field of art in that it's sometimes an uphill battle to convince people of the value of your services. Once you do, though, you may find yourself an indispensable member of the team. "Once you've got a client you've worked with a few times, she becomes reliant on you, and you're her go-to speechwriter for every possible occasion," says Barry. "It's great when that happens!"

TALENT AGENT

In my first job, I had lunch with another assistant at a different agency. In passing, I mentioned a big meeting my boss was having with a potential hot new client. Unfortunately, that hot new client was a current client at my friend's agency, and he had no choice but to go back and sound the alarm. The other agency was able to save the relationship with the wandering client, and my boss lost out. I was never found out, though the company-wide lecture about breaking confidentiality was not one of my finer moments. After that, I really learned the value of discretion.

—David, thirty, talent agent

IF YOU'VE EVER WATCHED the HBO show *Entourage,* you've glimpsed the world of Hollywood talent agents through the eyes of Ari Gold, the ballsy lead character who wheels and deals on behalf of A-list actor Vincent Chase. The talent agents I consulted for this section told me that the characterization of Ari Gold isn't too exaggerated. Talent agents represent actors and musicians, advising them on their careers, securing gigs, and negotiating contracts. High-stakes ones like Ari pay for their Ferraris by scoring huge deals for top celebrities and then pocketing a percentage of the stars' earnings. Gaining entrance to the übercompetitive, cutthroat agenting world, based in Los Angeles and New York, where most talent agents live, work, and schmooze, is a right of passage that only the best networkers survive. Do you have what it takes? Let's find out.

While established agents are extremely well connected—spending their days on the phone and lunching with studio, network, and record label executives, casting directors, managers, and clients—they don't start out that way. Nearly all agents, especially those in Hollywood, begin as unpaid interns in the mailrooms of established firms like ICM, William Morris, the Creative Artists Agency, or the Gersh Agency. However, even an oh-so-glamorous job like this mandates that you know someone in the industry who can place a phone call on your behalf. "Nepotism is a reality in Hollywood," says David, thirty, a talent agent in Los Angeles. "I got my first assistant job working for Jerry Bruckheimer because the girl scheduling the interviews also went to NYU and we bonded."

While it may be tempting to bypass this process and either launch your own agency or hook up with some inexperienced agents trying to gain momentum, you're probably better off paying your dues at a known firm. Most new agencies falter because they can't attract enough profitable clients, and you don't want to find yourself having to start all over. "It's best to make contacts at the big agencies," says David. "Get to know the assistants who are around your age and will give you a break and pass your résumé on. Also, go to the film festivals and chat up the agents after their panels. Show an interest in what they do, because your passion will come through."

Mailroom and intern work is thankless and grueling, but if you play your cards right, you'll use the time to meet and impress the right people, show them that you have drive and a natural instinct regarding what sells, and you will be able to position yourself well for the next available opening as an assistant agent in that firm. Some of the larger talent agencies now have official agent trainee programs, which require a bachelor's degree and are highly selective. Successful candidates have an enthusiasm for entertainment and some knowledge of how the industry works. If you're planning to apply for one of these programs, you should be prepared for a tough interview that will show what you're made of. With that in mind, pick up the industry's standard reading material, including books like *The Mailroom* (Rensin), *Reel Power* (Litwak), *The Agency* (Rose), and *The Last Mogul* (McDougal) before you show up.

Like assistant agents, agent trainees perform mostly administrative tasks. They serve as an agent's right hand, working the phones, writing memos, managing computer databases, and booking auditions. "Managing auditions is a big part of my job," says Clare, twenty-four, an agent trainee in New York. "I have to get all of the relevant information from the casting director and then put everything together in an easy-to-read format that tells the actor where she needs to be and when, and what script material she should prepare in advance." These entry-level positions often involve eighteen-hour days with no overtime and no breaks, but, fortunately, smart assistants usually advance quickly. "Assistants have the opportunity to scout out new talent," says Clare. "And once you're able to get a few clients of your own who are obviously on their way up, you're going to get promoted." Most assistants become full agents within one to three years—if they don't screw up. "You have to be really careful that you don't do anything early in your career, like leaking information, or bad-mouthing someone, that will jeopardize your chances," says David.

Although most talent agents don't pursue advanced degrees, they do have to be licensed. According to the Association of Talent Agents (www.agentassociation.com), which is a good organization for aspiring agents to become affiliated with, member agents are regulated by government agencies in California, New York, and the other parts of the country where agents do business. Additionally, talent agents who represent clients belonging to unions like the Screen Actors Guild and the Actors' Equity Association must have union franchises under which the agent abides by the unions' standards. Unlike other professions, however, the licensing process for talent agents is rather like getting your driver's license renewed and usually just consists of filling out some paperwork and paying the appropriate fees.

Talent agents pay a heavy price to play in Hollywood. Trainees and assistants only receive $400 to $600 a week, although a benefits package and vacation are typically included. Even after several years in the business, few talent agents are as well off as Ari Gold. Their annual salaries and bonuses vary considerably based on the commissions they bring into the agency (which amount to approximately 10 to 15 percent of each client engagement). And it's not just about the money. Talent agents lead exceedingly stressful lives. They must tread carefully between stroking their clients' egos and giving them the honest direction that's necessary to move careers forward. They jump through hoops to keep clients happy while looking over their shoulders to make sure another agency isn't trying to steal A-listers away. "The agent is the hub of the whole operation, the person who has to be able to interact with everyone, the person everyone wants to talk to," adds David.

Due to early burnout, agenting is often considered a young person's profession, though, ironically, twentysomething agents have to fight to be taken seriously. "Though I was a full agent at twenty-four, I didn't get any respect until I won a coveted industry award," says David. But despite the drawbacks, many consider the pressure and sacrifices worth it. "I get unbelievable perks—free movie screenings, parties with the stars, you name it," says Clare. "In order to make it in this business, you have to be resourceful, willing to work your butt off, and a great communicator. You've got to be able to keep track of a million things at once without missing a detail. But if you can do all these things, and you're willing to stick your neck out to get the job that you really want, agenting is going to offer more excitement and fun than any other career." Adds David: "I really enjoy feeling like I've changed someone's life, and built an important relationship. There's nothing like hanging out with a client over a few beers."

TELEVISION PRODUCER

While in high school, I was an intern at the CBS station in Philadelphia. The high schoolers were only allowed to intern in the sports department, so I spent hours a week listening to bad jokes and watching hours of games. I didn't realize it at the time, but I was learning how to choose the best pictures, memorable moments, and sound. On the weekends, I would work at the talk radio station down the hall for a sports call-in show. I barely knew what a jump ball was, but I was meeting Charles Barkley and learning the importance of screening out the wacky callers.

—Meredith, thirty-four, television producer

BEHIND EVERY SUCCESSFUL NEWSCAST, sitcom, drama, talk show, documentary, and commercial is a team of very busy producers. And nothing on television would happen without them. Responsible for coordinating programs from soup to nuts, they research topics; develop story angles; decide on-air look, format, and execution; write and edit scripts; hire on-air talent and other staff; coordinate with other departments such as distribution, accounting, and publicity; check facts; and supervise shooting. At the executive producer level, they may manage teams of segment, assistant, and associate producers and editorial staff.

Phil, thirty, is a producer responsible for the noon, five P.M., and six P.M. newscasts at the CBS affiliate in Columbus, Ohio, and he doesn't stop moving from early morning to long after dark. "My day begins with a look through the daybook, selecting stories for the noon broadcast," he says. "From there, it will be a flurry of activity talking to reporters and meteorologists, checking in on our regular features, writing the stories and the teasers for those stories, and getting the right graphics and video. And once one broadcast is over, we move on to the next one without missing a beat."

Television production's emphasis on teamwork is what appeals to many networkers. "I can plan a broadcast, but I count on my team to help me execute it," says Phil. "Though there are certainly personality clashes, there's something about the way that we run like a well-oiled machine in a breaking news situation, with everyone helping out, that is really rewarding for me." On the flip side, though, carrying the weight of an entire show, with unforgivable time pressures, can result in significant stress. "Our plan of attack can change fifty times in one day, and that's hard," says Phil. "But people are watching every second, and it's the producer's responsibility to get it right." Adds Meredith, thirty-four, a producer for Fox in New York: "The producer has to be calm and confident, the one who can make the decisions but is also willing to listen to various points of view."

So how does one get on the track to become a producer? Your education should start with a college degree, though what you major in isn't particularly important, and it isn't necessary to go to graduate school for journalism either. What is important is the experience you're able to obtain while you're in school or shortly thereafter. Official internships at news stations or at TV studios can be hard to come by, so instead you might try taking TV production classes (in editing and videography, for example) and/or volunteering at your local public access station. This will provide the material you need to put together a demo reel of broadcasts or programs you've worked on, which employers hiring for entry-level production assistant jobs will want to see.

In the event that you are able to secure a TV internship, make the most of it. "I convinced a college professor to allow me to take a graduate credit internship so I could work at the number one station in the Philadelphia market," says Meredith. "I had met a photographer there who said I should intern on the morning show, because I'd get a chance to do interviews, set up stories, and write. I did all that and more." While on the job, show the producers on staff that you are willing to work harder and faster than everyone else, no matter how menial the task. Do your best to establish the relationships that will lead to a full-time position at the conclusion of the internship, and if this isn't an option, at least make an effort to keep in touch with the contacts you've made

As this is a networking profession, association membership is also a valuable way to learn about the industry and meet seasoned producers. These organizations offer various seminars and events, as well as online publications and career resources to help you get started. Some of the major organizations for producers include:

- Academy of Television Arts and Sciences (www.emmys.com)
- American Women in Radio and Television (www.awrt.org)
- Broadcast Education Association (www.beaweb.org)
- National Association of Broadcasters (www.nab.org)
- National Association of Television Program Executives (www.natpe.org)
- Producers Guild of America (www.producersguild.org)
- Society of Motion Picture and Television Engineers (www.smpte.org)

Your first full-time, paying job in television production will likely be that of a production assistant (PA). According to the Princeton Review's paraphrasing of Thomas Hobbes, the life of the PA is "nasty, brutish, and short." Fierce competition results in low starting salaries and high burnout rates in the first two years. Work shifts can be sixteen hours or more, and when an emergency arises, PAs are expected to stay. Some may be assigned graveyard shifts, working from midnight to eight in the morning assembling data for morning newscasts and entering wire feeds into computers. Others will be responsible for mundane tasks such as proofreading copy for typos and making lunch or travel reservations. "The first jobs are low-paying and often can be considered grunt work, but if you're smart, you'll hang in there and utilize the access you gain to learn everything you can about how to be successful at the next stage," says Meredith. "Be patient, and always be open to and encourage critique because that's how you'll grow."

The PAs who see the light at the end of the tunnel are those who are creative, flexible, able to multitask and think on their feet, and have sound judgment regarding how material should be presented on air. They are promoted into assistant, associate, or segment producer positions, and their responsibilities and autonomy increase accordingly. Eventually, they might advance to the role of executive producer, or to a managerial position within a more prestigious show or station. No matter how senior they become, however, their salaries will never reach the level of some other careers in entertainment. The Princeton Review cites the annual starting salary for PAs as approximately $17K, with five-year producers making an average of $36K and ten- to fifteen-year producers earning a projected $72K. "Most producers will never hit six figures," says Phil. "However, since good ones are harder to find than, say, good on-air reporters, they generally make more." And most producers aren't in the business for the money anyway. "Nothing will ever be able to compare to the feeling I had when I won a Regional Emmy for best newscast," says Phil. "It was so incredibly humbling and exciting, and I went back to the newsroom with a new sense of confidence, because it was the ultimate confirmation that I'm good at my job."

WINE MERCHANT

> I work in a small, very hip wine shop on Magazine Street in New Orleans. I sell wine, I talk about wine, I pour wine, I teach people about wine, and I drink wine. I say "cheers" a lot, and I talk about anything and everything with lots of people every day. The job is mostly about having fun and enjoying life and getting others to do the same. I get a lot of cool schwag, I get to try a lot of new things—yesterday, sparkling sake—and I'm a neighborhood celebrity!
>
> —Catherine, twenty-seven, wine merchant

MANY PEOPLE ARE PASSIONATE about wine but few give serious thought to turning it into a career. A common misperception is that one has to have a cool million or two to purchase a vineyard on the West Coast, when in fact there are nearly as many types of wine careers as there are medical specialties. For example, as a laboratory enologist, you'd study the science of wine making. A tasting room manager at a vineyard hires tasting room staff, does state liquor reports and payroll, keeps inventory, and manages the wine club. Inside a winery, different individuals undertake the tasks of planting, fermentation, harvesting, bottling, and cellar work. Outside it, still others serve as distributors, importers, brokers, and wine writers. Wine educators and sommeliers (wine stewards) work in restaurants, retail shops, and private institutions teaching people about wine and making recommendations about what to drink.

The wine merchant, the job we will focus on in this section, either has his own retail shop or works for a shop or vineyard owner. His primary responsibility is to grow revenue through the retail sales of wine, which often involves purchasing merchandise, managing product and staff, helping customers with selections, running tastings, and implementing marketing programs and events. "The day-to-day operations are more labor-intensive than commonly assumed, since inventory is flowing into the store almost daily and must be checked in, priced, stocked, and displayed for sale," says John, thirty-seven, who owns the Wine Rack in Louisville, Kentucky. "More interesting is the process of hand selling to customers based on their likes, dislikes, and overall objectives. This is, for me, the best part of the business and gives me an ability to differentiate myself from competitors by offering a higher level of service."

While working as a merchant doesn't sound quite as glamorous as making wine, it requires much more knowledge of the trade than you might think. Wine customers like to ask lots of questions about how vines are pruned and where wines are stored, and as a merchant, you'd better have all the answers. "You have to be able to describe wines to people in an easy to understand, down-to-earth manner," says John. "Listening skills are very important, as most people have difficulty saying what they really mean about their taste in wines. It's your job to hear what they really mean and match them with a wine they will enjoy."

For these reasons, most wine merchants possess a combination of experience and education. If you're interested in a career in wine, however, it makes sense to get your feet wet first before investing several years in your training. Several seasoned wine merchants suggested getting a part-time job as an apprentice at a wine store, or doing a winery internship where you can learn the business from the ground up and get a feel for the aspects that appeal to you most. "I also recommend that prospective wine merchants spend a year or two in some type of sales position, no matter what the area, because sales skills transcend product lines," says John.

Winery internships are most plentiful during the harvest season of late August to November, otherwise known as "crush." You'll work very hard (think ten- to twelve-hour days, six days a week) and get paid very little doing a variety of semimenial tasks like cellar stocking and data collection in the lab, but if you have a positive attitude and take full advantage of the opportunity, you could easily use this as a jumping off point for a permanent career in the field. Sound good? Contact wineries, placement agencies, or some of the resources in this section during the late spring/early summer, and if you're able to secure a spot, do your homework before you arrive. "Learn all you can by tasting, reading, cooking, and being aware of the trends around you," advises John. You may also want to spend some time in a wine shop getting to know the inventory or take a tasting class so that you can show off your knowledge of pinot, merlot, and cabernet once on the job.

After you have some wine experience under your belt, you can apply for a full-time job as a merchant in a winery or retail shop. "I was able to get a job in a really cool, small wine store because I was one of the first people in my neighborhood to return home after Hurricane Katrina," says Catherine, twenty-seven, a wine merchant in New Orleans. "But it's usually tougher because there aren't many shops around, and the ones that exist generally don't have a lot of employees."

In order to qualify for a position like Catherine's, you'll need to be at least twenty-one and able to lift forty to fifty pounds. You'll have to work a flexible schedule that includes evenings, weekends, and holidays. And the more you know about grape varietals, countries, and regions, the more competitive you will be. At first, you'll likely receive an hourly wage of $10 to $20 an hour, but as you rise within that organization or another, your career as a wine merchant could potentially earn you high five figures and a generous benefits package. The following websites feature wine merchant job postings:

- Let's Talk Wine (www.letstalkwine.com)
- Washington Association of Wine Grape Growers (www.wawgg.org)

- Washington Wine Commission (www.washingtonwine.org)
- *Wine Business Monthly* (www.winebusiness.com)
- Wine and Hospitality Jobs (www.winecountryjobs.com)
- WinePro Recruiters (www.wineprorecruiters.com)
- *Wine Spectator* magazine (www.winespectator.com)

Formal education is not absolutely necessary for wine merchants with substantial hands-on experience, although the popularity of "wine schooling" has increased in recent years. The University of California at Davis's Department of Viticulture and Enology (wineserver.ucdavis.edu), for example, offers a program that teaches the wine life in its entirety, from grape consistency to sensory evaluation. At Walla Walla Community College in Washington (www.wwcc.edu), your study will consist of working in an actual winery, doing everything from planting the vines to bottling the finished product.

Depending on your focus, you may also want to consider obtaining the prestigious Master of Wine certification from the Institute of Masters of Wine (www.masters-of-wine.org). According to David Glancy, in an article he penned for *California Wine and Food Magazine*, candidates for the Master of Wine program first complete the study program offered by the Wine and Spirit Education Trust (WSET, www.wset.co.uk). WSET offers courses and exams in London and some other cities, as well as a home-study program. Then you must complete an application that requires proof of substantial work experience, a written tasting analysis, and an essay. If the Master of Wine's intensive, two-year program is not your cup of tea, Glancy also suggests another certification option from the Society of Wine Educators (wine.gurus.com). Based in Washington, D.C., this organization provides seminars and exams throughout the United States and in Tokyo and has two designations, Certified Wine Specialist (CWS) and Certified Wine Educator (CWE).

Successful merchants don't just love wine, they love the people who consume it. Superior customer service is one of the first attributes mentioned in nearly all job descriptions, and in a wine environment, strong communication and the ability to lead, listen, contribute, and follow through as part of a team is heavily emphasized. The wine world is only becoming more intimate and personal in nature, which may explain why more and more women are now joining what has traditionally been a male-dominated industry. But while women also excel at multitasking and attention to detail, two essential qualities, those with families may not be as well suited to the unpredictable nature of the wine merchant's schedule. As Catherine says, "It's a trade-off, but at least I keep my sanity and get lots of fun perks."

The Nurturer

My mother has always volunteered for our church and its various mission projects supporting children, the homeless, and Third World countries. I was raised knowing that I was fortunate and it was my earthly responsibility to give back through my career endeavors.

—Amber, twenty-three, nonprofit administrator

NURTURERS ARE SPECIAL PEOPLE, and fortunately for our world, history is full of them—from Jane Addams to Mother Teresa to Mahatma Gandhi. Most nurturers, however, aren't famous, because it is the role of the nurturer to stay on the sidelines and make a difference in her community, one person at a time. Hopefully, you can pick out a few nurturers in your own life. They are the ones who spend their free time with volunteer organizations, call to check up on you when you're sick, and never tire of giving you advice about the same problem.

The core personality of the nurturer is gentle, reliable, and warm, and nurturer jobs require the ability to communicate in a personal and trustworthy manner. "In my job, a professional demeanor does not equate to successful," says Anu, twenty-two, a nutritionist. "If you're cold and distant, you won't be able to affect people and invite them to open up to you." Christopher, a twenty-six-year-old social services caseworker, adds: "My clients don't trust many people, but I have to get them to somehow trust me. I have to get them to see potential in themselves that they never believed was there, or had given up hope of reaching." Many nurturer types have an innate ability to figure out others' needs and problem-solve if some of those needs aren't being met. "I've been able to cultivate a good BS detector and see who a person really is at the core," says Michael, twenty-nine, a life coach. "Then I cut through the things that are in the way in order to bring forth the best aspects of each client."

Not surprisingly, the nurturer's top priority is developing and sustaining the relationships she establishes through her empathetic nature and caretaking skills. Her sense of satisfaction with her life and her career comes from helping others and positively influencing lives. "The thing that I like about physical therapy compared to other health professions is the quality time we spend with clients," says Sean, twenty-six, a physical therapist. "I am able to develop one-on-one relationships with them and see them as individuals, which makes my job so much more enjoyable." But lest we box nurturers in too much, let's note that the lives they impact aren't necessarily human. "My dolphins are part of my family," says Kevin, twenty-seven, a zoologist. "I spend more time with them than I do with my parents. We trainers care so much for our animals and make sure they are as physically and mentally healthy as they can be."

The nurturer usually prefers to stay in the background and allow

> For the last three years, I've been through so many ups and downs. I quit my job to focus on my emotional well-being, and tried to understand all of the feelings I've had inside me for years. I'm amazed that so many of my friends have felt what I was feeling, and with my knowledge and experience, I've been able to advise them. They're grateful for my insights, and the mutual support and encouragement have really made my life proceed in a positive direction. That's why I think a life coach would be a dream job.
>
> —*Katrina, twenty-four*

others to take the spotlight, and is not a fan of confrontation. "I definitely don't like the conflict resolution aspect of my job," says Keya, a twenty-five-year-old nonprofit administrator. "Sometimes I have a volunteer who doesn't agree with the policies of our organization, which puts me in the uncomfortable position of trying to keep her happy so she will stay on." Traci, thirty, an elementary school teacher, also prefers helping children to other aspects of her job, like "family problems, difficult personalities, and political influences." Additionally, although the nurturer generally has a glass-half-full mentality, he tends to get angry and stressed when he encounters insensitive people or feels that his help or advice is being taken for granted. "I get really irritated when a patient doesn't follow the prescribed meal plan and I get blamed for her getting sick," says Ben, twenty-eight, a nutritionist.

"No matter how many times you tell a patient to avoid certain foods, sometimes she just won't listen, and that's pretty frustrating."

> When I was a kid, you could always find me in the woods or the water. Zoologist would be a great job, because learning about animal behavior would give me a better understanding of what people are like. Animals don't talk back. They aren't there to impress you, and you're guaranteed that they're not going to repeat what you tell them!
>
> —*Debi, twenty-four*

The nurturer is different from the other passion profiles in that she invests in the well-being of others ahead of her own needs—sometimes to a fault. Because she cares so deeply about others' lives, she can burn out easily. "A challenge is that I care too much about my clients," says Christine, a twenty-nine-year-old life coach. "I just want to help people, and so I don't charge enough and can't earn a living." Ben can relate. "You have to know when to say no," he says. "There is so much work out there that it's easy to take on too much and try to be all things to all people." Christopher suggests that nurturers avoid burnout by consciously making time for themselves and by setting limits for how they'll engage with, and what they'll do for, the people they serve. "It's tough to do, but it's essential," says Christopher. "You have to learn to be firm with your clients, your co-workers, and yourself. If you don't hold to the boundaries you set, it's worse than not having any at all."

Also, unlike some other passion profiles, the nurturer is not highly motivated by financial rewards. "The monetary compensation in this type of job is marginal compared to the extra hours put in," says Amber. "But it means more to me to grant wishes to deserving children than to have a fancy car or the $600 boots." In order to feel successful, however, nurturers need to be appreciated and know that their work is making a difference. Says Elyse, a twenty-two-year-old doula: "I love it when my mothering instincts switch into high gear and I feel like I'm needed and wanted. My ability to calm a woman and her partner down just by being there is very fulfilling." In his job as a social services caseworker, Christopher agrees. "The job itself is the biggest compensation. Helping people to help themselves and improving their quality of life is as rewarding as it gets."

This chapter will describe some of the most sought-after jobs for nurturer types, including doula, elementary school teacher, life coach, nonprofit administrator, nutritionist, physical therapist, social services caseworker, and zoologist. Read on to see how you might transform your caretaking abilities into a rewarding career.

> The doula job is cool because it represents women taking back the medical world in a very doable way. Not as much education or training is required, and it is very "woman to woman" in the age of cutthroat competition in corporate environments. Also, I had a home birth with a doula and feel I could provide similar positive experiences for other women.
>
> —Bekah, thirty-one

DOULA
• • • • • •

> Birth is an amazing experience, even second hand. It is something to
> be treasured and fully understood. To help and empower a mother
> through one of the most important events of her life gives me an enor-
> mous sense of accomplishment. It's really cool to see a baby born. I
> tear up every time.
>
> —Elyse, twenty-two, doula

THE DAY PARENTS GIVE BIRTH to a baby is one they'll remember forever. From that point on, their lives will be transformed, and nothing
will ever be, or look, the same. Can you imagine being a vital part of the
experience, taking care of parents' emotional needs during and after
childbirth and providing guidance and support as two people take the
huge step of becoming a family? If so, perhaps you could be a doula.

DONA International defines a doula as one who is trained and
knowledgeable about childbirth and the postpartum experience and
works within evidence-based standards of practice to improve out-
comes for mothers and babies. There are two types of doulas. Birth
doulas provide physical and emotional support and assistance to
women and their partners in gathering information about the course
of their labors and births and their options; offer help and advice on
comfort measures; and provide continuous emotional reassurance and
comfort throughout the childbirth experience. Postpartum doulas
provide education and nonjudgmental support and companionship;
assist with newborn care and family adjustment; and provide information on infant feeding, emotional and physical recovery from childbirth, infant soothing and coping skills, and referrals during the weeks
after birth, fostering maximum self-determination in the new parents.

You don't need a college degree to become a doula, but to be competitive in the field you should be certified by DONA. As this is a time-consuming process, you'll want to first familiarize yourself with what it means to be a DONA doula by spending some time on their website (www.dona.org). Here, you can review DONA's position papers, standards of practice, and code of ethics. By using the doula locator or joining in the Doula Talk discussion, you can ask a certified doula what the profession is like and decide for yourself if it's really for you. Pursuing certification mainly involves taking a DONA-approved birth or postpartum training workshop in your area. As a birth doula to be, after your sixteen hours of doula training and introduction to childbirth prerequisite, you must provide service to and receive positive evaluations from a minimum of three birthing mothers and their medical careproviders; participate in an online or in-person lactation workshop; and complete required reading, written essays, and a referral resource list. To complete the postpartum doula certification, the twenty-seven-hour doula workshop must be accompanied by participation in an online or in-person lactation workshop; CPR certification; completion of required reading, written essays, and a referral resource list; and good evaluations from at least three mothers for whom you've provided services as well as their partners or other support people and a recommendation from health care professionals who've seen you in action.

According to Childbirth International, most doulas are self-employed and responsible for finding their own clients, advertising and promoting their services, and managing their financial records, forms, and taxation. If you live in an area where women have not heard of doulas, your first and most important step will be to publicize the role and importance of a doula within your own community. Develop a flyer with statistics that show how having a doula can reduce your chance of needing a C-section and induction, and make sure local schools, libraries, and mom and baby groups are aware of your services. Use the online medium to your best advantage and create free listings on DoulaNetwork.com. Tell everyone you meet what you do for a living, but don't get carried away when talking to potential clients. "New doulas tend to give unsolicited advice to all the pregnant women they know, all the time," says Leann, thirty-three, a doula in Oregon. "But really, you should be doing the listening, not the talking. Let her be heard, show that you care, and she'll be more likely to consider having a doula."

The self-employed doula's next challenge is to decide what to charge. An article on Boston.com cites the median fee for a birth doula as $700 per birth, which includes several prenatal visits, twenty-four-hour-a-day on-call service for the months around the due date, continuous support throughout the entire labor, birth, and immediate postpartum period, and a postpartum follow-up visit. However, in determining your individual fee, you should take your level of experience and local competition into account.

Maybe you feel cut out for doula work but don't want to bother with your own business. In this case, you might try to get a job with a hospital, birth center, or doula agency. Here are some suggestions for making it happen:

- Search for local doula agencies on the Web and contact them about potential openings (New York University, for example, recommends fifteen doula agencies in Manhattan alone).

- Contact your local hospitals and birthing centers and find out if and how they employ doulas.

- Talk to local ob-gyns and representatives from your local chapter of La Leche League (a national breast-feeding advocacy organization).

- Become an active member of childbirth associations such as DONA, ICEA (International Childbirth Education Association, www.icea.org), and ALACE (Association of Labor Assistants and Childbirth Educators, www.alace.org).

- Get to know established midwives and doulas and determine if there are partnership opportunities.

- Scout out contacts and specific positions in publications such as *International Doula* magazine and DONA's *eDoula* newsletter.

Not surprisingly, doula is the "mother" of all the nurturing professions. Good listening was mentioned again and again as the most important skill a doula can have, and you must obviously be calm under pressure, compassionate, and emotionally available as well. You also have to be able to keep a smile on your face even when you're sleep-deprived. "Some labors will take a few hours, while others will have you going all night and into the next day," says Leann. But for many doulas, the hours spent caring for clients are the best part. "In many ways, being a doula doesn't feel like a job," says Elyse. "My compensation is emotional, and besides, something interesting is always happening. There's no monotony in the baby business."

ELEMENTARY SCHOOL TEACHER

I don't just teach. I nurture all day long. I have twenty-one little people who are still trying to learn the necessary skills to navigate through social situations. They also always have various ailments and injuries that need attention or just a hug and kiss. Do I love it? Sure. Where else can you fingerpaint and color as part of your job?

—Traci, thirty, elementary school teacher

TO BE HONEST, I was pretty surprised when the position of an elementary school teacher appeared on my list of the coolest jobs. Teaching is a noble and fulfilling profession, to be sure, but cool? Five hundred survey respondents can't be wrong, though, so schoolteacher has taken its place among the best jobs for nurturing personalities.

Since all of us attended elementary school, we presumably know what its teachers do. I'll provide a brief recap. Elementary school teachers typically instruct one class of around twenty children in several subjects, including reading, writing, math, science, and social studies. In some schools, a teacher will teach one special subject, such as music, art, or physical education, and in others, two or more teachers will form a team that is responsible for a group of students. Most teachers work a ten-month school year with a two-month vacation during the summer, but in some areas with a year-round schedule, the teachers will work eight weeks in a row with a one-week vacation and a five-week midwinter break.

Teaching elementary-age students, whether in a public or private school, is one of the most rewarding yet difficult jobs out there. Like many nurturing jobs, teaching children requires enormous patience, and while research has shown that there are many successful teaching styles, all good teachers must be diplomatic, inquisitive, trustworthy, and engaging. They are solid academic performers in their subject areas, know how to motivate others to achieve, and are committed to making a difference in their students' lives. Elementary school teachers in particular must have the emotional intelligence to understand students' unique needs, personalities, and backgrounds. Their communication skills must be outstanding, enabling them to work effectively with other teachers, administrators, support personnel, and parents. And if they want to have any free time, they'd better be efficient too. "Teaching elementary school is not nine to three," says Traci, thirty, a second grade teacher. "In business, people use work hours to put together presentations they're giving to a group. Teachers do presentations every day, but all of our preparation has to be done during lunch and after school. There's just no time during the workday."

I come from a family full of teachers, and I always used to think it was pretty easy to become one. But according to the U.S. Bureau of Labor Statistics' *Occupational Outlook Handbook,* all states require teachers to have a bachelor's degree and to have completed an approved teacher-training program with a prescribed number of subject and education credits, as well as supervised practice teaching. To teach in a public school, you must take a basic competency exam in order to be licensed by the state board of education or a licensure advisory committee. In most states, licensure is not required for private school teachers.

While it's easiest to complete these requirements as part of your undergraduate education, many teacher preparation programs are aimed at midcareer professionals from other fields. If you're interested in transitioning to a teaching career, take the time to investigate the certification process in your state. The American Federation of Teachers (www.aft.org) and the National Education Association (www.nea.org) websites are excellent places to begin your research. You may even find that your state, or one where you might be willing to relocate, offers accelerated licensure due to a shortage of qualified teachers.

Obtaining your teacher's license is a huge achievement, but it's not a golden key into the elementary school of your choice. Teaching positions, especially in the best districts, are competitive, and just like in any field, you must leverage resources such as the NEA's Student Program to network and build contacts. "Try to meet people working in districts or schools you've researched and identified as desirable," says Hillary, twenty-five, a first grade teacher. "Then, in the spring, ask them whom you should send your résumé and application to. Follow up via phone at the beginning of the summer. If you keep hitting dead ends, you might try contacting new schools or schools with new principals, which often yield great opportunities for new teachers."

Your next step will be acing the interview. First and foremost, prepare by doing your homework on the district and the school. Harry and Rosemary Wong of Teachers.Net recommend brushing up on the school's demographics, the district's mission, test scores, and curriculum before you meet with the principal. Ensure that you're getting yourself into a good situation by determining that the district has an induction program to support and train new teachers and a relatively low attrition rate. You should also put together a portfolio demonstrating your work with children (photos, student teaching assignments, et cetera), including as much technology-related material as possible. In coordinating each interview, "treat the principal's secretary with kid gloves," says Ileana, thirty-six, a fifth grade teacher, "because she rules the school!"

On the day of your interview, dress professionally and speak with confidence and passion. You don't need to spout dry educational theory like there's no tomorrow, but you should demonstrate that you take your job seriously and that you've thought about your own teaching methods and what life in your classroom will entail. Ileana advises: "Don't worry too much about your lack of experience. Many principals like young teachers because they fit in more easily and are willing to take on extra duties like coaching or chairing clubs."

By the time most elementary school teachers receive their first job offer, they are prepared for the low salary that goes with it. Using numbers from the American Federation of Teachers and the U.S. Bureau of Labor Statistics, I've determined that the average new teacher makes approximately $35K annually. From there, teaching generally offers a uniform salary schedule in which earnings are based on years of experience and training, and ongoing benefits typically include health insurance, paid sick leave, and retirement. Private school teachers generally earn less than public school teachers, but may get other perks such as free or subsidized housing.

Job security for teachers is better than in other nurturing professions because in most states, public school teachers receive tenure after a few years and cannot be fired without just cause and due process. And while most are happy to teach children for the whole of their careers, experienced teachers do have the opportunity to advance to a department chair, principal, superintendent, or other academic administrator. However, administrative positions at the principal level and above usually require a master's degree in education.

Many nurturing individuals—men and women—find lifelong satisfaction in the teaching profession. The job certainly has its frustrating aspects, from unruly students, parent and administrative politics, and large classes to heavy workloads and escalating accountability standards for performance on standardized tests. But with large numbers of baby boomer teachers retiring and an influx of students from other countries, the demand for qualified teachers is only increasing and opportunities abound. One thing's for sure: you'll never be bored. "This is not a stagnant job," says Traci. "You're a counselor to children and parents, a politician with the lawmakers, town residents, and the board of education, a nurse to sore bellies and broken bones, and teacher of all the major subjects. Since you are working with so many different personalities, learning styles, and family situations, every lesson and every comment needs to fit the situation. You're always learning."

LIFE COACH

My journey to become a life coach has not been a clear path—it has been a maze with a lot of unexpected twists and turns. If you want to be a life coach, live some life first. Find a coach or therapist you respond to and study with him or her, getting your own life tuned up and in focus so you have clarity down the road. And soak in as much information as possible, be it from books, lectures, or weekend seminars in the self-improvement world. Just learn as much as you can.

—Christine, twenty-nine, life coach

FOR SOME, MYSELF INCLUDED, giving advice is not a job, it's a way of life. I spend hours every week on the phone and on e-mail scrutinizing my friends' relationships and career choices, carefully considering decisions and developments from the perspective of an objective, third-party observer. Occasionally, I've thought about how wonderful it would be to get paid for my insights, except I don't have five years to devote to a Ph.D. in psychology. As I was researching this book, however, I met several caring individuals who love talking to people and figuring out what makes them tick. These people have gotten around the doctoral requirement and are making excellent money every day helping people succeed. They are life coaches.

A life coach is a person who provides an environment to help clients produce fulfilling results in their personal and professional lives. She is trained to listen, to observe, and to customize her approach to individual client needs. Like true nurturers, good life coaches believe in the potential of the people with whom they work. Their job is to provide support and enhance the skills, resources, and creativity the client already has. The process typically begins with a short interview over the phone or in person so that the coach can assess the person's current challenges, priorities, and desired results. Subsequent sessions may last about sixty minutes, and between scheduled meeting times, the coach may ask the client to complete specific exercises or read materials that support behavior change and goal achievement.

Sounds easy enough, right? But lest you think that life coaches simply sit in a room or on the phone with their clients and chat away freely, licensed coaches are actually required to possess and adhere to a structured set of competencies advocated by the International Coach Federation (ICF). These include:

- **Establishing Trust and Intimacy.** Creating a safe, supportive environment that produces ongoing mutual respect and trust

- **Active Listening.** Focusing completely on what the client is and is not saying, and supporting client self-expression
- **Powerful Questioning.** Asking questions that reveal the information needed for maximum benefit to the client
- **Designing Actions.** Creating opportunities for ongoing learning, during coaching and in work/life situations
- **Planning and Goal Setting.** Developing and maintaining an effective coaching plan for each client
- **Managing Progress and Accountability.** Holding attention on what is important for the client, and leaving responsibility with the client to take action

Acquiring these competencies and determining how to integrate them into your own trademark process must be your first order of business as you set out to become a life coach. You can do this in two ways, the first of which is to hire your own life coach so that you can gain an in-depth understanding of the coach-client relationship. This step will also help you ensure that you actually enjoy life coaching before you invest too much time and money. The next phase of your journey involves completing an ICF-accredited training program (www.coachfederation.com), which, in addition to teaching you the competencies listed above, also prepares you for the challenges of a coaching career, including building your practice and persuading others of the value of your services. In a self-regulating field, you can rest easy knowing that your ICF-accredited program must be regularly reviewed to ensure that it demonstrates a commitment to the highest standards in the profession. There are three ICF credentials that you can pursue through the organization's training programs: associate certified coach (ACC), professional certified coach (PCC), and master certified coach (MCC). Each requires hours of coach-specific training and coaching experience, and any will give you a leg up as you establish your reputation, for they communicate that you are experienced, responsible, and recognized internationally for your skills.

Once you've completed your training program, you're ready for the significant challenge of attracting enough clients to make a living. Steve Mitten, a life coach and a past president of ICF, says that the first thing you must realize is that life coaching is a new phenomenon. Since few people even know what it is, a straightforward sales pitch won't work. Instead, you must actively market your services as a solution to problems people already have and are spending money on, such as career uncertainty or relationship difficulties. Then, you'll want to develop a business plan in which you select a competitive niche, or an area where your experience and strengths meet a unique marketplace need and will allow you to target a specific segment of the population. For example, Christine, a twenty-nine-year-old life coach in California, had previously written a self-help book for young women in the throws of a quarterlife crisis called *20 Something, 20 Everything.* The book's success made Christine credible with and appealing to twentysomething females, and so she developed her life coaching business plan to focus on the requirements of her built-in audience.

As part of your business plan, you will also need to decide how much to charge for your services, so that you can generate an income as a coach. People always want to know about averages, so I'll tell you that according to the Coaches Training Institute, a graduate certified coach with one year of experience averages about $6,200 a month. This rate of $39 an hour assumes that you are servicing a new client every hour of every business day, which of course isn't the case. You will probably charge more per hour but will spend a large chunk of time generating business for your fledgling practice, especially in the beginning. "Be prepared that it takes most coaches three years to become profitable. Most coaches who leave coaching do so because they haven't been able to build a sustainable business, not because of the quality of their coaching," says Michael, twenty-nine, a life coach in New York. "Have a great team behind you that can offer help and support during the tough times—financial and otherwise."

When it comes to marketing your new coaching practice, the life coaches I talked to had lots of good advice (of course, they're life coaches!). Among their wise words: give free introductory sessions so clients can try coaching and realize how much they love it, do workshops or other speaking engagements in your community, establish your presence online with a strong website and expert articles, form partnerships with other coaches, and get involved with your local ICF chapter. You can give incentives to clients for referring their friends and offer group coaching for those who cannot afford one-to-one sessions. "I also make myself competitive by staying current on industry trends and expanding my coaching skills and tools," says Michael. "As a coach, you're always working on yourself."

Want to learn more before you take the plunge? David Wood, founder of the International Coach Academy, has a great website (www.life-coaching-resource.com) that offers a monthly e-newsletter, a mentoring program for new coaches, and a step-by-step guide to establishing your practice. One thing's for sure: as the world gets more stressful, life coaching as a profession is only going to grow. Are you a born nurturer—naturally curious about people, sensitive, and empathetic? Do you have some solid problem-solving and entrepreneurial skills mixed in? If this sounds about right, and you're willing and able to invest some resources up front, you might think about taking advantage of one of the hottest career trends today: life coaching.

NONPROFIT ADMINISTRATOR

> My father passed away from colon cancer when I was fourteen. Before he died, my dad told me that making happiness real for others is truly the greatest gift because it provides the foundation for the celebration of life. While filming *Survivor* in Africa, I had the opportunity to visit a small village called Wamba. I played hacky sack with a group of HIV-positive children, and seeing the joy in these children's eyes made me realize something had to be done to stop the deadly path of this disease. I've been given many gifts: money, celebrity, soccer talent—and to just sit back and watch people die was not an option for me.
>
> —Ethan, thirty-two, nonprofit administrator

WOULD IT BE EASIER to get up in the morning knowing that everything you'll do at work that day would positively impact people's lives or improve our society for future generations? Would it be easier to toil in a windowless cube if your personal values and your professional responsibilities were perfectly in line? I believe that nonprofit administrators have a motivational edge on the rest of us, because even when they're making cold calls and stamping letters, they know they're making a difference and doing meaningful work. Since the events of September 11, 2001, the number of U.S.-based organizations needing capable staff has increased exponentially, and twenty- and thirtysomethings disillusioned with the priorities of the for-profit world are turning to nonprofit careers in droves. Should you be one of them? Let's take a look at what a nonprofit job looks like.

According to career website Vault (www.vault.com), the nonprofit sector is hugely diverse, both in terms of types of organizations and types of positions available. Some nonprofits employ thousands of paid workers through a well-defined organizational structure, while others consist of one paid executive director who coordinates volunteers. The type of organization most commonly associated with the term *nonprofit* is the community-based organization, or CBO. CBOs respond to basic unmet needs within a community, providing direct services such as meals-on-wheels, job-placement assistance, and child care. Other types of organizations that fall under the nonprofit umbrella are concerned with arts and culture (such as the Whitney Museum of American Art), advocacy and social policy (such as Mothers Against Drunk Driving), scientific research (such as the CATO Institute), and international outreach (such as UNICEF). The larger organizations consist of several staff roles, including the executive director, who is essentially the CEO; the director of development, who oversees fund-raising; the director of programming, who designs programs and services; and the director of marketing, who oversees communication with the public. Varying numbers of staffers and volunteers, who spend the majority of their time in offices functioning in a team environment, round out the typical nonprofit organization. New college graduates typically enter the nonprofit workforce at the coordinator level, while individuals with private sector experience may be hired directly into an executive position. Regardless of official titles, however, everyone who works in a nonprofit has a wide array of responsibilities.

As the co-founder of the nonprofit organization Grassroot Soccer, which uses a sporting environment to further education and awareness of HIV/AIDS, thirty-two-year-old Ethan spends his days organizing fund-raising dinners and celebrity soccer tournaments, calling corporations, giving lectures, and traveling to Africa to see his programs literally play out there. "I had to figure out how to start a

501(c)(3), select a board of directors, write grants, and make bylaws," says Ethan of his role at the helm of the organization. "I had to learn what was out there, what worked, and what didn't. It's very much like running a business." Amber, twenty-three, is an assistant with the Make-A-Wish Foundation and does a lot of important work for someone at her level. "I do a lot of writing and editing—preparing and updating marketing, fund-raising, and informational documents," says Amber. "I also assist the chief executive officer with fund-raising plans and ventures, and form and release communication to the governing board of directors."

The nonprofit world is similar to the private sector with respect to recruiting and hiring. Most entry-level positions require a bachelor's degree and some senior-level positions require a master's or Ph.D. The application and interview process is normally handled through a human resources department. How can you make yourself stand out in a field of young and passionate candidates? "Take business, finance, and marketing classes, and pertinent seminars to stay one step ahead," suggests Amber. "Do an internship in a small nonprofit and look for opportunities to better the organization before you leave. If the files need a major overhaul, then spend an entire Saturday reorganizing them; it will make the office more efficient and you more competitive on the job market." And don't forget to network. "I fell in love with Make-A-Wish when my cousin was a wish child. I heavily pursued a pro bono internship while I was in college and then kept in close contact with the chief operating officer and human resources manager after I left," says Amber. "I expressed my interest in working for the organization every month via e-mail and phone, and eventually I was hired for a full-time job that started after I graduated."

Here are some helpful resources to check out as you prepare to dive into your nonprofit job or internship search:

- GuideStar (www.guidestar.org)
- Idealist (www.idealist.org)
- Independent Sector (www.independentsector.org)
- Nonprofit Career Network (www.nonprofitcareer.com)
- Philanthropy Careers (www.philanthropy.com/jobs)
- Professionals for NonProfits (www.nonprofitstaffing.com)
- VolunteerMatch (www.volunteermatch.org)

If you are one of those nurturers with a strong moral compass, the gift of persuasion, and dogged determination, then a career in nonprofit administration could be for you. These jobs are not perfect, though, and you should be aware of the drawbacks before jumping in. First, compensation is fairly low across the board. Most nonprofit workers make under $50K, and entry-level positions typically do not exceed $30K. Executives can earn six-figure salaries, but those positions are few and far between. If you're fresh out of college, a nonprofit environment may not provide much career guidance or mentoring because there are so few people on your precise path. And finally, many nonprofit organizations are perpetually understaffed, causing stress and burnout among employees. But many nonprofit administrators maintain that these disadvantages are worth it. For as the website Vault says, this career involves interactions with a broad array of people from all class levels and executive levels and engenders a tremendous amount of prestige and respect in the community.

NUTRITIONIST
• • • • • • • • • • • • •

> My job is very personal. I work intimately with people, learning about their lives and concerns. As a nutritionist, I empathize with people who live alone while working two to three jobs to pay the rent and eat poorly as a result, and those who have a family to feed and neglect themselves in order to make sure everyone else is taken care of. I try to help these people overcome the overwhelming amount of stress they endure daily and show them how to treat their bodies right.
>
> —Anu, twenty-two, nutritionist

TO MANY WHO HAVE CHOSEN this path, nutrition is not a career but a way of life. It affects everyone equally, regardless of race, background, or socioeconomic status, and what we feed our bodies is relevant to everything we do. Nutritionists have the ability to improve people's long-term health and overall quality of life with a few simple suggestions, and so the knowledge they hold and the work they do is empowering and significant.

Nutritionists also have the advantage of being qualified to do a whole range of jobs. According to the U.S. Bureau of Labor Statistics' *Occupational Outlook Handbook,* nutritionists plan food and nutrition programs, supervise the preparation and serving of meals, prevent and treat illnesses by promoting healthy eating habits, and recommend dietary modifications. Clinical dietitians provide nutritional services for patients in hospitals and nursing care facilities. Community dieticians, working in public health clinics, home health agencies, and fitness centers, counsel individuals on nutritional practices that prevent disease and promote health. They may also be employed in the food manufacturing, service, and marketing sectors—analyzing foods, preparing literature, or reporting on the nutritional content of certain ingredients or recipes. Management dietitians oversee large-scale meal planning, budgeting, sanitation, and preparation in health care facilities, company cafeterias, prisons, and schools. Consultant dietitians work under contract with health care facilities, sports teams, or supermarkets, or in their own private practices. They perform nutrition screenings and offer advice on diet-related concerns such as weight loss and cholesterol reduction.

As a community nutritionist at the Cross Island YMCA in Bellerose, New York, twenty-two-year-old Anu has the type of job that first comes to mind when you think about this profession. "I sit down with a client, one-on-one, and find out about her living situation," says Anu. "Does she live alone or with a big family to feed? Does she have a really long commute to work? Is she up and active all day long, or does she barely get enough exercise? Based on this information, I come up with specific suggestions (for example, meals that take half the time to prepare) and ways the client can change poor habits (like how to shop for whole-grain items, or items low in saturated fats). Then, I follow up so that I can monitor the results."

Because there isn't a regulatory body for nutritionists, anyone can claim to be one regardless of their education. However, most legitimate nutritionists are also registered dietitians (RDs). Registered dietitians must complete a bachelor's degree in dietetics, foods and nutrition, or food service systems management, and coursework approved by the Commission on Accreditation for Dietetics Education (CADE) of the American Dietetic Association (ADA). They must also do a full- or part-time CADE-accredited supervised practice program, or internship, at a health care facility, community agency, or food service corporation. Finally, they have to pass a national examination administered by the Commission on Dietetic Registration.

Many aspiring nutritionists have undergraduate degrees in other fields and fear having to start all over to secure RD status. If this is your situation, the ADA recommends having your college transcripts evaluated by the directors of a few different CADE-accredited programs. These directors can advise you on the additional coursework you'll need to complete in order to meet the requirements, and you'll be able to select a school that offers the best and most affordable option.

Once you are affiliated with a dietetics program, that institution will guide you through the process of applying for what many say are competitive internships, and later, jobs. You can supplement your school's efforts on your behalf by becoming a student member of the world-renowned ADA, which will open doors to valuable networking opportunities and career-building resources. Developing a relationship with the ADA early on is a smart move, because in order to maintain your RD status over time, you'll need to take advantage of the organization's high-quality continuing education offerings, including multidisciplinary programs, conferences, webinars, and publications.

The ADA website (www.eatright.org) has a comprehensive internship and job search tool, and sites such as DieticianCentral.com (www.dieticiancentral.com), GovernmentJobs (www.governmentjobs.com), USAJOBS (www.usajobs.gov), and Govtjobs.com (www.govtjobs.com) feature nutrition job listings as well. Since state and local government agencies supposedly provide one in five nutrition-related jobs, these last two sites in particular are worth a look. If you are targeting a specific location for your search, you might contact the human resources departments in nearby hospitals, schools, and nursing homes.

Although internships might be tough to obtain, most people with the RD certification don't have too much trouble finding employment. A quick Google search reveals hundreds of openings for RDs, and the U.S. Bureau of Labor Statistics suggests that the nutrition field will grow quickly through 2014 as a result of increasing emphasis on disease prevention through improved dietary habits. The money is better than in some other nurturer occupations—the ADA cites the median annual salary for RDs as around $55K—and the nutrition field offers plenty of advancement opportunities. With experience or graduate-level study, nutritionists can hold management positions, such as director of a dietetic department, can become specialists in areas such as renal or diabetic dietetics, or can become involved in university teaching or research.

If you're thinking about becoming a nutritionist, you need to have an encyclopedic knowledge of how nutrition affects certain age groups, body systems, and conditions, and you should also possess sound judgment and an innate understanding of human nature. As in other nurturer fields, a never-ending supply of patience and compassion is required. "Many of my patients are struggling with life-threatening diagnoses, while others have already tried dozens of methods—from strange diets to experimental drugs—in order to improve their health. It's critical that I not only hear them out, but also really listen to them," says Ben, twenty-eight, a clinical nutritionist and RD in St. Louis.

Solid communication skills enable the good nutritionist to teach abstract concepts in a way that's easy to understand, and to encourage cooperation. "I have the occasional nonmotivated client who is unwilling to change her lifestyle. But the upside is, at one point she did want to, and that's why she came to see me," says Anu. "The number of diseases, symptoms, and complications that can be cured by nutrition is amazing. I love it when I get a referral from a happy client, because I know my advice worked and that she feels comfortable enough to allow me to help someone she cares about."

PHYSICAL THERAPIST

> The biggest challenge I face is communicating to parents that their child may never walk independently while at the same time encouraging them to hope. I can't see into a crystal ball to predict what the future holds for a child, but even if she doesn't walk, she can have such a fulfilling life, so I want to do everything I can to help families maintain a positive outlook.
>
> —Miriam, thirty-six, physical therapist

PHYSICAL THERAPY IS CURRENTLY one of the fastest-growing professions, so it's hard to believe it didn't exist until the early twentieth century. In 1921, Mary McMillan and several other women dedicated to improving rehabilitation initiatives founded the first physical therapy professional association, the American Women's Physical Therapeutic Association. World War II and the polio epidemic popularized the use of physical therapy and increased the need for trained clinicians. Today, the demand for physical therapists continues to rise as the baby boomers reach senior-citizen status and seek treatment for age-related disabilities or impaired functioning.

For those of you who have never injured a bone or muscle and haven't been privy to the secrets of the physical therapist's office, allow me to explain what a physical therapist (PT) does. In their book *50 Best Jobs for Your Personality*, J. Michael Farr and Laurence Shatkin describe the PT as one who assesses, plans, and participates in rehabilitative programs that improve mobility, relieve pain, increase strength, and decrease or prevent deformity of patients suffering from disease or injury. After performing an initial exam measuring the patient's strength, motor development and function, sensory perception, functional capacity, and respiratory and circulatory efficiency, the PT determines a diagnosis and designs an individual program of physical treatment. These programs usually involve manual exercises, massage and/or traction, moist packs, ultraviolet and infrared lamps, and ultrasound machines. PTs may direct and supervise PT aides or assistants, who help with treatments and perform routine tasks.

Some physical therapists are general practitioners and treat a wide range of ailments, while others specialize in geriatrics, orthopedics, sports medicine, or cardiopulmonary physical therapy, among other subfields. Miriam, thirty-six, is a pediatric physical therapist in New Jersey. "The best and hardest part of my job is that I play with children all day long. Actually, I have to trick the children into thinking that therapy is playtime. While most of my day is hands-on, I do spend time writing patient notes; communicating with doctors, patients, and families; attending planning meetings; and ordering equipment." Miriam has worked in a variety of settings including a hospital, a school, and her home, seeing patients on an outpatient basis. The U.S. Bureau of Labor Statistics' *Occupational Outlook Handbook* states that nearly six out of ten PTs work in hospitals or in solely or jointly managed PT offices, and the others are employed with home health care services, nursing care facilities, outpatient care centers, and adult day care programs. Approximately 25 percent of American PTs currently work part-time. "Physical therapy is a fantastic career for a woman with kids because there's a lot of flexibility in scheduling patients," says Leah, twenty-nine, a PT student in California. Most PTs make good money too. Farr and Shatkin cite average annual earnings as approaching $60K, and those numbers are only increasing.

A common misperception is that one can become a physical therapist by starting as a PT assistant. In fact, according to the U.S. Bureau of Labor Statistics' *Occupational Outlook Handbook*, there is really only one way into the profession, and that's through an accredited physical therapist educational program that takes two to three years to complete. Such programs offer degrees at the master's and doctoral levels, and include coursework in biology, chemistry, neuroanatomy, biomechanics, examination techniques, and human growth and development. Besides getting classroom and laboratory instruction, students receive supervised clinical experience so that they are prepared to practice immediately upon graduation. PT programs tend to be competitive, so to bolster your chances of getting in you should take the Graduate Record Examination (GRE) and aim for a score of 500 or better on the verbal and quantitative section with a 3.5 or better on the writing assignment. The American Physical Therapy Association (APTA, www.apta.org), the main professional organization representing PTs nationwide, says that admissions officers also look for volunteer experience as a PT aide or assistant, involvement in school and community activities, and letters of recommendation from physical therapists or science teachers.

Securing that all-important hands-on experience is the biggest hurdle for many prospective PTs. When Leah wanted to apply to PT school, she leveraged the career center at her undergraduate institution to learn about health care and community volunteer opportunities. She also contacted the athletic departments and health care facilities on the campus, as well as the offices of her own physicians, to see if anyone could use an extra pair of hands. Once you have all of the prerequisites under your belt, you'll be ready to select your accredited PT program. Several PTs cited the APTA website as a terrific place to begin your search. As you investigate different options, this site recommends that you talk with current students about their experiences and contact recent graduates to see how quickly they passed the licensure exam and how quickly they found a job.

Throughout your life as a PT, the APTA will continue to serve as a critical resource. While you're in school, the organization will do a great deal to provide you with the tools for a successful career, including events, job fairs, an online job bank, a mentoring program, and a student assembly for networking and learning about contemporary PT issues. And once you've graduated, you'll likely turn to the APTA again and again, as licensed PTs move up through participating in continuing education courses and workshops. "Advancement into management comes with experience and further training," says Sean, a twenty-six-year-old PT. A management position, such as the chief of physical therapy at a hospital or the head of your own practice, might involve increased responsibility for patient care, additional supervision of students or other personnel, development and/or marketing of new physical therapy programs, and quality assurance.

Before you plow through the layers of education required to enter this field, you'll want to think hard about whether the profession is a good fit. Exceptional bedside manner is not necessarily a requirement for MDs anymore, but it's essential for PTs. "A good PT is empathetic and a good listener," says Sean. Miriam concurs. "PTs should be highly altruistic, should love spending time with people, and should be able to maintain a clear line of communication with doctors, other therapists, and families," she says. "I'm my patients' cheerleader, and the most fulfilling part of my job is when a parent approaches me and just says 'thank you.' "

SOCIAL SERVICES CASEWORKER

One thing I can say for sure is that every day is different. Some cases are more predictable, while others are more involved and complex. You can never predict a client's needs on a daily basis, and it has been my experience that there is no general formula to follow. You have to look at each case on an individual basis, keeping in mind that each client has her own unique strengths and limitations.

—Meg, twenty-four, social services caseworker

THE SOCIAL SERVICES CASEWORKER ensures that troubled or vulnerable individuals receive the assistance they need to function effectively in society. She is the supreme nurturer: compassionate, trustworthy, patient, and possessing a strong sense of responsibility. Inspiring confidence and respect, the caseworker thrives on using her unique set of skills and talents to transform lives for the better. She is rewarded not with generous financial compensation (the average annual salary for a caseworker is around $27K), but with the knowledge that every day, in service to her community, she helps a person or a family who might be otherwise neglected.

Social services caseworkers usually work with professionals from a variety of fields, such as nursing, psychiatry, psychology, rehabilitative or physical therapy, or social work. They're responsible for intervening in and managing aspects of clients' lives including food supply, shelter, medical care (mental and physical), personal hygiene, finances, and transportation. Caseworkers may coordinate specific benefits and services, mediate relationships with other providers, and talk with family members and others to gain insight into clients' backgrounds and needs. They usually provide emotional support and help clients become involved in pursuits that will improve their long-term well-being. Working alternately in offices and in the field, the typical caseworker keeps detailed records on each client and regularly reports progress to supervisors.

Christopher, twenty-six, is a behavioral health caseworker for Montgomery County, Maryland. "I spend most days meeting with clients to assist them in obtaining entitlements such as Medical Assistance, SSI/SSDI, and food stamps, or to help them get into programs for treatment or residence," he says. "Sometimes I also participate in trainings so that I can better serve my clients, or complete paperwork that can't be done where I'm meeting with people back-to-back. Seeing clients is certainly the most rewarding part, since I get to speak with the person I'm trying to help and find out exactly what they want and need."

The U.S. Bureau of Labor Statistics' *Occupational Outlook Handbook* says that more than half of social services workers are in the health care and social assistance industries. One in three is employed by state and local governments, primarily in public welfare agencies and facilities for mentally disabled and developmentally challenged individuals. Meg, twenty-four, a caseworker for a state rehabilitation agency, helps disabled individuals secure gainful employment. "I provide daily counseling and guidance, and facilitate services, so that the client can choose a vocation," Meg says. "I enjoy my job because of the gratification I receive when a client achieves a job goal, and because of the personal fulfillment that comes from helping others."

A bachelor's degree is generally the minimum educational requirement for an entry-level position as a social services caseworker, although licenses or certificates in subfields such as human services, addictions, or gerontology can be helpful as well. Nowadays, social services employers increasingly prefer a master's degree in social work or a related field, especially for autonomous positions with less direct supervision. The job outlook for caseworkers is projected to be excellent through the next five years, especially for individuals with a background in gerontology and substance abuse treatment.

As in many other fields, an internship or volunteer position is the best way to break into social services, and a short-term assignment will provide an ideal opportunity to see how you would handle a highly rewarding but emotionally draining career in the field. "Very few people attempt a job in this field before their college graduation, but that's what I did," says Christopher. "I applied for and got a position as a mental health counselor who met with and made referrals for kids who had been arrested." In case you're not as lucky as Christopher, though, you might try a volunteer position to get your foot in the door. One of the thousands of U.S.-based nonprofit organizations would probably be happy to provide you with valuable experience in lieu of a paycheck.

Here are some resources you might use to locate a social service internship, or, if you've already worked in the field, a paying job:

- American Counseling Association (www.counseling.org)
- AmeriCorps (www.americorps.org)
- Good Works (www.goodworks.org)
- Human Services Career Network (www.hscareers.com)
- National Association of Social Workers (www.naswdc.org)
- SocialServices (www.socialservice.com)
- U.S. Department of Health and Human Services (www.os.dhhs.gov)

As you go through the process of interviewing for a social services caseworker position, there are a few things you should keep in mind, including:

- Can you answer behavioral-based questions about specific client cases you've worked on in the past?
- Have you taken the time to research the organization's community clientele and work conditions?
- Will the organization assist you in obtaining the necessary certification or licensing?

Once you land a job as a social services caseworker, I'm sure you'll find your desire to nurture others consistently realized. Recognize, however, that social services is a field prone to burnout. "From the beginning, I wanted to save the world, like most fledgling counselors do," says Christopher. "I worked more than I should, I put more of my own energy into a client's problems than the client was putting in, and I just plain tried too hard. You have to know your limits." Other caseworkers agree. There is always more that could be done, but cut yourself some slack, set a clear boundary between your work and personal lives, and take the time to consciously value your own contributions. Doing these things successfully will ensure your promotion into more senior positions in case management, supervision, and administration, where you'll have the opportunity to make an even greater impact on your community and on the world.

ZOOLOGIST

It's an incredible feeling when you've made a connection with one of the dolphins and you can see that it is eager to work with you. My job definitely has its share of dirty work, but nothing beats getting in the water with the dolphins and just having fun. And I'll never forget the time I got to witness the birth of a dolphin. It's one of the most amazing things I've ever seen.

—Kevin, twenty-seven, zoologist

WHEN MOST PEOPLE THINK OF ZOOLOGISTS, they imagine animal caregivers in zoos or other habitats. I've since learned that a zoologist may actually hold a variety of positions. According to the Princeton Review, most zoologists are involved in curating, directing, or zookeeping. The curator oversees the care and distribution of animals in the zoo, coordinates animal loans with other zoos, and writes scientific papers, while the director performs more administrative duties, such as fund-raising, budgeting, and planning exhibitions. Curators and directors work closely to determine the best way to contain the animals, maintain their habitats, and manage the facility. The zookeeper provides the daily care of feeding, training, cleaning, and monitoring of the animals and their environments.

The zoologists I spoke with mostly fall into the zookeeping category. Some aspire to be curators or directors someday, while others are content to stay in their zookeeping positions, possibly advancing to head keeper or head trainer. Depending on the size of the zoo or habitat, zookeepers may work with all of the animals, or may specialize in a certain species, such as dolphins or gorillas.

Zookeeping is a rewarding but weighty profession, as zookeepers are solely responsible for the health and well-being of the animals in their care. They must possess a keen understanding of animal behavior, keep highly detailed records, and train the animals so they can interact with veterinarians and the public. While zookeepers do spend a lot of time physically working in the cages with the animals, they are also tasked with communicating with their co-workers and the zoo's human visitors. "Talking to the public and showing people the animals is a very important part of my job," says Tiffany, twenty-seven, a zookeeper in Atlanta. "If people aren't able to see these animals and learn about them, they have no reason to care about them and want to save them in the wild." As you can probably guess, most zookeepers do not work a nine-to-five schedule, because animals must be cared for 24/7 and you never know when an emergency may arise.

It takes a special type of nurturer to be a zookeeper. First and foremost, she must be able to develop an exceptional rapport with her animals. "A zookeeper must be able to read and understand the animals because they can't tell you how they feel or what they want. And zoo animals are not like pets. You can't force wild animals to do anything, so you have to be a patient person," says Tiffany. "You have to be able to stay calm under stressful circumstances and gain trust from animals who have bad histories with people. And like raising children, there is no handbook. Just when you think you've got things figured out, the animals completely change the routine and you have to start all over again!"

So let's say that you love animals and you've decided that you're willing to perform the less glamorous aspects of zookeeping, like cleaning, bathing, and picking up after your charges. How might you get a job as a zookeeper? Well, let's start with the educational requirements. A bachelor's degree in zoology or a biological science is preferred, and some colleges offer specific programs oriented toward a zoo career. The Santa Fe Community College in Florida, for example, has a teaching zoo, while Moorpark College in California offers an exotic animal training management program.

If you are finished with school and majored in something unrelated, you'll need to have solid experience working with large populations of nondomesticated animals. Most zoos and animal care facilities have volunteer programs and internships, and some even offer paid part-time positions. To find these jobs, you might visit your local zoo, vet, or wildlife rehabilitation center and talk to the employees there, check out the job sections of the American Association of Zoo Keepers (www.aazk.org) and the Association of Zoos and Aquariums (www.aza.org) websites, or attend one of these organizations' events or conferences.

Unfortunately, entry-level zookeeping jobs and internships are more competitive than ever, and old-fashioned networking is the best way of all to obtain one. "One of my professors was the nutritionist at the Denver Zoo. I really wanted to work with gorillas, so I pleaded my case with her," says Tiffany. "She helped me by letting me work with her on a seal and sea lion study, which was the experience I needed to get an internship at the Fossil Rim Wildlife Center." Kevin, twenty-seven, a marine mammal trainer at the National Aquarium in Baltimore, says it also helps if you're willing to move anywhere for a job. "There are a lot of people who want a very limited number of positions. It's all about being in the right place at the right time, and since you never know where a job may open up, you have to be flexible with location."

Finally, there's the issue of pay. Nearly all of the zookeepers I spoke with said their jobs are a labor of love. Several sources cite the average annual salary for zookeepers as $28K to $49K, but some entry-level positions pay even less than the bottom of this range. "As a zookeeper, you'll never get an amazing salary or a bonus for a job well done," says Tiffany. "Your compensation will be having happy and healthy animals that are thriving. And when you develop that special relationship with them, it's the world."

Afterword

IF YOU'RE CURRENTLY FEELING unfulfilled in your job situation, or are looking to explore other options, I hope that this book has given you some good leads. Whether you're thinking of checking out two of the jobs or twenty, it may seem daunting to take the necessary steps to find out if one of them is the right fit for you—and with good reason. "Getting the career you want involves preparation, tuning in to your inner cravings, and evaluating what is in your best physical and financial interest," says Christine Hassler, the author of *20 Something, 20 Everything.* "There will be bumps and rough times, and some sacrifice might be necessary."

Throughout your process of exploration, it's important to have realistic expectations of "dream careers." Although the individuals profiled in this book love their jobs, even they don't believe there's such a thing as the perfect work situation. Every job has its ups and downs, and aspects they love and aspects they don't love. "If we expect our jobs to fulfill us, if we expect to not have to work that hard, if we expect to jump out of our beds every day bursting with excitement about going to work, we're kidding ourselves," says Hassler. Add Abby Wilner and Catherine Stocker, authors of *The Quarterlifer's Companion*: "There's a reason it's called work. It's not always going to be fun." This is a hard but necessary lesson that I had to learn when I succeeded in my dream job of being a book author.

Within each chapter, I made a point of including concrete tips for how you can get started in certain fields. Generally, though, you should not be deterred by a lack of relevant experience. In developing a résumé and other promotional materials for the field you want to pursue, think about how your current skills and talents apply to the responsibilities you'll hold in the new job. "Don't forget that there are some skills that are valued in any field, such as your ability to manage people or projects or your ability to work on a team. Maybe you are very good at generating creative ideas or have great organizational skills. Look outside your current job for skills that you have picked up through activities in the community," recommend Wilner and Stocker.

It's a smart idea to ease into a new career one foot at a time. Perhaps this means earning a paycheck at your current job while doing a part-time internship in your new field, conducting informational interviews over your lunch break, or taking an adult education class or workshop on the weekend. The only way to find out if you're passionate about something is to try it. Making a spur-of-the-moment decision to enroll in a full-time graduate program is probably not the best way to do so, however. Say Wilner and Stocker: "You should try out a graduate field of study in the real world first, because it's a huge commitment both in terms of time and money, and the job itself will not necessarily be the same in practice as the graduate program curriculum."

Remember that any progress is good progress. Even confident twenty- and thirtysomethings stay in unsatisfying jobs because they feel safe, and because they're afraid of making a bad decision about a new career. But in the quest to uncover a source of meaningful work, your worst enemy is inertia. "Deciding what kind of work will make you happy is a choice, a big one," says Julie Jansen, author of *I Don't Know What I Want, But I Know It's Not This*. "Today, there are so many choices that sometimes it may seem easier to sit still and not make any at all. But you have a clear choice—you can either decide to begin the process of change, or you can continue doing something that doesn't make you happy."

It's possible to pursue your dream job whether you're twenty-two or eighty-two, but there's no doubt that twenty- and thirtysomethings have more flexibility when it comes to test-driving different careers. The process of self-discovery is much easier when you're unencumbered by family responsibilities and substantial financial burdens, and when you haven't yet reached a level in a career where it's tougher to turn back. Now really is the best time, so what are you waiting for? I'll see you in your next gig.

Acknowledgments

How'd You Score That Gig? has been several years in the making, since my first book, *They Don't Teach Corporate in College,* led me to develop my own "cool job" as a twenty- and thirtysomething career expert. My sophomore effort would not have been possible without the more than five hundred people who generously responded to my research survey and the more than one hundred inspiring individuals who agreed to be interviewed and share their trade secrets.

A special thanks to my agents: Alex Glass, who was instrumental in fleshing out the initial concept, and Michelle Wolfson, who lent a supportive ear during the production phase. Thanks to my editor, Christina Duffy, who believed in the book from the start and is wise beyond her years. And it has been an honor and a pleasure to work with such a wonderful team at Random House, especially Jane von Mehren, Sanyu Dillon, Brian McLendon, Patty Park, Ashley Gratz-

Collier, Avideh Bashirrad, Beth Pearson, Mark Maguire, Gene Mydlowski, and Carol Russo—I couldn't have done it without you!

More appreciation goes out to David Dunne and the team at Edelman, who have made it possible for me to do what I love while having the opportunity to work with savvy marketing folks every week; the students and professionals who attend my seminars and encourage me to keep giving them; and the other career and twentysomething bloggers who have opened their virtual homes to me.

Last but not least, I thank my wonderful husband, Stewart Shankman, and our talented network of friends, who share stories of their own gigs daily.

Bibliography

ADVENTURER SOURCES

American Society of Limnology and Oceanography. Working in the Aquatic Sciences. aslo.org/career/aquaticcareer.html, accessed 2006.

Bureau of Labor Statistics, U.S. Department of Labor. *Occupational Outlook Handbook, 2006–07 Edition*. "Conservationist Scientists and Foresters." www.bls.gov/oco/ocos048.htm, accessed 2006.

Bureau of Labor Statistics, U.S. Department of Labor. *Occupational Outlook Handbook, 2006–07 Edition*. "News Analysts, Reporters, and Correspondents." stats.bls.gov/oco/ocos088.htm, accessed 2006.

Burgett, Gordon. *Travel Writer's Guide*, 3rd ed.. Novato, Calif.: Communication Unlimited, 2002.

CollegeBoard.com. "Career: Conservation Scientists." www.collegeboard.com/csearch/majors_careers/profiles/careers/104812.html, accessed 2006.

Conservation International's Investigate Biodiversity. "Conservation Careers: Tips for Getting Started." investigate.conservation.org/xp/IB/conservationcareers/getting_started.xml, accessed 2006.

Ford, Nancy. "Photojournalism as a Career." www.nlford.com/career, accessed 1999.

Monster.com. "Career Advice: Adventure Travel Guide." jobprofiles.monster.com/Content/job_content/JC_PersonalCareand Service/JSC_Travel/JOB_AdventureTravelGuide/jobzilla_html?job profiles=1, accessed 2006.

Office of Naval Research. "Oceanography/Marine-Related Careers." www.onr.navy.mil/careers/ocean_marine/, accessed 2004.

O'Neil, L. Peat. "Breaking into Travel Writing." www.adventuretravelwriter.com/Breakin.htm, accessed 2000.

SchoolsintheUSA.com. "Career Search: Photojournalist." www.schoolsintheusa.com/careerprofiles_details.cfm?carid=1108, accessed 2006.

Sea Grant Marine Careers. "Occupation Salaries." www.marinecareers.net/employment_academic.html, accessed 2005.

SoYouWanna.com. "SoYouWanna Teach English Abroad?" www.soyouwanna.com/site/syws/englishabroad/englishabroad.html, accessed 2006.

St. John, Warren. "A Job with Travel but No Vacation." travel2.nytimes.com/2006/07/09/fashion/sundaystyles/09TRAVEL. html, accessed 2006.

TeachAbroad.com. "Is Teaching Abroad for You?" www.teachabroad.com/teach-article.cfm, accessed 2006.

U.S. Department of State. "What Does a Foreign Service Officer Do?" careers.state.gov, accessed 2006.

Voyt, Peter. "Are You Cut Out for an Adventure Career?" featuredreports.lycos.monster.com/adventurersjobs/cutout, accessed 2006.

Wilson, Bradley. "Careers in Photojournalism." www.nppa.org, accessed 2006.

CREATOR SOURCES

American Society of Interior Designers. "Is Interior Design for You?" www .asid.org/become/Is+Interior+Design+for+You.htm, accessed 2006.

Animation Arena. "Game Design Salaries." www.animationarena.com /game-design-salaries.html, accessed 2006.

Bureau of Labor Statistics, U.S. Department of Labor. *Occupational Outlook Handbook, 2006–07 Edition.* "Landscape Architects." www.bls.gov/oco/ocos039.htm, accessed 2006.

CookingSchools.com. "Top 10 Qualities of a Great Culinary Professional." www.cookingschools.com/articles/culinary-top-10.html, accessed 2006.

Designaré Interior Design Collective. "No Experience and Looking for Work." www.dezignare.com/newsletter/work.html, accessed 2006.

Fashion Group International. "Careers." newyork.fgi.org/index.php, accessed 2006.

Fashion Net. "How to Become a Fashion Designer." www.fashion.net/howto/fashiondesigner/index.html, accessed 2006.

FashionSchools.org. "Fashion Designer." www.fashion-schools.org/fashion-designer.htm, accessed 2006.

Hoffman, W. Randy. "Learning to Serve, Serving to Learn." www.cookingschools.com/introduction, accessed 2006.

Knab, Christopher. "10 Essential Tips for Making a Living with Your Music." www.musicbizacademy.com/knab/articles/10makealiving.htm, accessed 2006.

Marley, Phil. *FabJob Guide to Become a Video Game Designer.* Seattle: FabJob, 2005.

Mayfield, Katherine. *Acting A to Z.* Washington, D.C.: Backstage Books, 1998.

National Association for Music Education. "Careers in Music." www.menc.org/industry/job/careers/careers.html, accessed 2006.

Princeton Review, The. "Career: Fashion Designer." www.princetonreview.com/cte/profiles/facts.asp?careerID=63, accessed 2006.

Princeton Review, The. "Career: Landscape Architect." www.princetonreview.com/cte/profiles/dayInLife.asp?careerID=179, accessed 2006.

Screen Actors Guild. "Getting Started as an Actor." www.sag.org, accessed 2006.

Warren, Lissa. *The Savvy Author's Guide to Book Publicity.* New York: Carroll & Graf, 2004.

Wright, Lenore. *Common Script Mistakes (and Misconceptions).* www.breakingin.net/Script_faq.htm, accessed 2006.

DATA HEAD SOURCES

American Association of Pharmaceutical Scientists. "Is a Career in Pharmaceutical Sciences Right for Me?" www.aapspharmaceutica .com/careercenter/resources/isacareer.asp, accessed 2006.

American Meteorological Society. "A Career Guide for the Atmospheric Sciences." www.ametsoc.org/atmoscareers/index.html, accessed 2006.

American Planning Association. "Considering a Career in Planning." www.planning.org/careers/index.htm, accessed 2006.

Bureau of Labor Statistics, U.S. Department of Labor. *Occupational Outlook Handbook, 2006–07 Edition.* "Atmospheric Scientists." www.bls.gov/oco/ocos051.htm, accessed 2006.

Bureau of Labor Statistics, U.S. Department of Labor. *Occupational Outlook Handbook, 2006–07 Edition.* "Computer Software Engineers." www.bls .gov/oco/ocos267.htm, accessed 2006.

Bureau of Labor Statistics, U.S. Department of Labor. *Occupational Outlook Handbook, 2006–07 Edition.* "Computer Support Specialists and Systems Administrators." www.bls.gov/oco/ocos268.htm, accessed 2006.

Bureau of Labor Statistics, U.S. Department of Labor. *Occupational Outlook Handbook, 2006–07 Edition.* "Engineers." www.bls.gov/oco/ocos027.htm, accessed 2006.

Bureau of Labor Statistics, U.S. Department of Labor. *Occupational Outlook Handbook, 2006–07 Edition.* "Financial Analysts and Personal Financial Advisors." www.bls.gov/oco/ocos259.htm, accessed 2006.

Bureau of Labor Statistics, U.S. Department of Labor. *Occupational Outlook Handbook, 2006–07 Edition.* "Urban and Regional Planners." www.bls .gov/oco/ocos057.htm, accessed 2006.

Career Prospects in Virginia. "Computer Security Specialists." www.career prospects.org/briefs/A-D/ComputerSecurity.shtml, accessed 2006.

Golden, Daniel. "No Longer Just Eggheads, Linguists Leap to the Net." www.unh.edu/linguistics/Resources/techling.htm, accessed 2006.

(ISC)[2]. *Career Guide: Decoding the Information Security Profession.* www .securitymanagement.com/library/careerguide_technofile0906.pdf, accessed 2006.

Junior Engineering Technical Society, The. "Environmental Engineering." www.jets.org/publications/environmental.cfm, accessed 2006.

McCook, Alison. "Big Makeover for Big Pharma." www.the-scientist .com/2005/06/20/S6/1/, accessed 2006.

National Society of Professional Engineers. "Becoming Licensed as a Professional Engineer." www.nspe.org/lc1-how.asp, accessed 2006.

Princeton Review, The. "Career: Financial Planner." www.princeton review.com/cte/profiles/dayInLife.asp?careerID=176, accessed 2006.

Sightseer's Guide to Engineering, A. "Roosevelt Lake Visitor Center." www.engineeringsights.org/SightDetail.asp?Sightid=21&id=6&view =d&name=Civil%2FEnvironmental&page=1&image=0, accessed 2006.

Tittel, Ed. "Building a Career in Information Security." www.certmag .com/articles/templates/cmag_feature.asp?articleid=659&zoneid=9, accessed 2006.

Wikipedia. "Computational Linguistics." en.wikipedia.org/wiki /Computational_linguistics, accessed 2006.

ENTREPRENEUR SOURCES

Arneson, Elizabeth. "Before You Buy a Bed and Breakfast." bandb.about .com/cs/beforeyoubuy/bb/byb-bandb.htm, accessed 2006.

———. "What Every Aspiring Innkeeper Should Know." bandb.about.com/cs/aspiring/a/advice.htm, accessed 2006.

Arvidson-Dailey, Peggy. "How to Start a Pet Sitting Business." www.bark talk.com/newsletter031506.html, accessed 2006.

BedOwner.co.uk. "Decorating Your B&B." bedowner.co.uk/Articles /Decorating_your_B&B.htm, accessed 2006.

BedOwner.co.uk. "Marketing Your B&B." bedowner.co.uk/Articles /Marketing_your_B&B.htm, accessed 2006.

Benjamin, Robert. "Pet Sitting: Start Your Own Business." www.buzzle .com/editorials/1-8-2006-85796.asp, accessed 2006.

Creative Solutions for Home and Office. "Frequently Asked Questions About Becoming an Organizer." onlineorganizing.com/BecomeAn Organizer.asp?content=C11BeAnOrganizerFAQs, accessed 2006.

Elms, Janelle. "How to Start an eBay Business." www.entrepreneur.com /ebusiness/gettingstarted/article83068.html, accessed 2006.

Entrepreneur Magazine. *How to Start a Retail Store* (specialty publication) www.entrepreneur.com, accessed 2006.

Fitness Consulting Group. "New Health Club Business Mistakes #1." www.fitnessconsultinggroup.com/new-health-club.html, accessed 2006.

Gracia, Maria. "First-time Visitor Letter." www.getorganizednow.com /po-introduction.html, accessed 2006.

International Health, Racquet & Sportsclub Association. "10 Million Americans Forecasted to Join a Health Club in 2006." www.fit commerce.com/Blueprint/WebControls/Announcements/ViewAnnoun cement.aspx?ItemID=956&mid=112&portalId=2&cid=112, accessed 2006.

Jasmine, Grace. *FabJob Guide to Become a Professional Organizer*. Seattle: FabJob, 2005.

Lander, Jack. "Should You License or Manufacture Your Invention?" smallbusiness.yahoo.com/r-article-a-41032-m-4-sc-25-should _you_license_or_manufacture_your_invention-i, accessed 2006.

Meeting Professionals International. Career Resources. www.mpiweb .org/cms/mpiweb/default.aspx, accessed 2006.

Meeting Professionals International. Integrated Marketing Demographic Information. www.mpiweb.org/cms/mpiweb/default.aspx, accessed 2006.

Monosoff, Tamara. "Selling Your Invention." www.entrepreneur.com /startingabusiness/inventing/inventionscolumnisttamaramonosoff /article159558.html, accessed 2006.

National Association of Professional Organizers. "Code of Ethics." www .napo.net/get_organized/ethics.html, accessed 2006.

National Association of Professional Organizers. Recommended Exam Study Resources. www.napo.net, accessed 2006.

National Association of Professional Organizers. "So You Want to Be an Organizer?" www.napo.net/faqs/want.to.be.organizer.html, accessed 2006.

National Association of Professional Pet Sitters. Frequently Asked Questions. www.petsitters.org/, accessed 2006.

National Retail Federation. "Trends and Statistics." www.nrf.com/, accessed 2006.

Pavlina, Steve. "How to Make Money from Your Blog." www.stevepavlina .com/blog/2006/05/how-to-make-money-from-your-blog/, accessed 2006.

Rincon, Ana. "Online Business 101." onlinebusiness.about.com/cs /startingup/a/101.htm, accessed 2006.

Rowse, Darren. "How Bloggers Make Money from Blogs." www.problogger .net/archives/2005/12/06/how-bloggers-make-money-from-blogs, accessed 2006.

Salary.com. "Job Valuation Report: Meeting/Event Planner." secure
.salary.com/jobvaluationreport/docs/jobvaluationreport/jobsellhtmls/
Meeting-Event-Planner-salary-job-description.html, accessed
2006.

Sloan, Paul, and Paul Kaihla. "Blogging for Dollars." money.cnn.com
/magazines/business2/business2_archive/2006/09/01/8384325,
accessed 2006.

INVESTIGATOR SOURCES

American Psychological Association. "Careers in Psychology." www.apa
.org/topics/psychologycareer.html, accessed 2006.

American Society of Crime Laboratory Directors. "Learning About
Forensic Science." www.ascld.org/visitors/resources.php, accessed 2006.

Association of Professional Futurists. "FAQs: About the Futures Field."
profuturists.org/content/category/3/18/42, accessed 2006.

Bev, Jennie S., and Leslie Poston. "Breaking into and Succeeding as an
Antiques Dealer." www.stylecareer.com/antiques_dealer.shtml, accessed
2006.

British Antique Dealers' Association. "Making a Career in Antiques." www
.bada.org/index.pl?id=2199, accessed 2006.

Bureau of Labor Statistics, U.S. Department of Labor. *Occupational Outlook
Handbook, 2006–07 Edition.* "Archivists, Curators, and Museum
Technicians." www.bls.gov/oco/ocos065.htm, accessed 2006.

Bureau of Labor Statistics, U.S. Department of Labor. *Occupational Outlook
Handbook, 2006–07 Edition.* "Automative Service Technicians and
Mechanics." www.bls.gov/oco/ocos181.htm, accessed 2006.

Bureau of Labor Statistics, U.S. Department of Labor. *Occupational Outlook
Handbook, 2006–07 Edition.* "Social Scientists." www.bls.gov/oco
/ocos054.htm, accessed 2006.

Career Prospects in Virginia. "Overview of Careers in Forensics." www
.careerprospects.org/briefs/P-S/SummaryForensics.shtml, accessed 2006.

Coates, Joseph. "On Being a Futurist." josephcoates.com/pdf_files/220_OBF
.pdf, accessed 2006.

CriminalJusticeUSA.com. "Criminologist." www.criminaljusticeusa.com
/criminologist.html, accessed 2006.

Drummer, Alan. "Auto Technician Careers: Your Fast Track to Success."

encarta.msn.com/encnet/departments/careertraining/?article=autotech, accessed 2006.

Hirst, K. Kris. "Field Technician." archaeology.about.com/od/alternate careers/p/fieldtech.htm, accessed 2006.

Midwest Forensics Resource Center. "Frequently Asked Questions About Training and Careers in Forensic Science." www.mfrc.ameslab.gov /FAQ_Forensic_Science_Student.php, accessed 2006.

Princeton Review, The. "Career: Antiques Dealer." www.princetonreview .com/cte/profiles/dayInLife.asp?careerID=9, accessed 2006.

Princeton Review, The. "Career: Criminologist." www.princetonreview .com/cte/profiles/dayInLife.asp?careerID=47, accessed 2006.

Princeton Review, The. "Career: Curator." www.princetonreview.com/cte /profiles/dayInLife.asp?careerID=48, accessed 2006

Schulz, Constance, et al. "Careers for Students of History." www.historians .org/pubs/careers/index.htm, accessed 2006.

Society for American Archaeology. *The Path to Becoming an Archaeologist.* www.saa.org/public/resources/SAA_PathBrochure.pdf, accessed 2006.

Victoria University Career Development and Employment. "Career View: Criminology." www.vuw.ac.nz/st_services/careers/resources /career_publications/career_views/criminology.pdf, accessed 2006.

NETWORKER SOURCES

Association of Image Consultants International. "Overview of Image Consulting." www.aici.org, accessed 2006.

Association of Talent Agents. "Frequently Asked Questions." www.agent association.com, accessed 2006.

Birnbaum, Jeffrey H. "The Road to Riches Is Called K Street." www .washingtonpost.com/wp-dyn/content/article/2005/06/21 /AR2005062101632.html, accessed 2006.

Cottingham, Rob. "Five Ways to Break into Speechwriting." www.social signal.com/speechlist/issues/7, accessed 2006.

Field, Shelly. *Career Opportunities in the Sports Industry.* New York: Checkmark Books, 2004.

Glancy, David. "Launching Your Wine Career." www.californiawineand food.com/wine/wine-career.htm, accessed 2006.

Goulet, Tag, and Rachel Gurevich. *FabJob Guide to Become an Image Consultant.* Seattle: FabJob, 2006.

Johns Hopkins University School of Advanced International Studies. *Career Opportunities on Capitol Hill.* www.sais-jhu.edu, accessed 2006.

Opportunities in Public Affairs. "Capitol Hill Job Guide." www.brubach.com/capitolhilljobguide.htm, accessed 2006.

Princeton Review, The. "Career: Lobbyist." www.princetonreview.com/cte/profiles/dayInLife.asp?careerID=88, accessed 2006.

Princeton Review, The. "Career: Marketing Executive." www.princetonreview.com/cte/profiles/dayInLife.asp?careerID=93, accessed 2006.

Princeton Review, The. "Career: Television Producer." www.princetonreview.com/cte/profiles/dayInLife.asp?careerID=156, accessed 2006.

Vault. "Career Profiles: Book Editor." www.vault.com, accessed 2006.

Vault. *Vault Guide to Capitol Hill Careers.* www.vault.com/store/book_preview.jsp?product_id=25654, accessed 2006.

Wasnak, Lynn. "How Much Should I Charge?" www.njcreatives.org/members_only/reference/how-much.htm, accessed 2006.

NURTURER SOURCES

American Dietetic Association. FAQs for Career Changers. www.eatright.org, accessed 2006.

American Federation of Teachers. "2005 Survey & Analysis of Teacher Salary Trends." www.aft.org/salary/index.htm, accessed 2006.

American Physical Therapy Association. Physical Therapy Education FAQ. www.apta.org, accessed 2006.

Bureau of Labor Statistics, U.S. Department of Labor. *Occupational Outlook Handbook, 2006–07 Edition.* "Dietitians and Nutritionists." www.bls.gov/oco/ocos077.htm, accessed 2006.

Bureau of Labor Statistics, U.S. Department of Labor. *Occupational Outlook Handbook, 2006–07 Edition.* "Physical Therapists." www.bls.gov/oco/ocos080.htm, accessed 2006.

Bureau of Labor Statistics, U.S. Department of Labor. *Occupational Outlook Handbook, 2006–07 Edition.* "Social and Human Service Assistants." www.bls.gov/oco/ocos059.htm, accessed 2006.

Bureau of Labor Statistics, U.S. Department of Labor. *Occupational Outlook*

Handbook, 2006–07 Edition. "Teachers: Preschool, Kindergarten, Elementary, Middle, and Secondary." www.bls.gov/oco/ocos069.htm, accessed 2006.

Childbirth International. *Guide to Becoming a Doula.* www.childbirth international.com, accessed 2006.

Coaches Training Institute. "CTI Database Survey." www.thecoaches .com/info/stats.html, accessed 2006.

Doulas of North America. "Doula FAQs." www.dona.org, accessed 2006.

Farr, J. Michael, and Laurence Shatkin. *50 Best Jobs for Your Personality.* Indianapolis: Jist Works, 2005.

HSPeople.com. "Human Service Workers and Assistants." www.hspeople .com, accessed 2006. (HSPeople.com now redirects to Jobscience.com, which is apparently a different company.)

International Coach Federation. "Coaching Core Competencies." www .coachfederation.org/ICF, accessed 2006.

International Coaching Federation. "Why Pursue an ICF Credential?" www.coachfederation.org/ICF, accessed 2006.

Legnos, Jessica. *Boston Globe Job Explainer: Doula.* www.boston.com/jobs, accessed 2006.

Mitten, Steve. "Top 10 Marketing Tips for Coaches." www.acoach4u.com /marketing_tips_for_life_coaches.htm, accessed 2006.

Princeton Review, The. "Career: Zoologist." www.princetonreview.com/cte /profiles/dayInLife.asp?careerID=166, accessed 2006.

Vault. "Nonprofit." www.vault.com/articles/Nonprofit-22089848.html, accessed 2006.

Wong, Harry, and Rosemary Wong. "Applying for a Teaching Job in a Tight Market." www.teachers.net/gazette/MAY03/wong.html, accessed 2006.

ALEXANDRA LEVIT thinks she has a pretty cool job. She's the founder and president of Inspiration @Work, a career consulting firm, and has authored several books, including the popular *They Don't Teach Corporate in College: A Twenty-Something's Guide to the Business World* and the forthcoming *Success for Hire* from ASTD Press.

Levit's career advice has been featured in more than five hundred media outlets including ABC News, Fox News, the Greg Behrendt Show, the *Wall Street Journal*, the *New York Times*, National Public Radio, *Fortune*, the Associated Press, Yahoo!, and MSN. Known as one of the premiere career spokespeople of her generation, she regularly speaks at corporations and universities around the country about business issues facing young employees.

She graduated from Northwestern University and resides in Chicago, Illinois, with her husband, Stewart. Visit her website and blog at www.alexandralevit.com and the book website at www.scorethatgig.com.